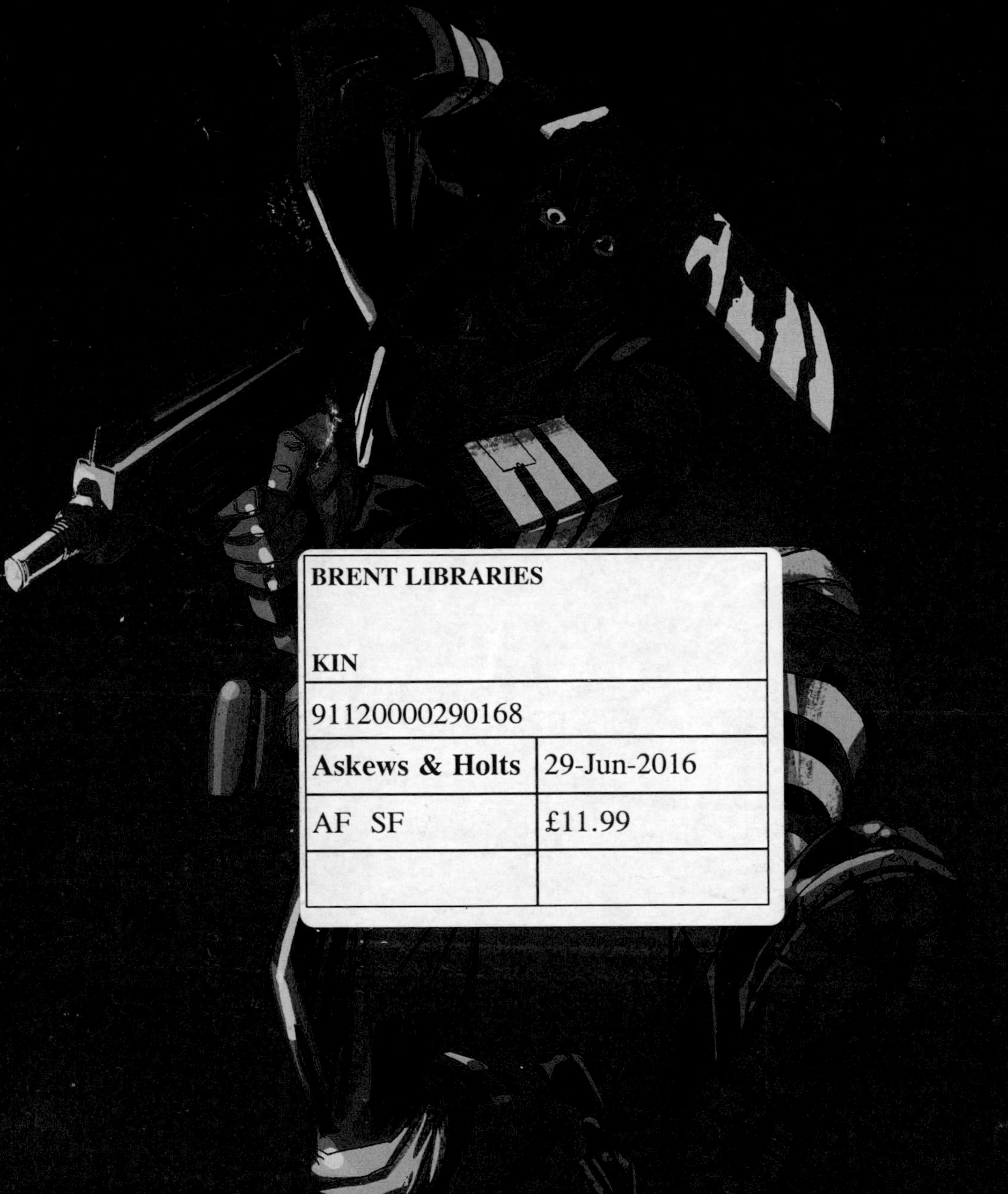

# THE WORLD'S GREATEST COMIC MAGAZINE!

# DEADPOOL

## GERRY DUGGAN
### WITH BRIAN POSEHN [#3.1]
writers

## SCOTT KOBLISH
artist

## NICK FILARDI
color artist

---

# TALES OF THE MERCS FOR MONEY

## CULLEN BUNN, BEN ACKER, BEN BLACKER, AMY CHU, TIM SEELEY, MIKE HAWTHORNE and GERRY DUGGAN
writers

## TYLER CROOK, DANILO BEYRUTH, EMILIO LAISO, MIKE NORTON, MIKE HAWTHORNE & TERRY PALLOT and PHIL NOTO
artists

## TYLER CROOK, VERONICA GANDINI, ISRAEL SILVA, JORDIE BELLAIRE and PHIL NOTO
color artists

---

## VC's JOE SABINO
letterer

## FRANCISCO HERRERA & FERNANDO RIZO [#3.1], SCOTT KOBLISH & GURU-eFX [#6] and TONY MOORE [#7]
cover art

---

## HEATHER ANTOS
assistant editor

## JORDAN D. WHITE
editor

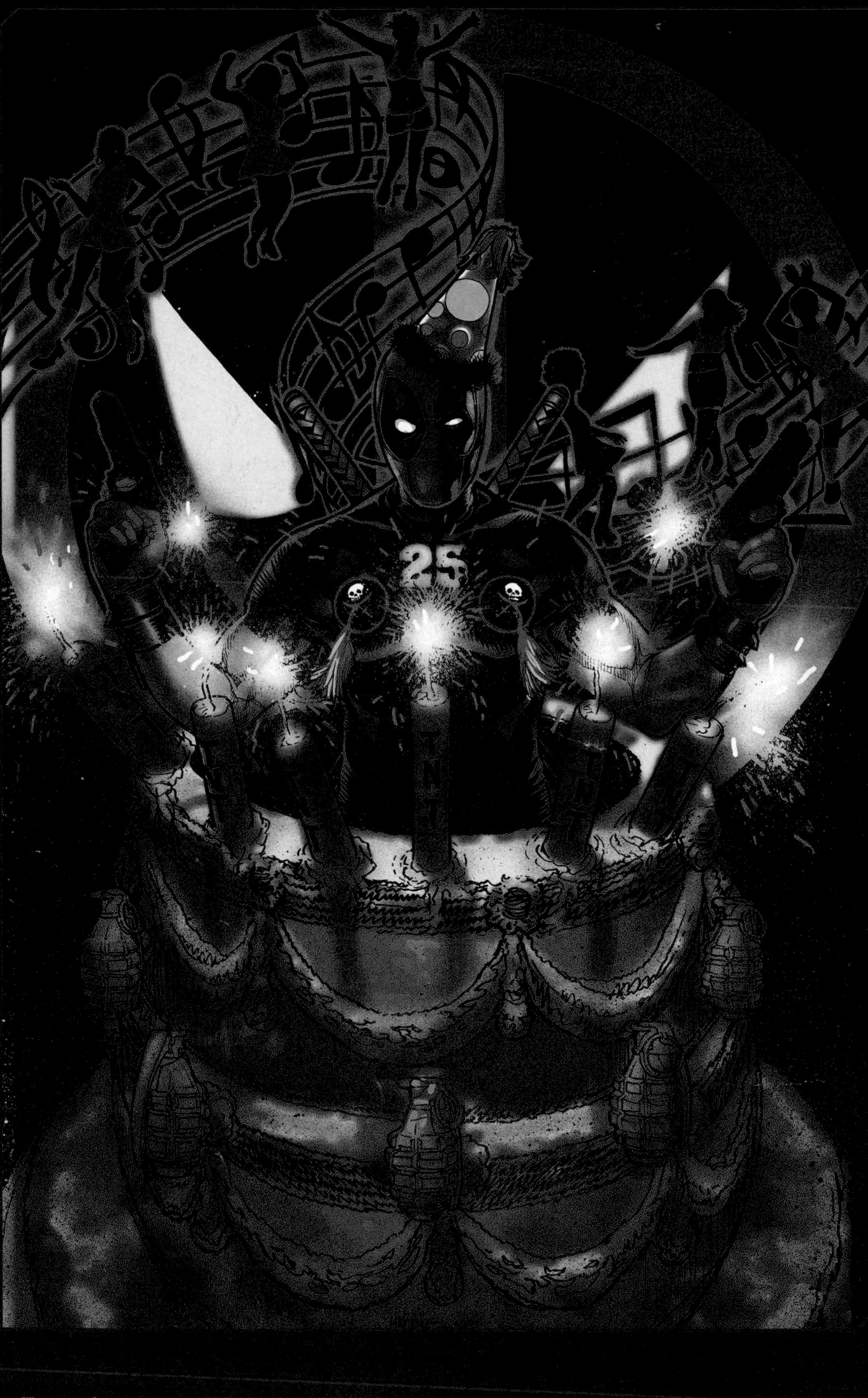
25

#7 variant by TONY HARRIS

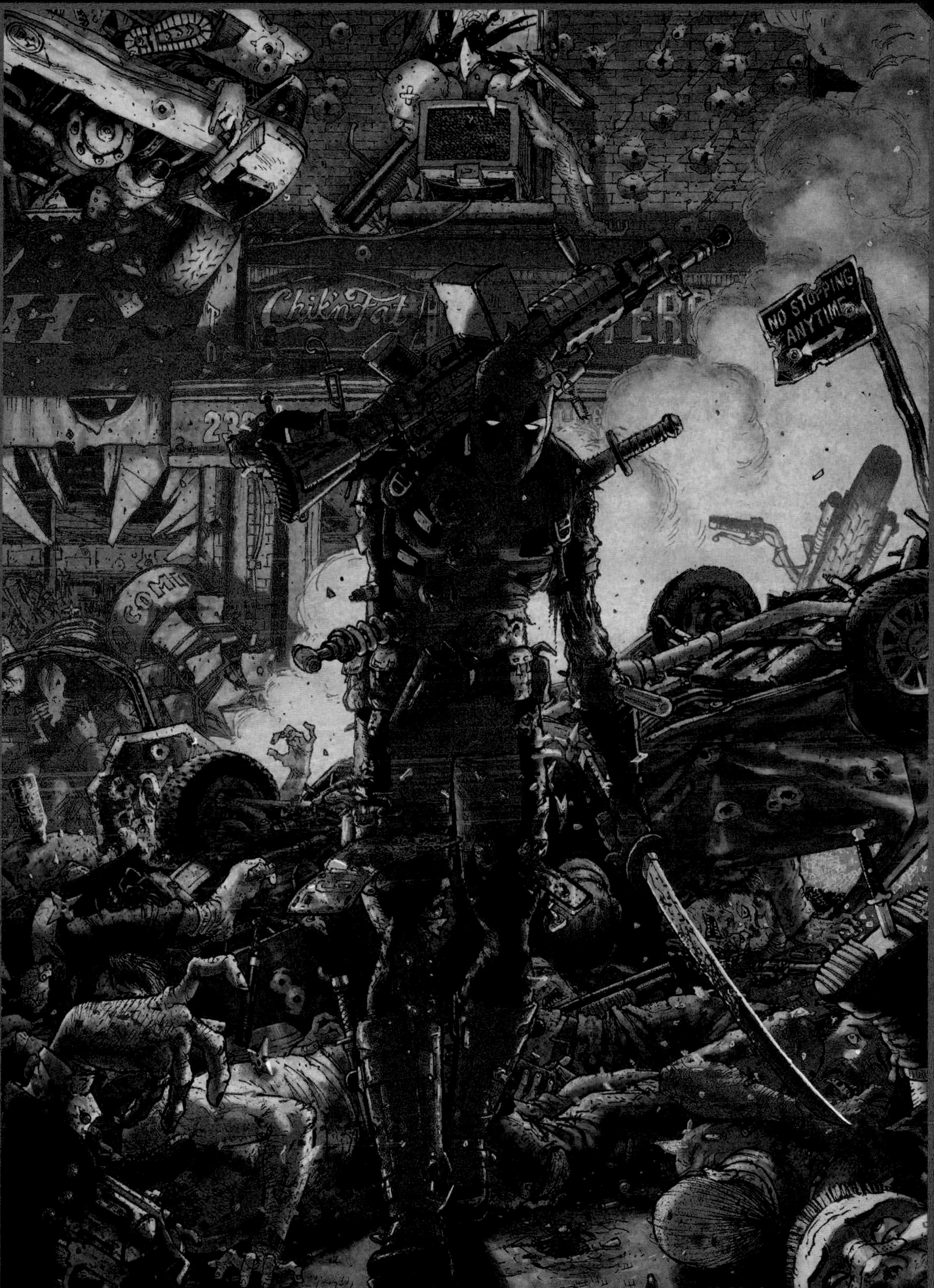
ChiknFat
NO STOPPING ANYTIME

# THE END OF AN ERROR

Avenger...Assassin...Superstar...Smelly person...Possibly the world's most skilled mercenary, definitely the world's most annoying, Wade Wilson was chosen for a top-secret government program that gave him a healing factor allowing him to heal from any wound. Somehow, despite making his money as a gun for hire, Wade has become one of the most beloved "heroes" in the world. Call him the Merc with the Mouth...call him the Regeneratin' Degenerate...call him...

# DEADPOOL

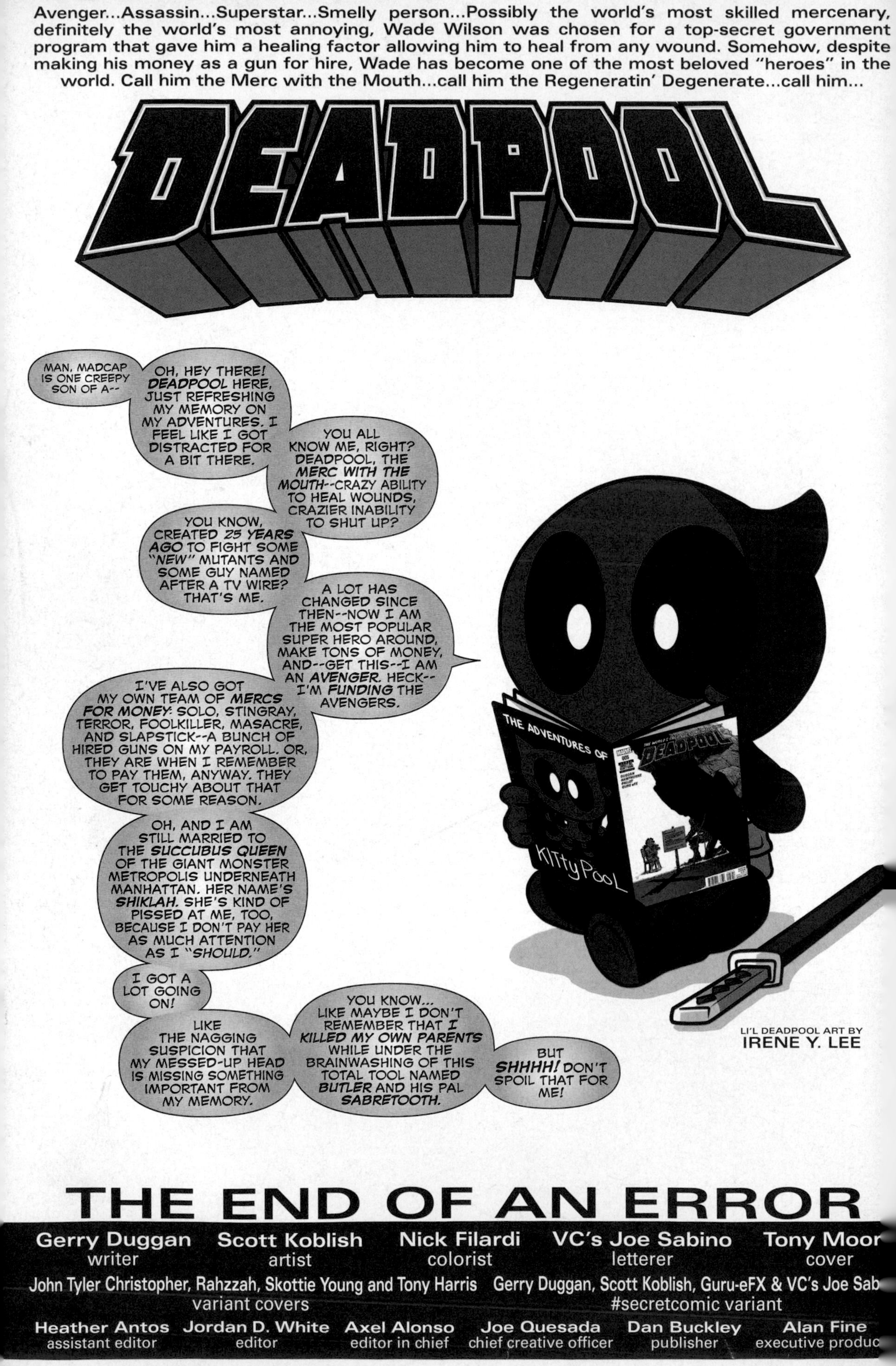

MAN, MADCAP IS ONE CREEPY SON OF A--
OH, HEY THERE! DEADPOOL HERE, JUST REFRESHING MY MEMORY ON MY ADVENTURES. I FEEL LIKE I GOT DISTRACTED FOR A BIT THERE.
YOU ALL KNOW ME, RIGHT? DEADPOOL, THE MERC WITH THE MOUTH--CRAZY ABILITY TO HEAL WOUNDS, CRAZIER INABILITY TO SHUT UP?
YOU KNOW, CREATED 25 YEARS AGO TO FIGHT SOME "NEW" MUTANTS AND SOME GUY NAMED AFTER A TV WIRE? THAT'S ME.
A LOT HAS CHANGED SINCE THEN--NOW I AM THE MOST POPULAR SUPER HERO AROUND, MAKE TONS OF MONEY, AND--GET THIS--I AM AN AVENGER. HECK--I'M FUNDING THE AVENGERS.
I'VE ALSO GOT MY OWN TEAM OF MERCS FOR MONEY: SOLO, STINGRAY, TERROR, FOOLKILLER, MASACRE, AND SLAPSTICK--A BUNCH OF HIRED GUNS ON MY PAYROLL. OR, THEY ARE WHEN I REMEMBER TO PAY THEM, ANYWAY. THEY GET TOUCHY ABOUT THAT FOR SOME REASON.
OH, AND I AM STILL MARRIED TO THE SUCCUBUS QUEEN OF THE GIANT MONSTER METROPOLIS UNDERNEATH MANHATTAN. HER NAME'S SHIKLAH. SHE'S KIND OF PISSED AT ME, TOO, BECAUSE I DON'T PAY HER AS MUCH ATTENTION AS I "SHOULD."
I GOT A LOT GOING ON!
LIKE THE NAGGING SUSPICION THAT MY MESSED-UP HEAD IS MISSING SOMETHING IMPORTANT FROM MY MEMORY.
YOU KNOW... LIKE MAYBE I DON'T REMEMBER THAT I KILLED MY OWN PARENTS WHILE UNDER THE BRAINWASHING OF THIS TOTAL TOOL NAMED BUTLER AND HIS PAL SABRETOOTH.
BUT SHHHH! DON'T SPOIL THAT FOR ME!
THE ADVENTURES OF
KITty PooL
DEADPOOL


LI'L DEADPOOL ART BY
IRENE Y. LEE

# THE END OF AN ERROR

**Gerry Duggan** writer · **Scott Koblish** artist · **Nick Filardi** colorist · **VC's Joe Sabino** letterer · **Tony Moor** cover

John Tyler Christopher, Rahzzah, Skottie Young and Tony Harris variant covers · Gerry Duggan, Scott Koblish, Guru-eFX & VC's Joe Sab #secretcomic variant

**Heather Antos** assistant editor · **Jordan D. White** editor · **Axel Alonso** editor in chief · **Joe Quesada** chief creative officer · **Dan Buckley** publisher · **Alan Fine** executive produc

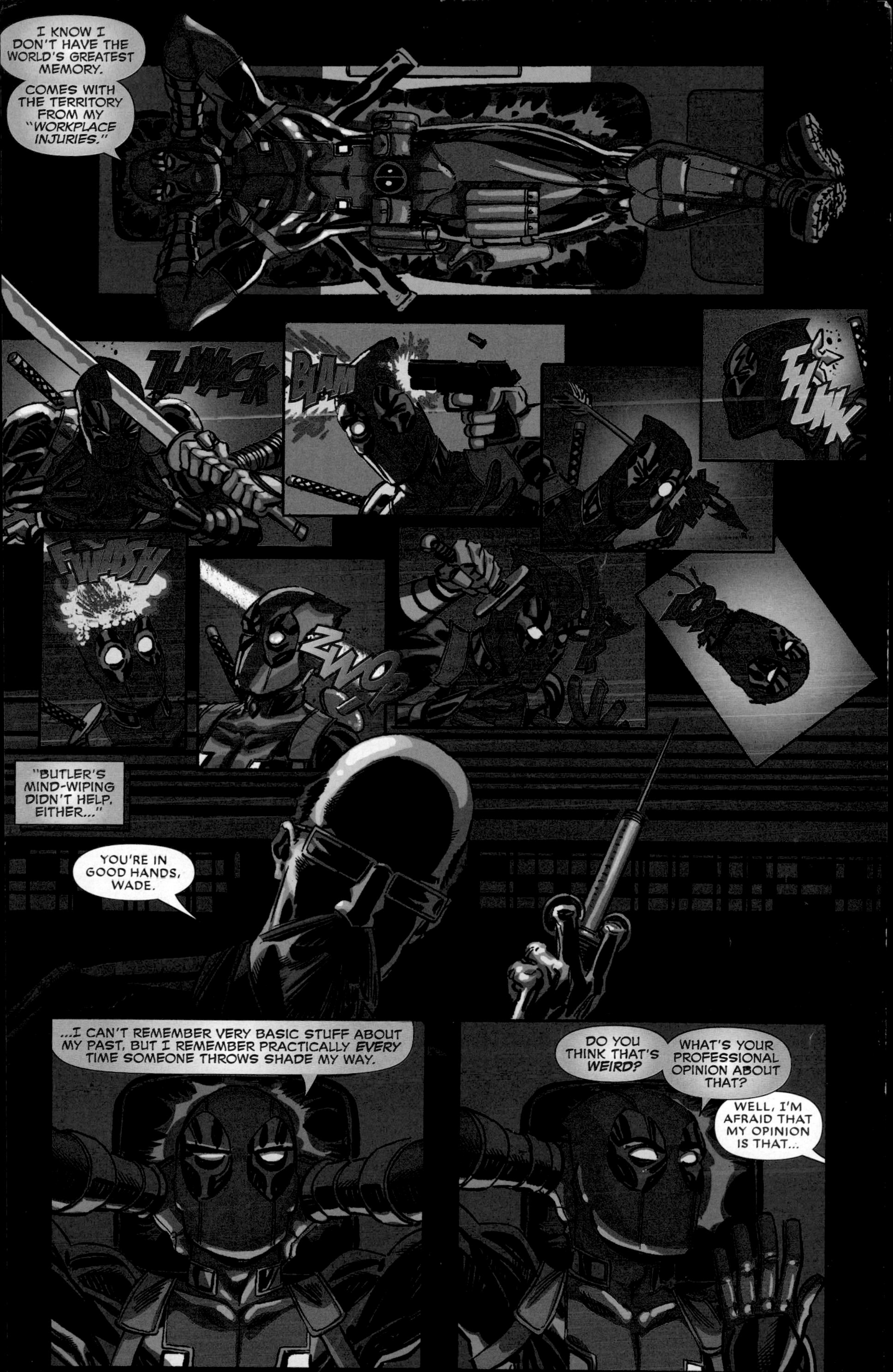
I KNOW I DON'T HAVE THE WORLD'S GREATEST MEMORY.
COMES WITH THE TERRITORY FROM MY "WORKPLACE INJURIES."
THWACK
BLAM
THUNK
FWASH
ZWOP
"BUTLER'S MIND-WIPING DIDN'T HELP, EITHER..."
YOU'RE IN GOOD HANDS, WADE.
...I CAN'T REMEMBER VERY BASIC STUFF ABOUT MY PAST, BUT I REMEMBER PRACTICALLY EVERY TIME SOMEONE THROWS SHADE MY WAY.
DO YOU THINK THAT'S WEIRD?
WHAT'S YOUR PROFESSIONAL OPINION ABOUT THAT?
WELL, I'M AFRAID THAT MY OPINION IS THAT...

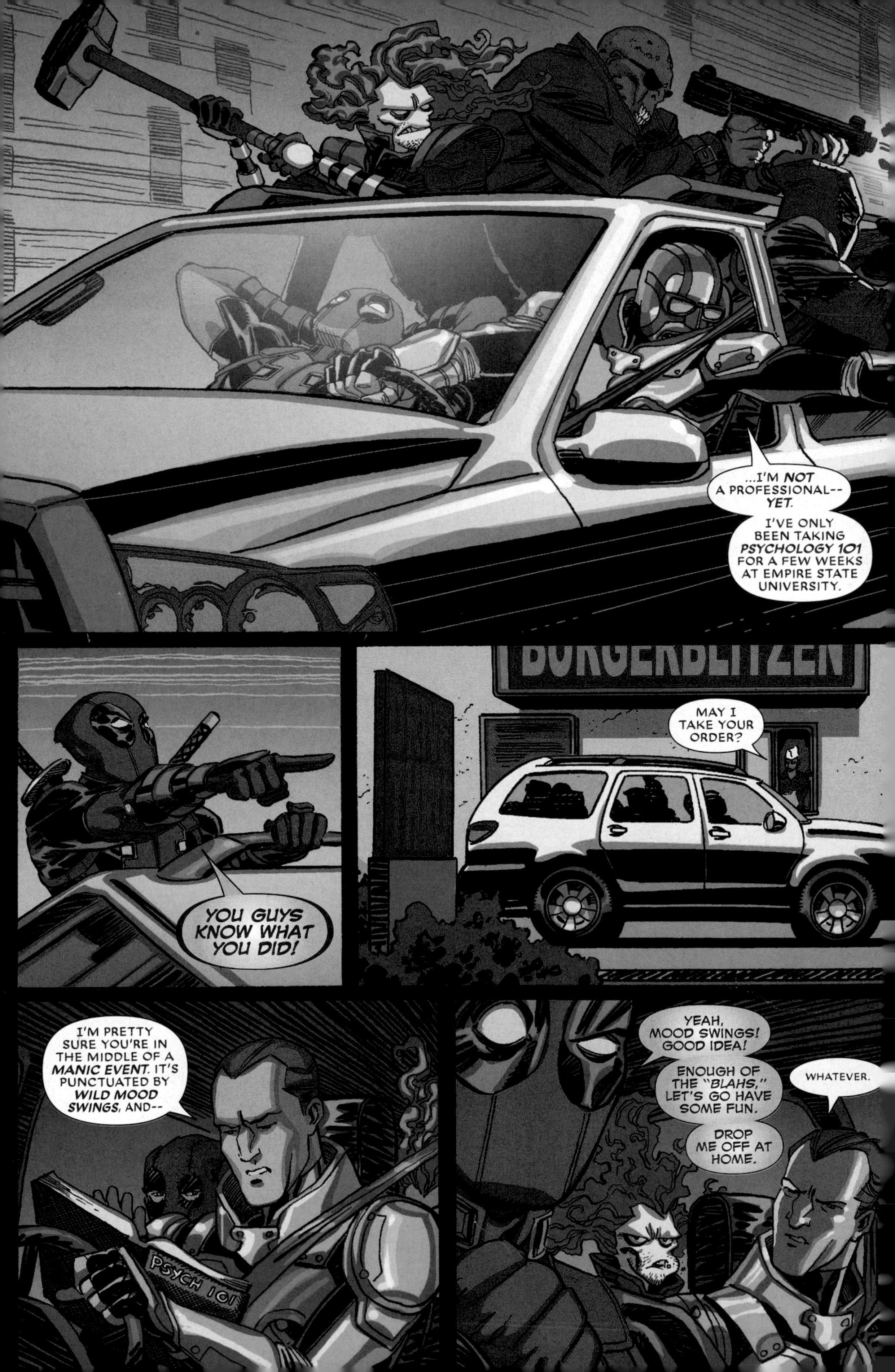
...I'M NOT A PROFESSIONAL-- YET.
I'VE ONLY BEEN TAKING PSYCHOLOGY 101 FOR A FEW WEEKS AT EMPIRE STATE UNIVERSITY.
YOU GUYS KNOW WHAT YOU DID!
BURGERBLITZEN
MAY I TAKE YOUR ORDER?
I'M PRETTY SURE YOU'RE IN THE MIDDLE OF A MANIC EVENT. IT'S PUNCTUATED BY WILD MOOD SWINGS, AND--
PSYCH 101
YEAH, MOOD SWINGS! GOOD IDEA!
ENOUGH OF THE "BLAHS," LET'S GO HAVE SOME FUN.
DROP ME OFF AT HOME.
WHATEVER.

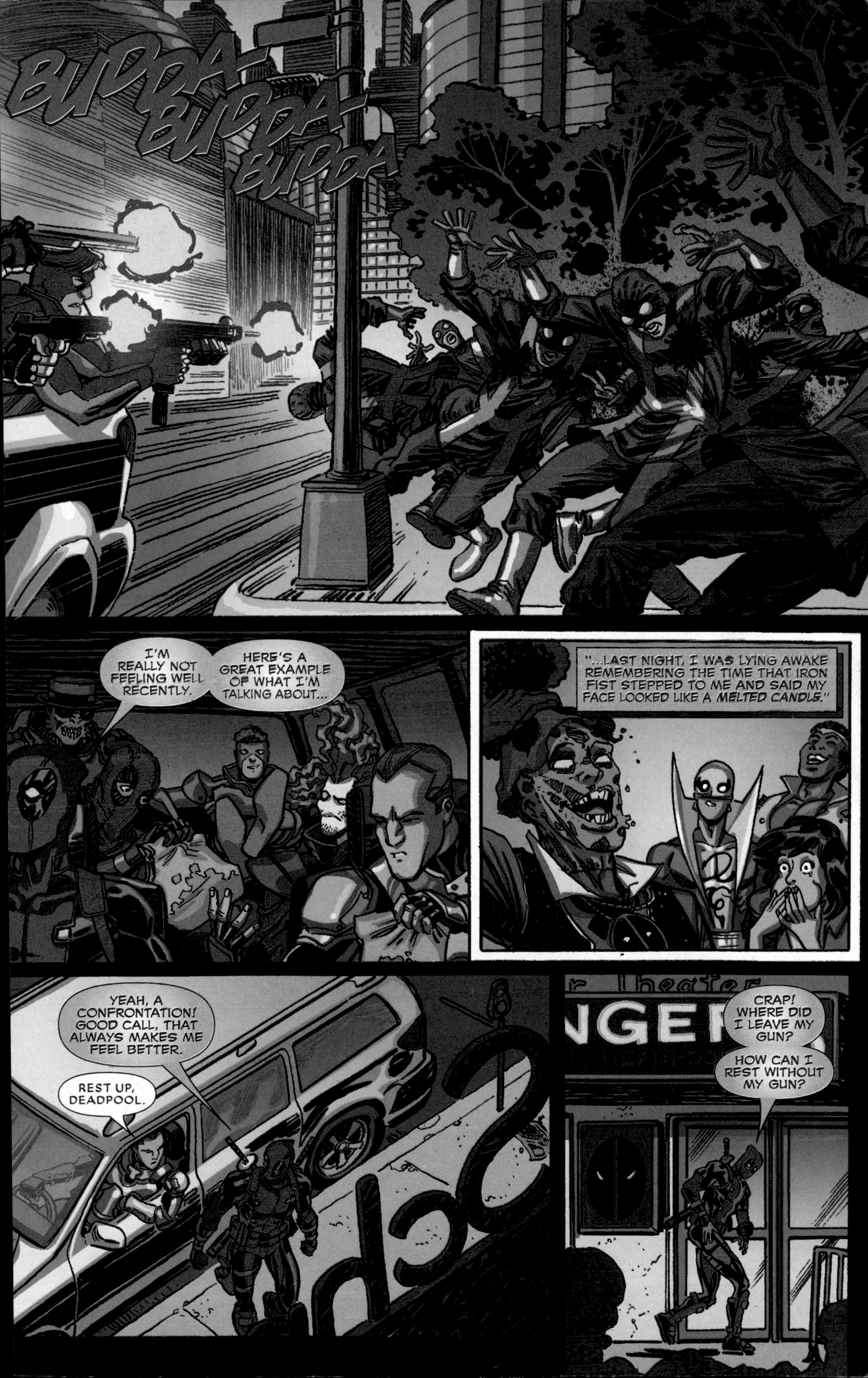
BUDDA-BUDDA-BUDDA
I'M REALLY NOT FEELING WELL RECENTLY.
HERE'S A GREAT EXAMPLE OF WHAT I'M TALKING ABOUT...
"...LAST NIGHT, I WAS LYING AWAKE REMEMBERING THE TIME THAT IRON FIST STEPPED TO ME AND SAID MY FACE LOOKED LIKE A MELTED CANDLE."
YEAH, A CONFRONTATION! GOOD CALL, THAT ALWAYS MAKES ME FEEL BETTER.
REST UP, DEADPOOL.
CRAP! WHERE DID I LEAVE MY GUN?
HOW CAN I REST WITHOUT MY GUN?

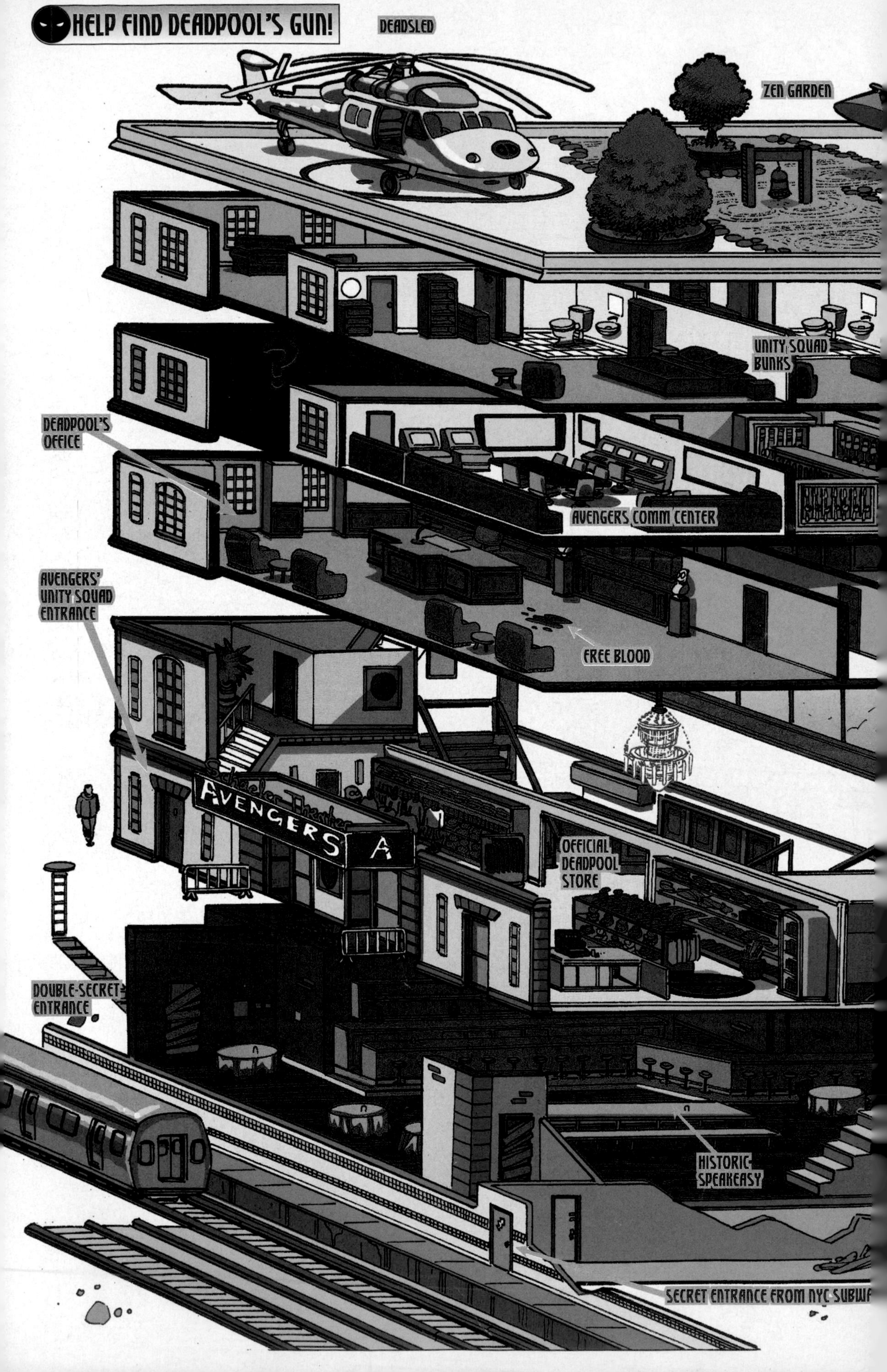
HELP FIND DEADPOOL'S GUN!
DEADSLED
ZEN GARDEN
UNITY SQUAD BUNKS
DEADPOOL'S OFFICE
AVENGERS COMM CENTER
AVENGERS' UNITY SQUAD ENTRANCE
FREE BLOOD
AVENGERS
A
OFFICIAL DEADPOOL STORE
DOUBLE-SECRET ENTRANCE
HISTORIC SPEAKEASY
SECRET ENTRANCE FROM NYC SUBWA

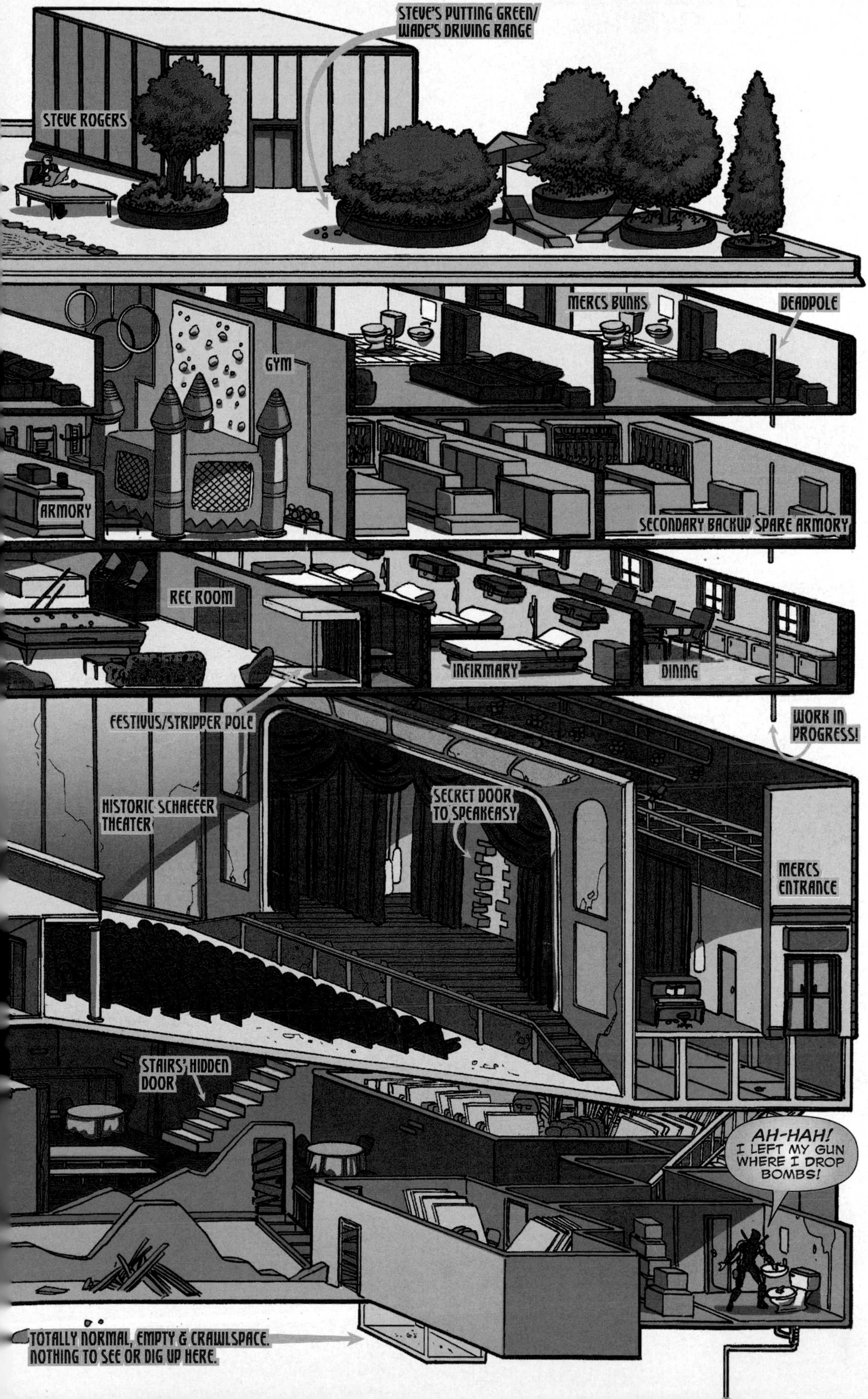
STEVE'S PUTTING GREEN/
WADE'S DRIVING RANGE
STEVE ROGERS
MERCS BUNKS
DEADPOLE
GYM
ARMORY
SECONDARY BACKUP SPARE ARMORY
REC ROOM
INFIRMARY
DINING
FESTIVUS/STRIPPER POLE
WORK IN PROGRESS!
HISTORIC SCHAEFER THEATER
SECRET DOOR TO SPEAKEASY
MERCS ENTRANCE
STAIRS' HIDDEN DOOR
AH-HAH! I LEFT MY GUN WHERE I DROP BOMBS!
TOTALLY NORMAL, EMPTY & CRAWLSPACE.
NOTHING TO SEE OR DIG UP HERE.

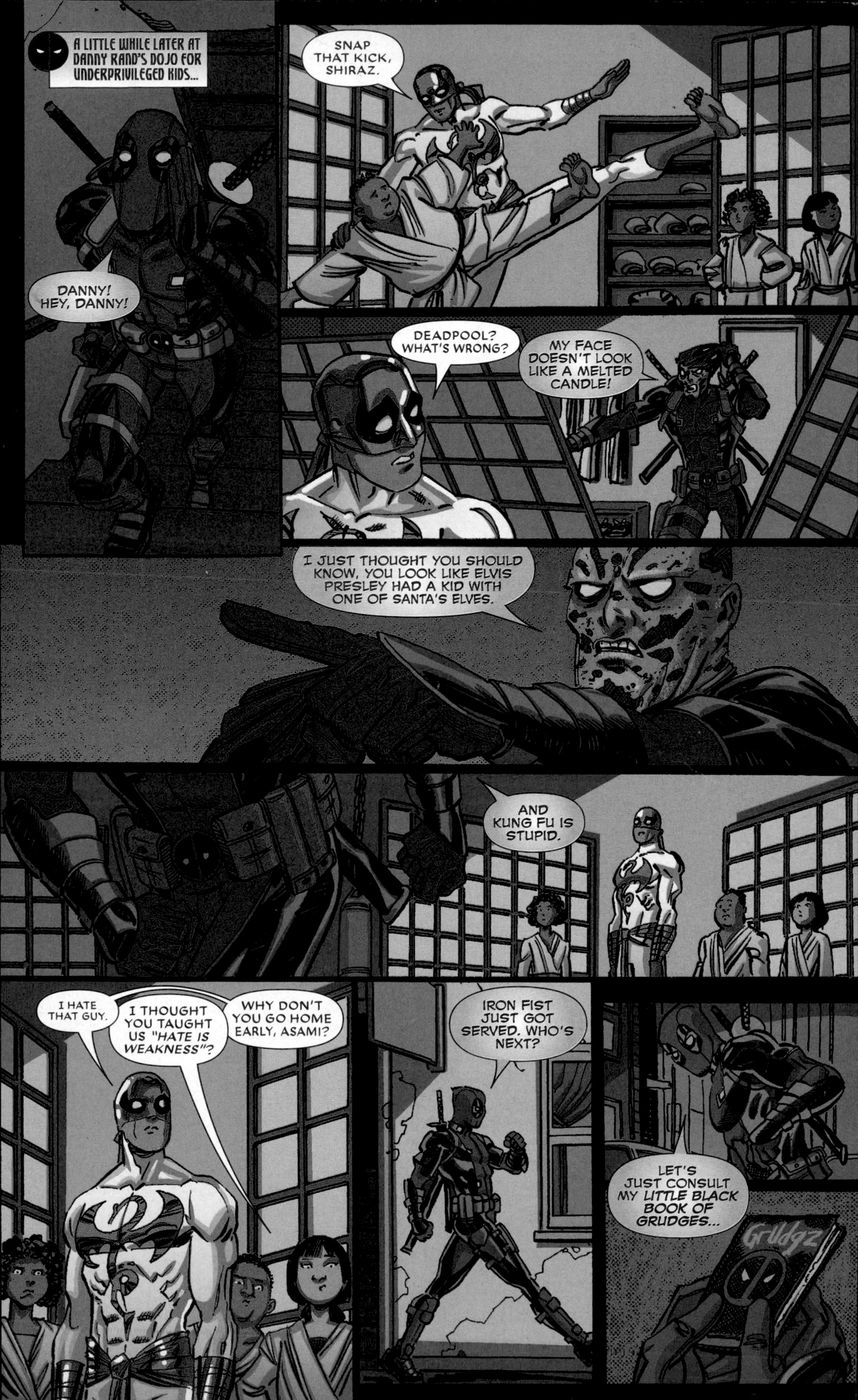
A LITTLE WHILE LATER AT DANNY RAND'S DOJO FOR UNDERPRIVILEGED KIDS...
DANNY! HEY, DANNY!
SNAP THAT KICK, SHIRAZ.
DEADPOOL? WHAT'S WRONG?
MY FACE DOESN'T LOOK LIKE A MELTED CANDLE!
I JUST THOUGHT YOU SHOULD KNOW, YOU LOOK LIKE ELVIS PRESLEY HAD A KID WITH ONE OF SANTA'S ELVES.
AND KUNG FU IS STUPID.
I HATE THAT GUY.
I THOUGHT YOU TAUGHT US "HATE IS WEAKNESS"?
WHY DON'T YOU GO HOME EARLY, ASAMI?
IRON FIST JUST GOT SERVED. WHO'S NEXT?
LET'S JUST CONSULT MY LITTLE BLACK BOOK OF GRUDGES...
GRUDGZ

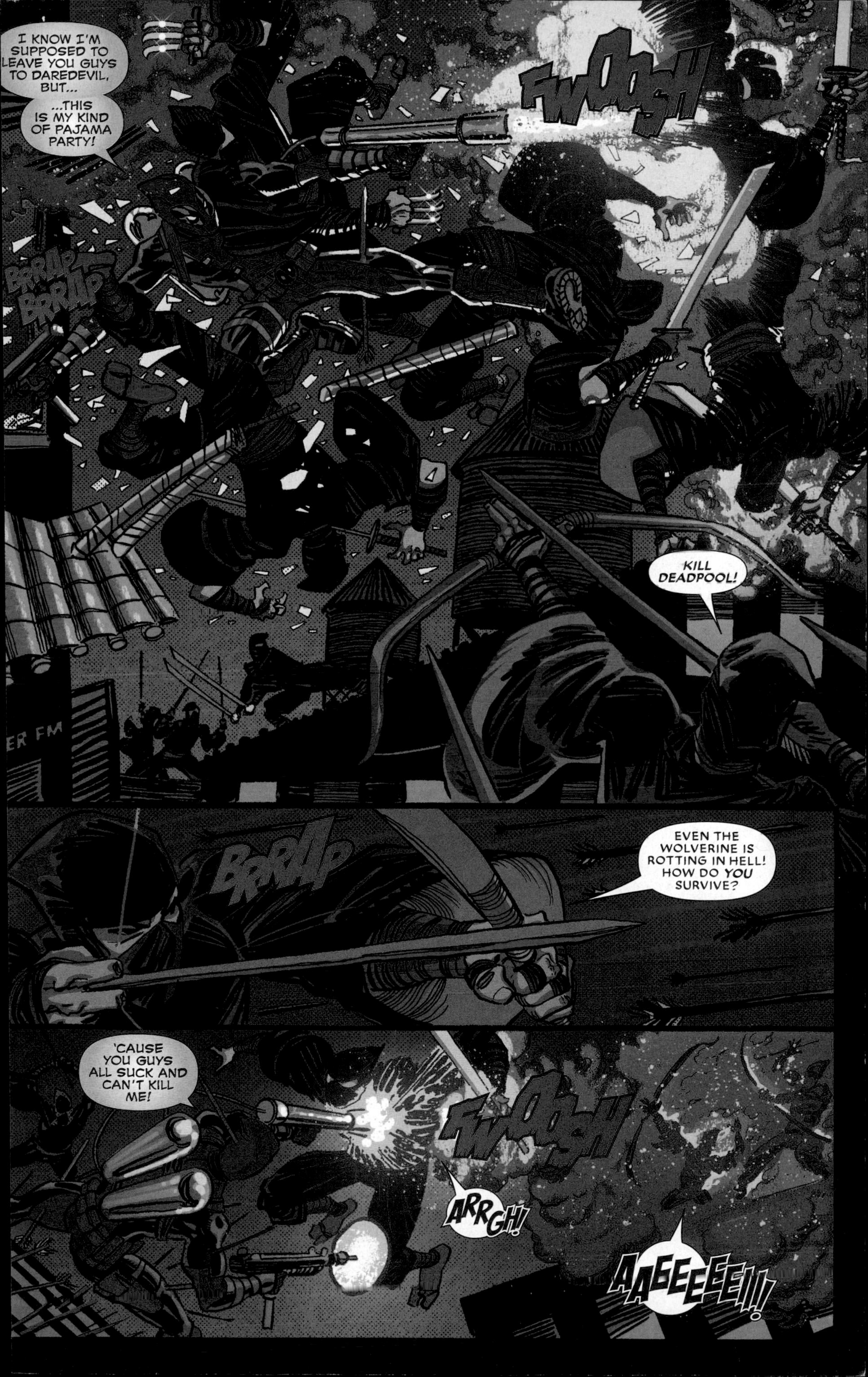
I KNOW I'M SUPPOSED TO LEAVE YOU GUYS TO DAREDEVIL, BUT...
...THIS IS MY KIND OF PAJAMA PARTY!
FWOOSH
BRRAP BRRAP
KILL DEADPOOL!
ER FM
BRRAP
EVEN THE WOLVERINE IS ROTTING IN HELL! HOW DO YOU SURVIVE?
'CAUSE YOU GUYS ALL SUCK AND CAN'T KILL ME!
FWOOSH
ARRGH!
AAEEEEE!!!

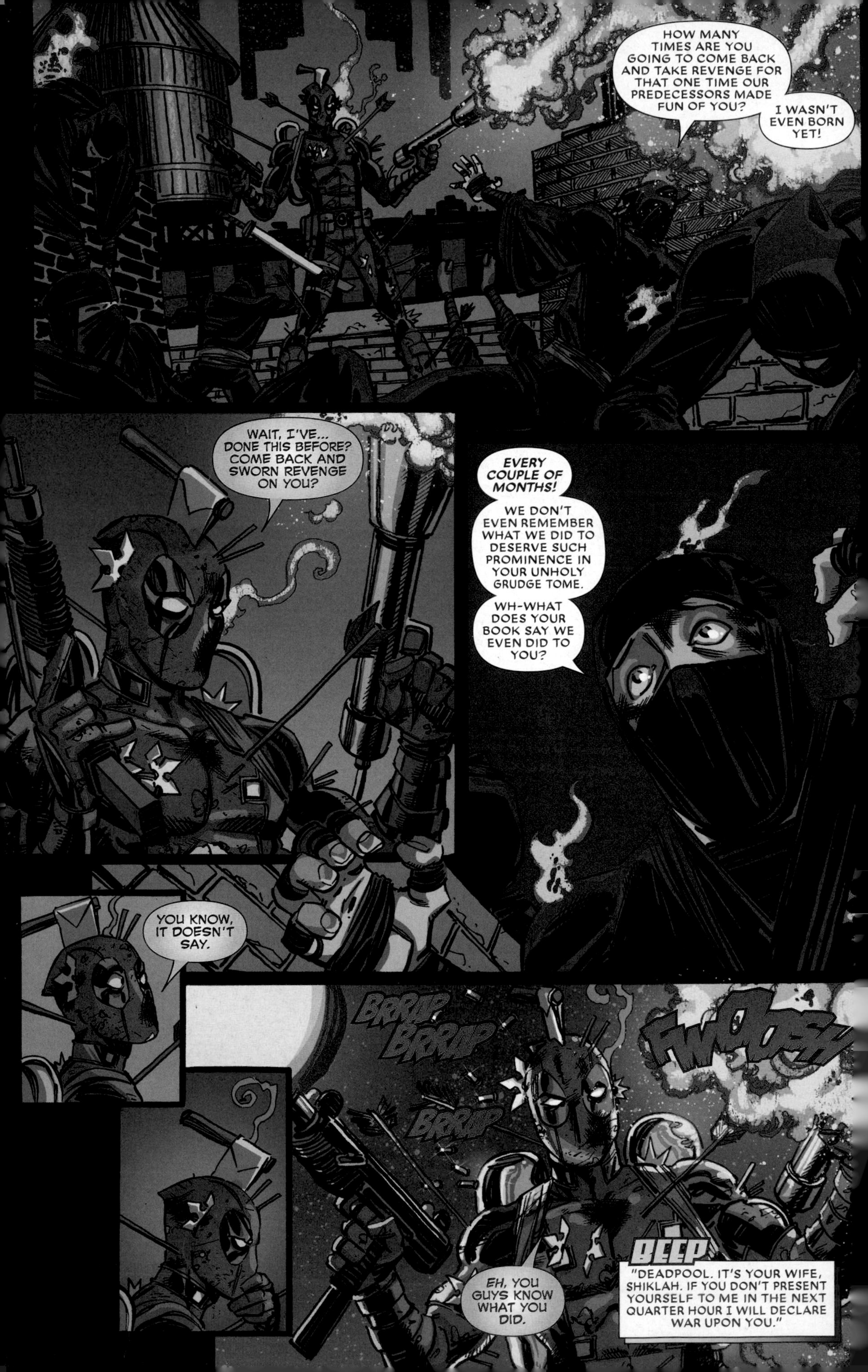
HOW MANY TIMES ARE YOU GOING TO COME BACK AND TAKE REVENGE FOR THAT ONE TIME OUR PREDECESSORS MADE FUN OF YOU?
I WASN'T EVEN BORN YET!
WAIT, I'VE... DONE THIS BEFORE? COME BACK AND SWORN REVENGE ON YOU?
EVERY COUPLE OF MONTHS!
WE DON'T EVEN REMEMBER WHAT WE DID TO DESERVE SUCH PROMINENCE IN YOUR UNHOLY GRUDGE TOME.
WH-WHAT DOES YOUR BOOK SAY WE EVEN DID TO YOU?
YOU KNOW, IT DOESN'T SAY.
BRRAP BRRAP
FWOOSH
BRRAP
EH, YOU GUYS KNOW WHAT YOU DID.
BEEP
"DEADPOOL. IT'S YOUR WIFE, SHIKLAH. IF YOU DON'T PRESENT YOURSELF TO ME IN THE NEXT QUARTER HOUR I WILL DECLARE WAR UPON YOU."

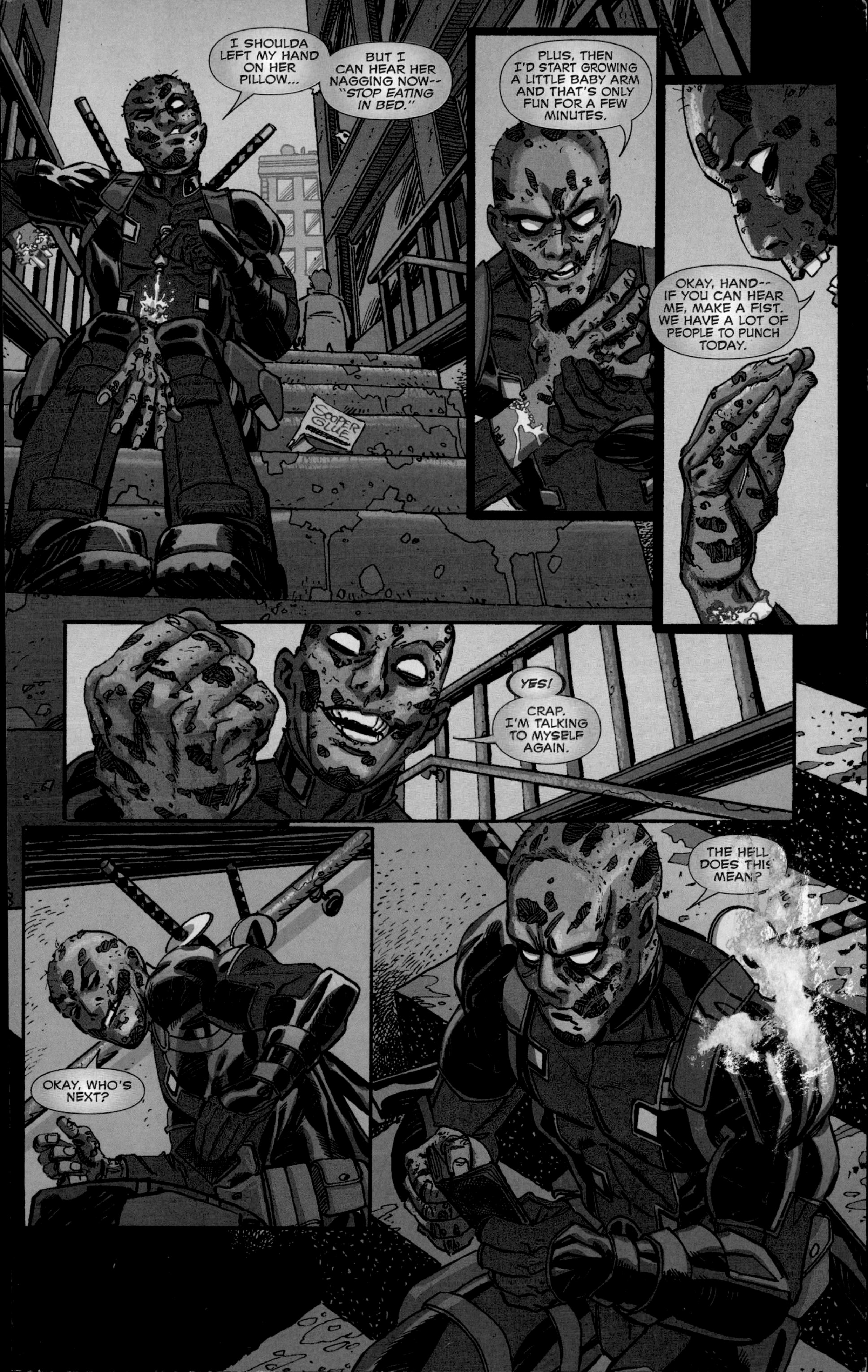
I SHOULDA LEFT MY HAND ON HER PILLOW...
BUT I CAN HEAR HER NAGGING NOW-- "STOP EATING IN BED."
SOOPER GLUE
PLUS, THEN I'D START GROWING A LITTLE BABY ARM AND THAT'S ONLY FUN FOR A FEW MINUTES.
OKAY, HAND-- IF YOU CAN HEAR ME, MAKE A FIST. WE HAVE A LOT OF PEOPLE TO PUNCH TODAY.
YES!
CRAP. I'M TALKING TO MYSELF AGAIN.
OKAY, WHO'S NEXT?
THE HELL DOES THIS MEAN?

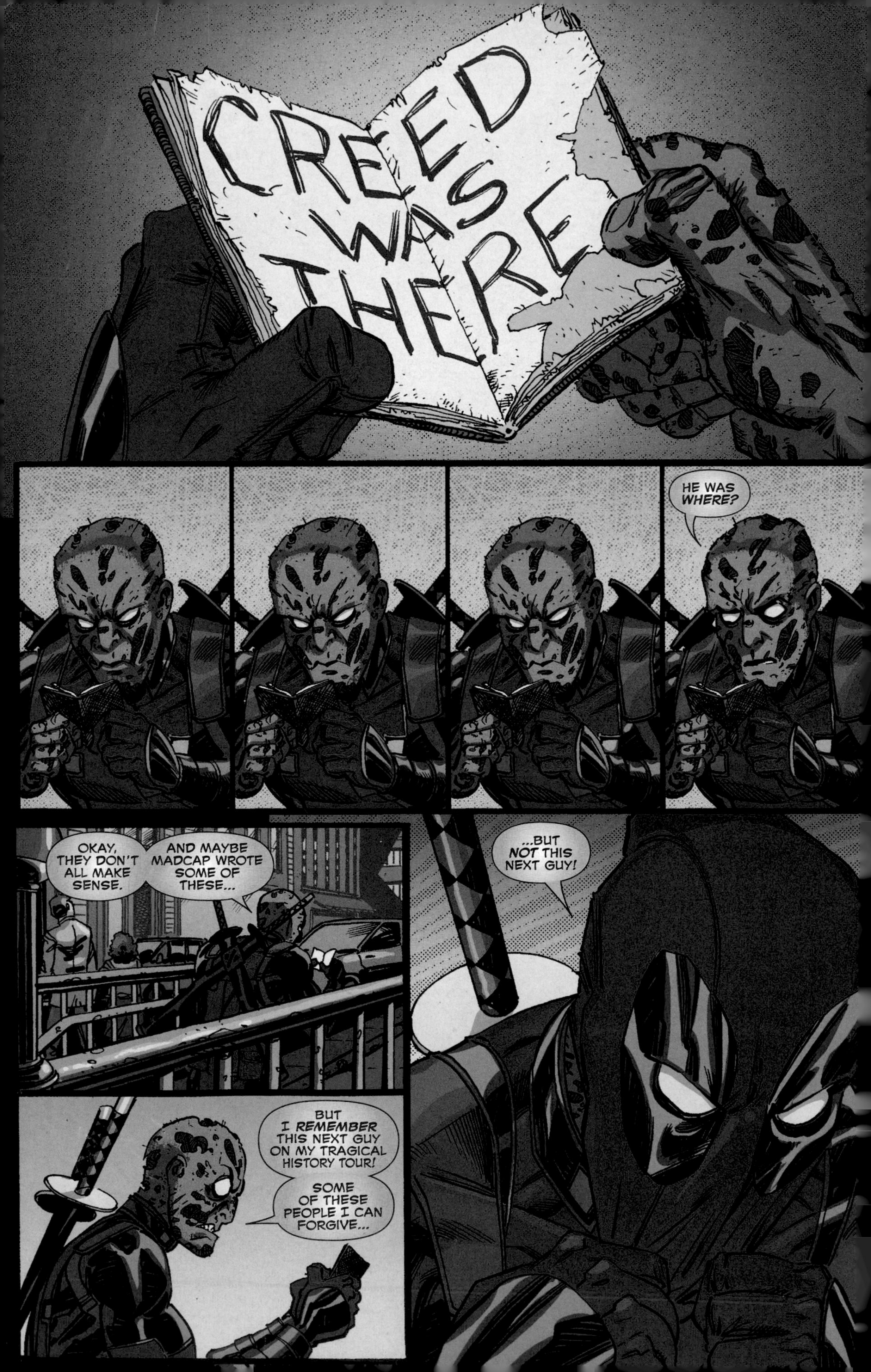
CREED WAS THERE
HE WAS WHERE?
OKAY, THEY DON'T ALL MAKE SENSE.
AND MAYBE MADCAP WROTE SOME OF THESE...
BUT I REMEMBER THIS NEXT GUY ON MY TRAGICAL HISTORY TOUR!
SOME OF THESE PEOPLE I CAN FORGIVE...
...BUT NOT THIS NEXT GUY!

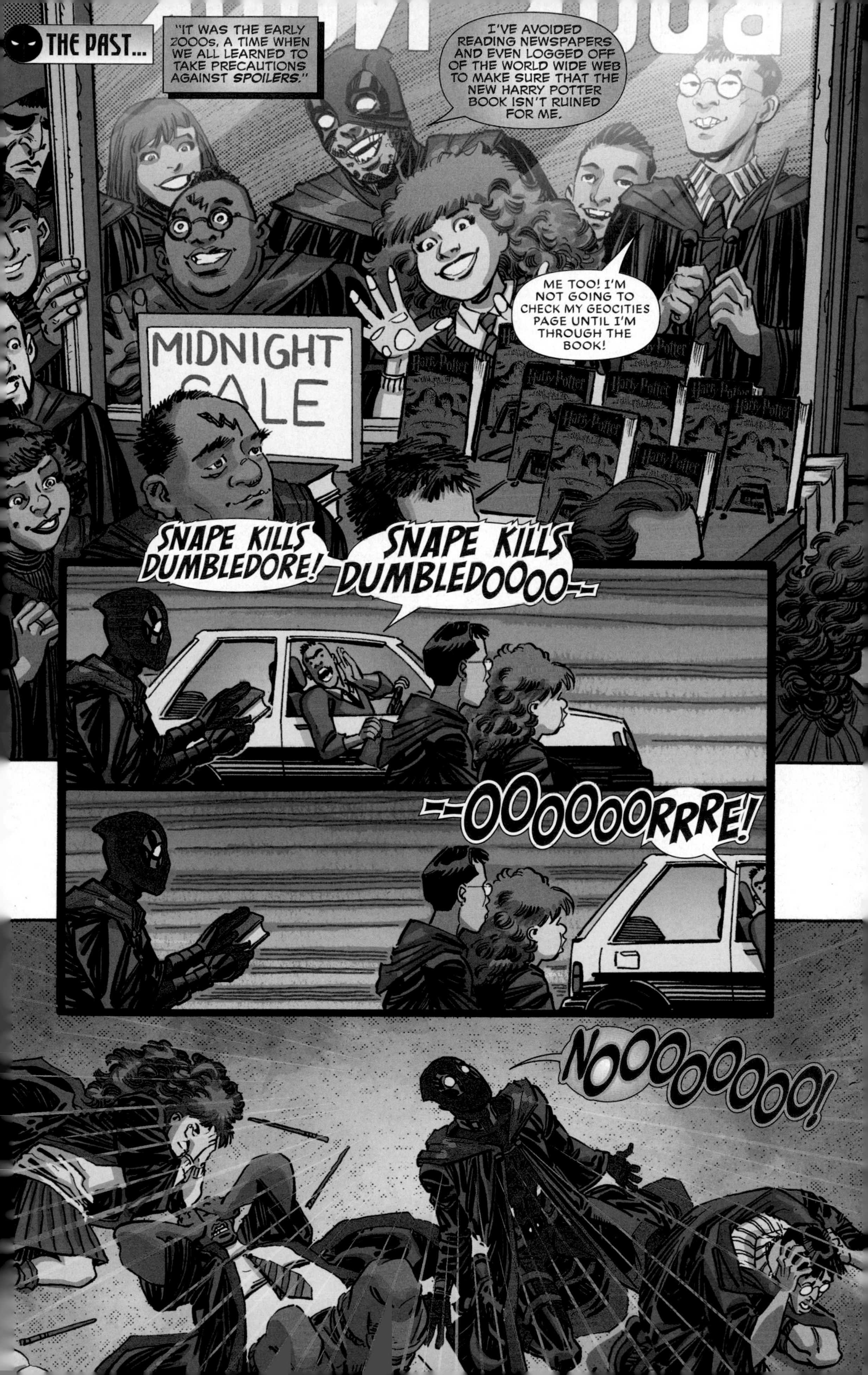
THE PAST...
"IT WAS THE EARLY 2000s, A TIME WHEN WE ALL LEARNED TO TAKE PRECAUTIONS AGAINST SPOILERS."
I'VE AVOIDED READING NEWSPAPERS AND EVEN LOGGED OFF OF THE WORLD WIDE WEB TO MAKE SURE THAT THE NEW HARRY POTTER BOOK ISN'T RUINED FOR ME.
ME TOO! I'M NOT GOING TO CHECK MY GEOCITIES PAGE UNTIL I'M THROUGH THE BOOK!
MIDNIGHT SALE
Harry Potter
SNAPE KILLS DUMBLEDORE!
SNAPE KILLS DUMBLEDOOOO--
--OOOOOOORRRE!
NOOOOOOOOO!

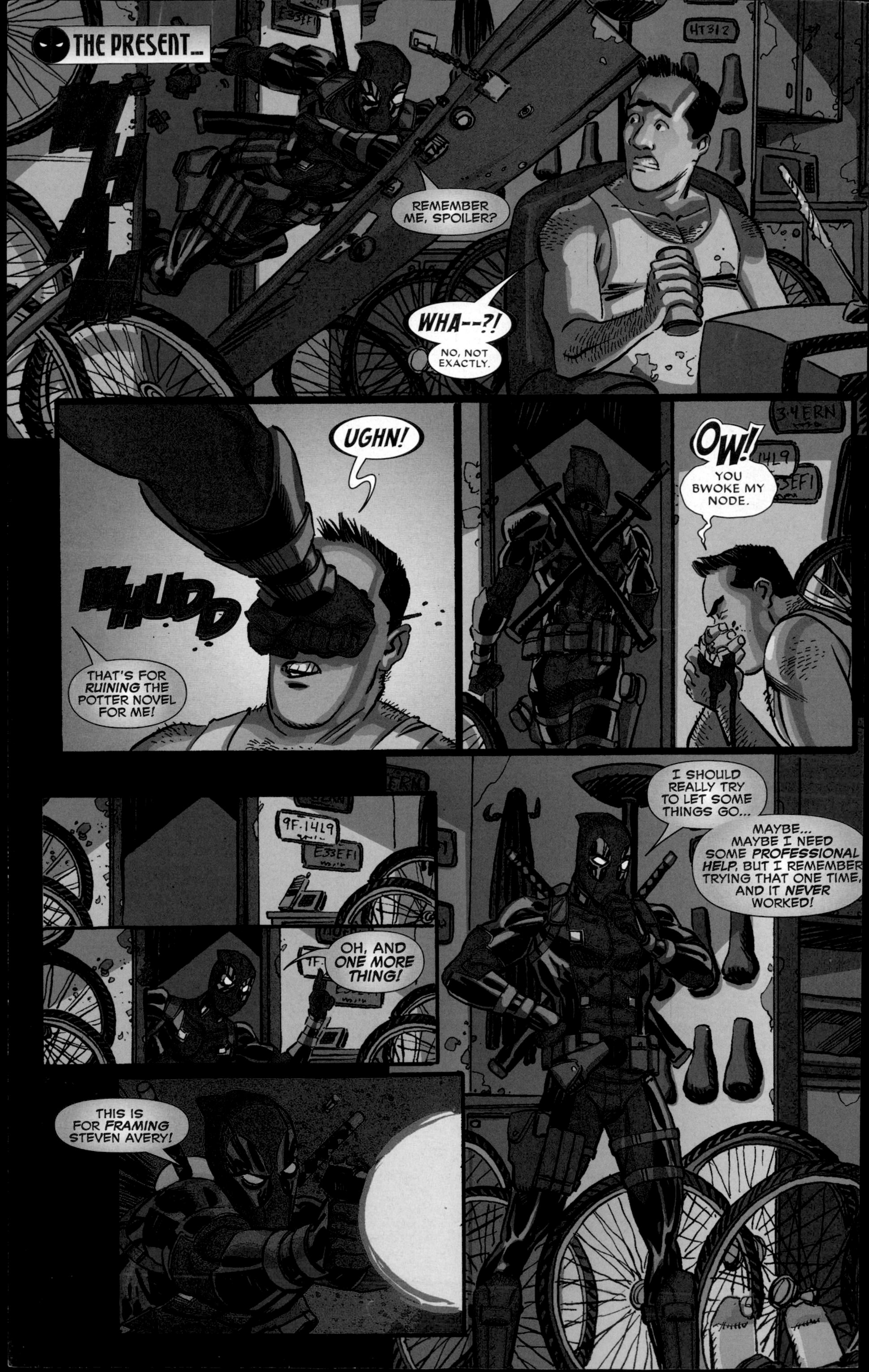
THE PRESENT...
REMEMBER ME, SPOILER?
WHA--?!
NO, NOT EXACTLY.
UGHN!
THAT'S FOR *RUINING* THE POTTER NOVEL FOR ME!
OW!
YOU BWOKE MY NODE.
OH, AND *ONE MORE THING!*
THIS IS FOR *FRAMING* STEVEN AVERY!
I SHOULD REALLY TRY TO LET SOME THINGS GO...
MAYBE... MAYBE I NEED SOME *PROFESSIONAL HELP*, BUT I REMEMBER TRYING THAT ONE TIME, AND IT *NEVER* WORKED!

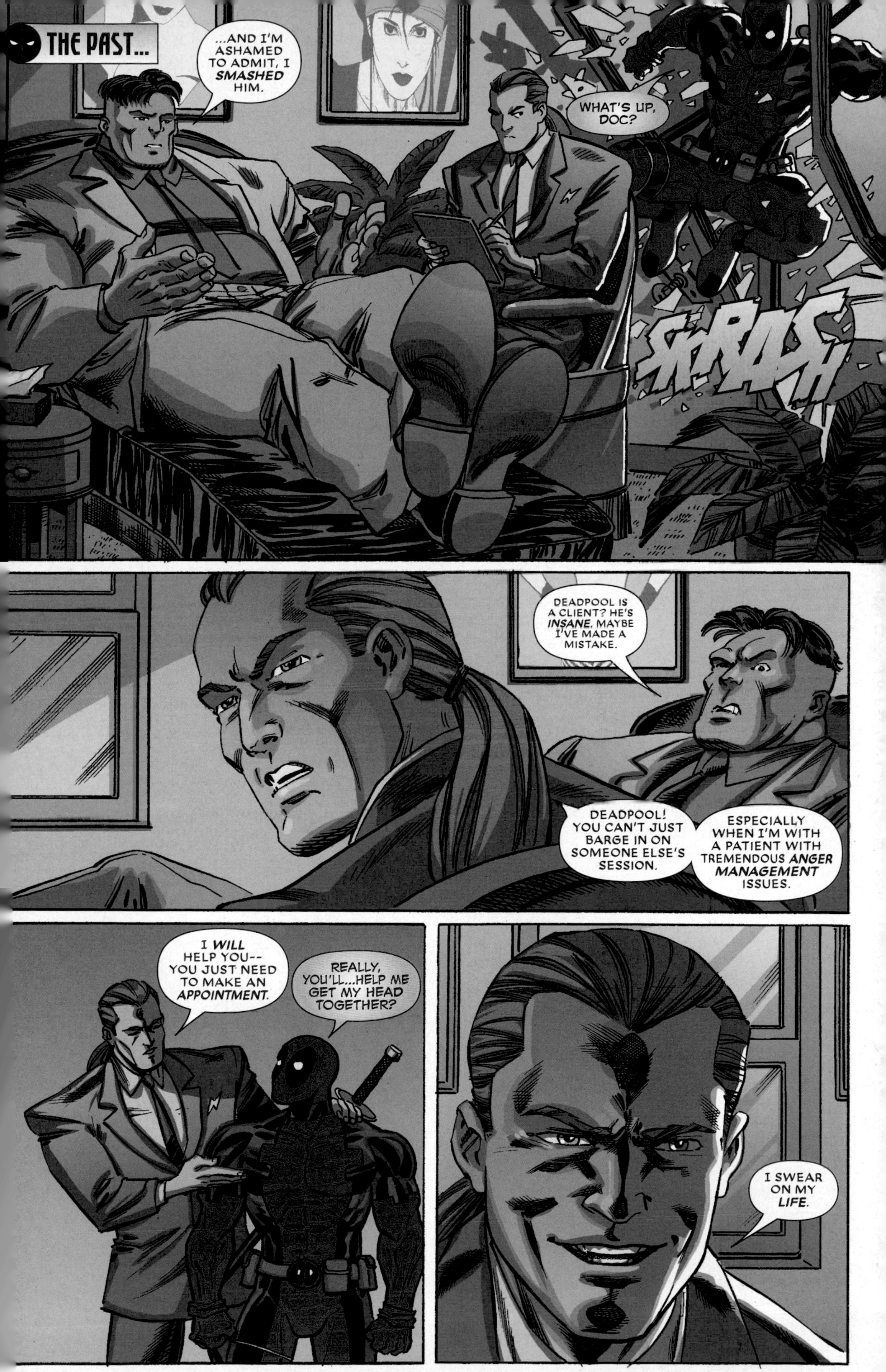
THE PAST...
...AND I'M ASHAMED TO ADMIT, I SMASHED HIM.
WHAT'S UP, DOC?
SKRASH
DEADPOOL IS A CLIENT? HE'S INSANE. MAYBE I'VE MADE A MISTAKE.
DEADPOOL! YOU CAN'T JUST BARGE IN ON SOMEONE ELSE'S SESSION.
ESPECIALLY WHEN I'M WITH A PATIENT WITH TREMENDOUS ANGER MANAGEMENT ISSUES.
I WILL HELP YOU-- YOU JUST NEED TO MAKE AN APPOINTMENT.
REALLY, YOU'LL...HELP ME GET MY HEAD TOGETHER?
I SWEAR ON MY LIFE.

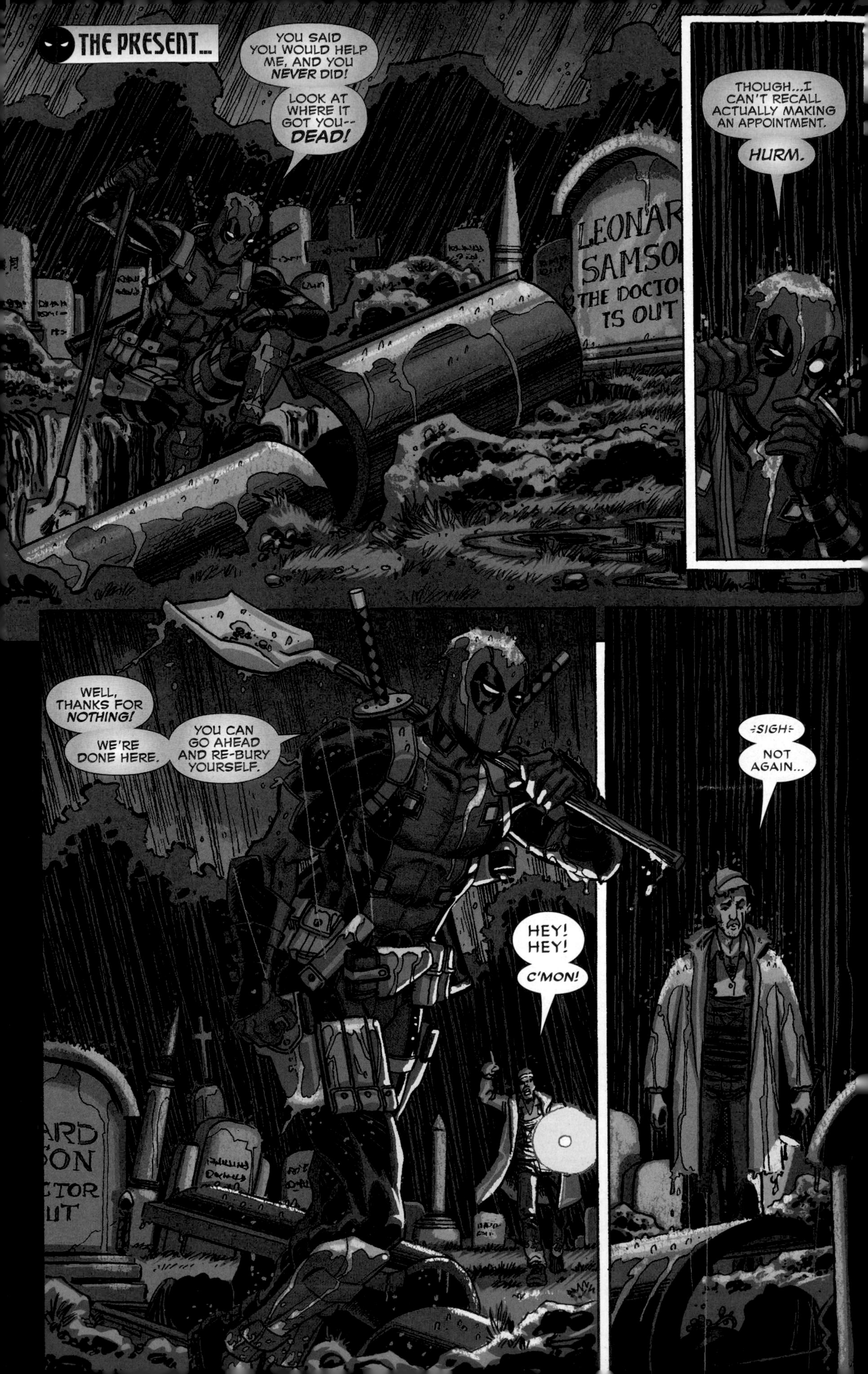
THE PRESENT...
YOU SAID YOU WOULD HELP ME, AND YOU NEVER DID!
LOOK AT WHERE IT GOT YOU-- DEAD!
LEONAR SAMSO THE DOCTO IS OUT
THOUGH...I CAN'T RECALL ACTUALLY MAKING AN APPOINTMENT.
HURM.
WELL, THANKS FOR NOTHING!
WE'RE DONE HERE.
YOU CAN GO AHEAD AND RE-BURY YOURSELF.
HEY! HEY!
C'MON!
ARD SON CTOR UT
=SIGH=
NOT AGAIN...

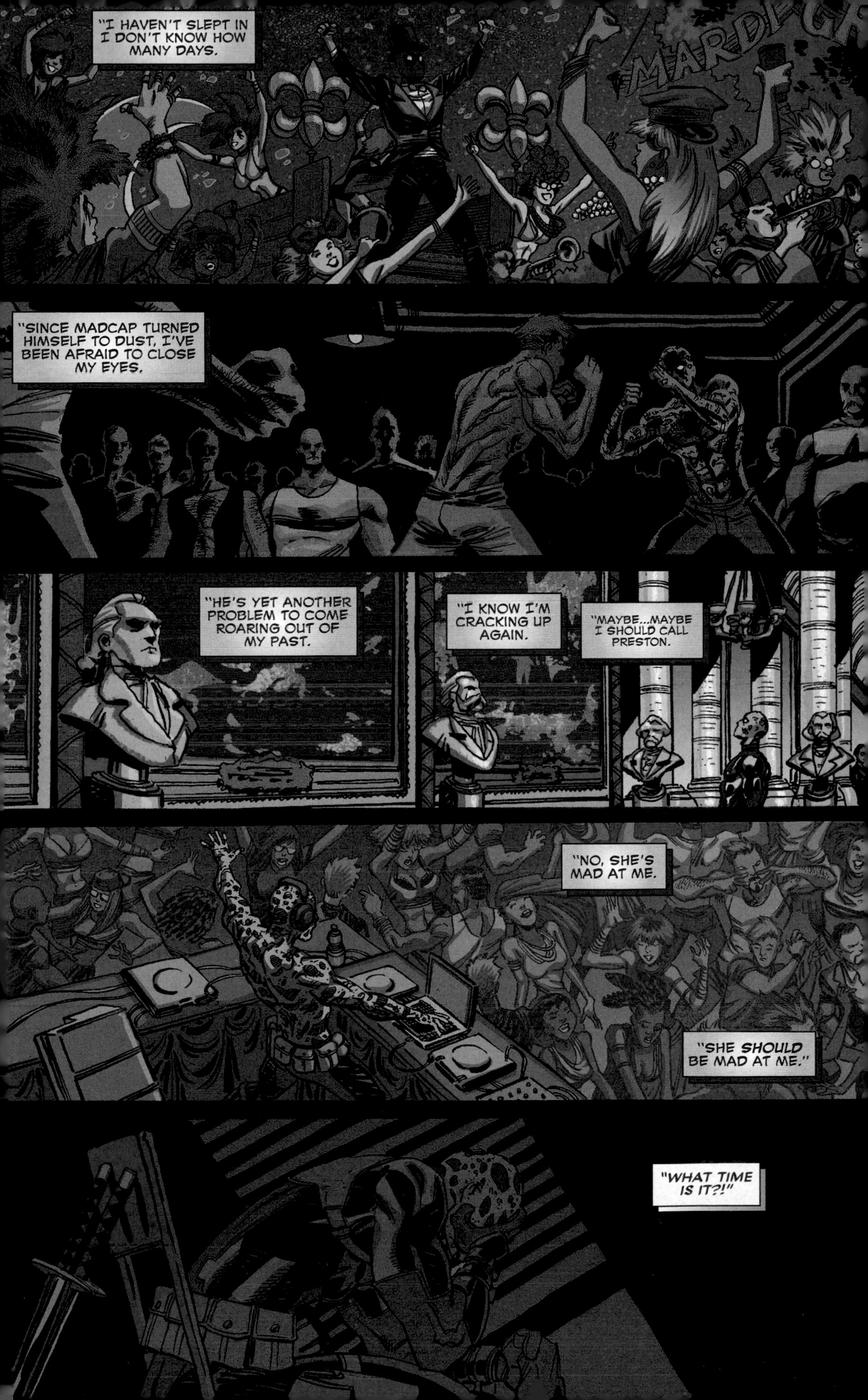
"I HAVEN'T SLEPT IN I DON'T KNOW HOW MANY DAYS.
MARDI GR
"SINCE MADCAP TURNED HIMSELF TO DUST, I'VE BEEN AFRAID TO CLOSE MY EYES.
"HE'S YET ANOTHER PROBLEM TO COME ROARING OUT OF MY PAST.
"I KNOW I'M CRACKING UP AGAIN.
"MAYBE...MAYBE I SHOULD CALL PRESTON.
"NO, SHE'S MAD AT ME.
"SHE *SHOULD* BE MAD AT ME."
*"WHAT TIME IS IT?!"*

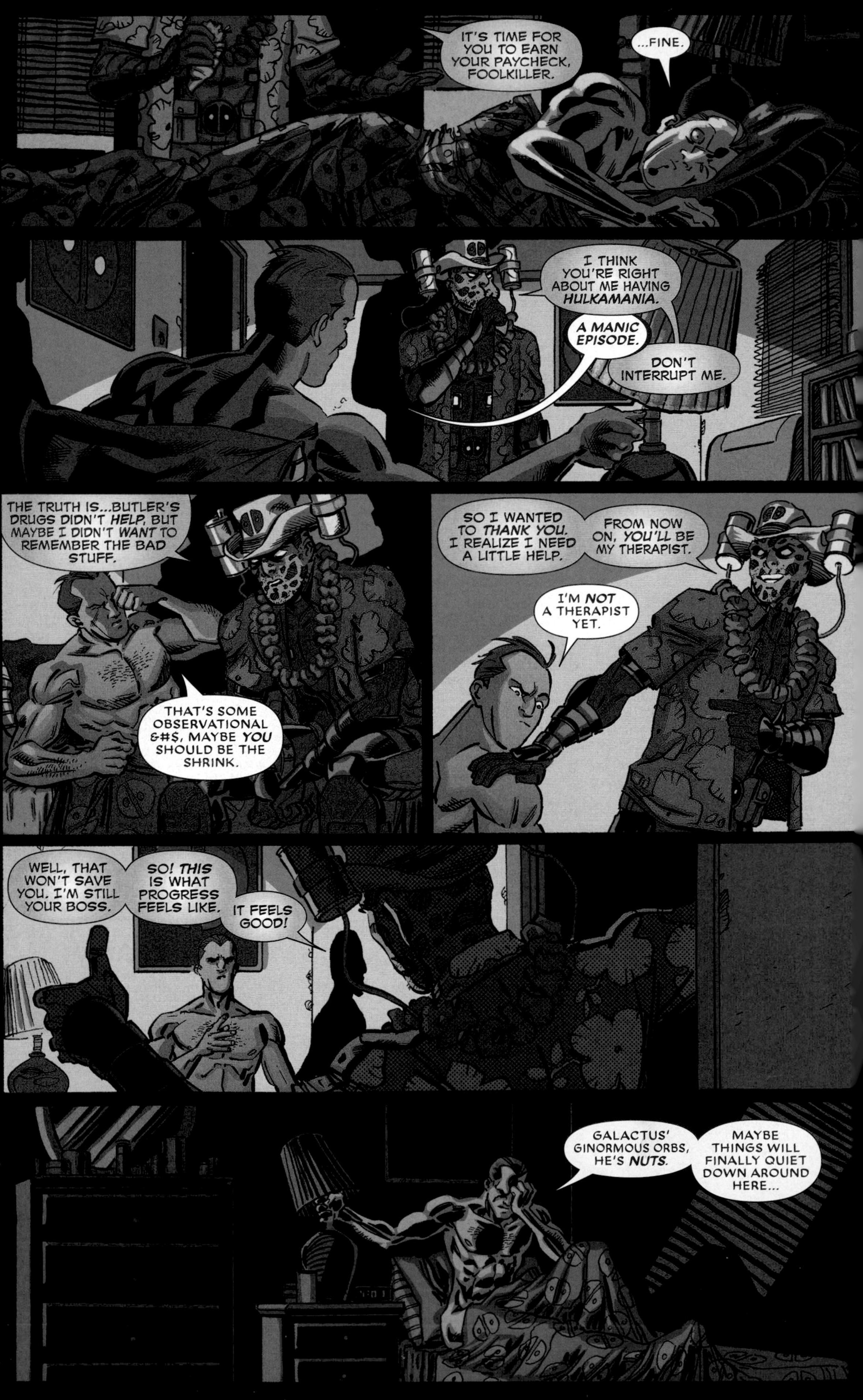
IT'S TIME FOR YOU TO EARN YOUR PAYCHECK, FOOLKILLER.
...FINE.
I THINK YOU'RE RIGHT ABOUT ME HAVING HULKAMANIA.
A MANIC EPISODE.
DON'T INTERRUPT ME.
THE TRUTH IS...BUTLER'S DRUGS DIDN'T HELP, BUT MAYBE I DIDN'T WANT TO REMEMBER THE BAD STUFF.
THAT'S SOME OBSERVATIONAL &#$, MAYBE YOU SHOULD BE THE SHRINK.
SO I WANTED TO THANK YOU. I REALIZE I NEED A LITTLE HELP.
FROM NOW ON, YOU'LL BE MY THERAPIST.
I'M NOT A THERAPIST YET.
WELL, THAT WON'T SAVE YOU. I'M STILL YOUR BOSS.
SO! THIS IS WHAT PROGRESS FEELS LIKE.
IT FEELS GOOD!
GALACTUS' GINORMOUS ORBS, HE'S NUTS.
MAYBE THINGS WILL FINALLY QUIET DOWN AROUND HERE...

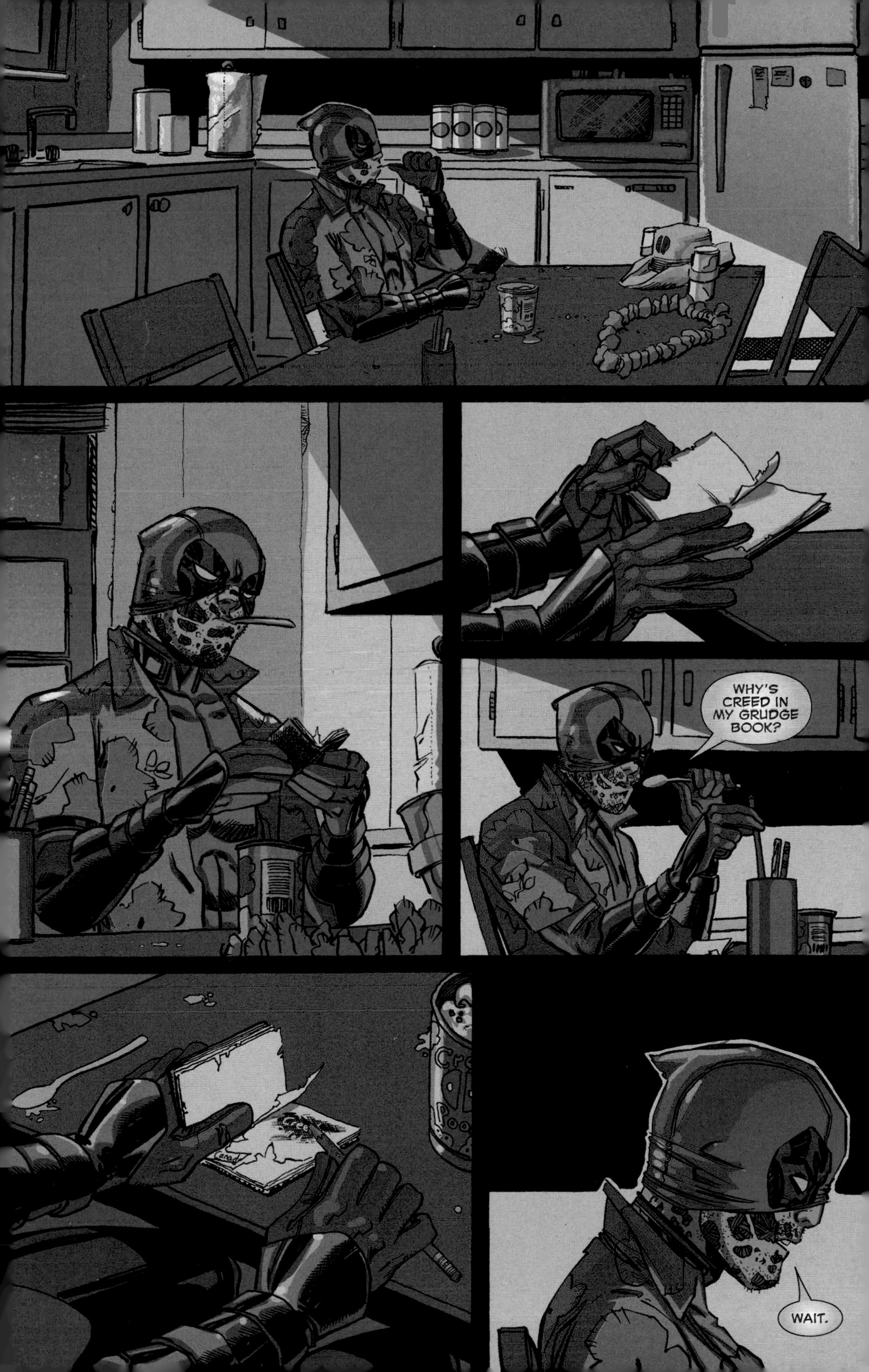
WHY'S CREED IN MY GRUDGE BOOK?
WAIT.

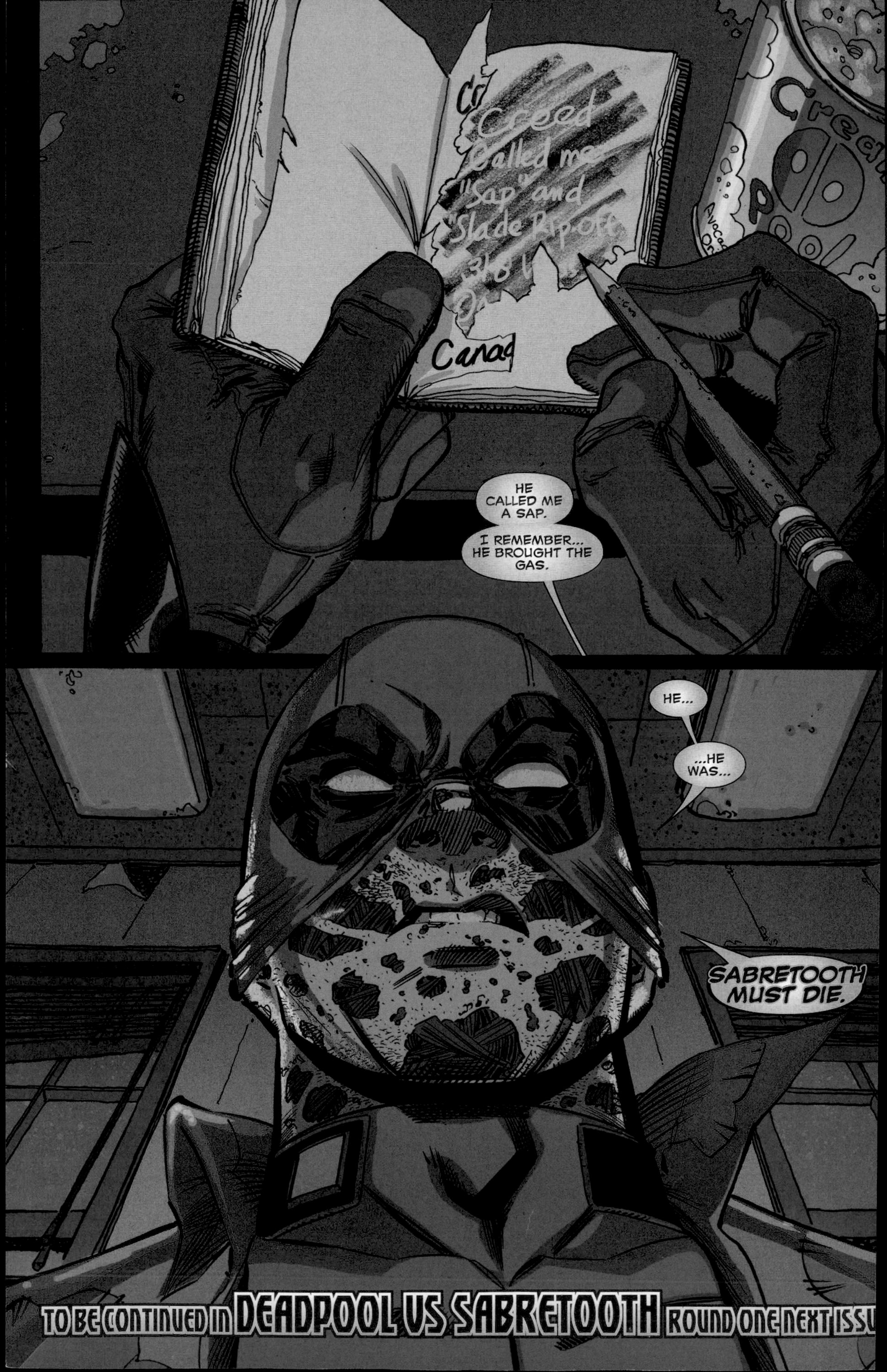
Creed
Called me
"Sap" and
"Slade Rip-Off"
Canad
HE CALLED ME A SAP.
I REMEMBER... HE BROUGHT THE GAS.
HE...
...HE WAS...
SABRETOOTH MUST DIE.
TO BE CONTINUED IN DEADPOOL VS SABRETOOTH ROUND ONE NEXT ISSU

# DEADPOOL

## PROUDLY PRESENTS:
## TALES OF THE
## MERCS FOR MONEY

# TERROR
An ancient warrior cursed with immortality in a rotting body, Terror can replace body parts and take on memories from those new parts.

## ARMED AND DANGEROUS

**Cullen Bunn**
writer

**Tyler Crook**
artist

# SLAPSTICK
Transformed by an alien artifact into a malleable, "cartoony" form, Steven Harmon uses objects pulled from a subspace pocket to battle evil.

## SLAPSTICK MEETS THE FORGOTTEN

**Ben Acker & Ben Blacker**
writers

**Danilo Beyruth**
artist

**Veronica Gandini**
colorist

# FOOLKILLER
Inspired to kill those he deems "fools" by his own criteria, Gregory Salinger uses his "purification guns" and other weapons to "better" the world.

## FOOLKILLER GOES BACK TO SCHOOL

**Amy Chu**
writer

**Emilio Laiso**
artist

**Israel Silva**
colorist

**VC's Joe Sabino**
letterer

# DEADPOOL

## PROUDLY PRESENTS:
## TALES OF THE
## MERCS FOR MONEY

### STINGRAY
Scientist Walter Newell invented the Stingray armor for underwater research...but also uses its myriad abilities to fight for what's right.

## BENEATH THE SURFACE

**Tim Seeley**
writer

**Mike Norton**
artist

**Veronica Gandini**
colorist

### MASACRE
A mysterious former priest from Mexico was inspired by Deadpool to take up machetes for justice as the Spanish-speaking Masacre

## EL DIABLO EMPUJÓ

**Mike Hawthorne**
writer/artist

**Terry Pallot**
inker

**Jordie Bellaire**
colorist

### SOLO
With short-range teleportation powers and special forces training, James Bourn has dedicated himself to eradicating Terror...and making a few bucks.

## SOLO'S SOLO MISSION

**Gerry Duggan**
writer

**Phil Noto**
artist

**Heather Antos**
assistant editor

**Jordan D. White**
editor

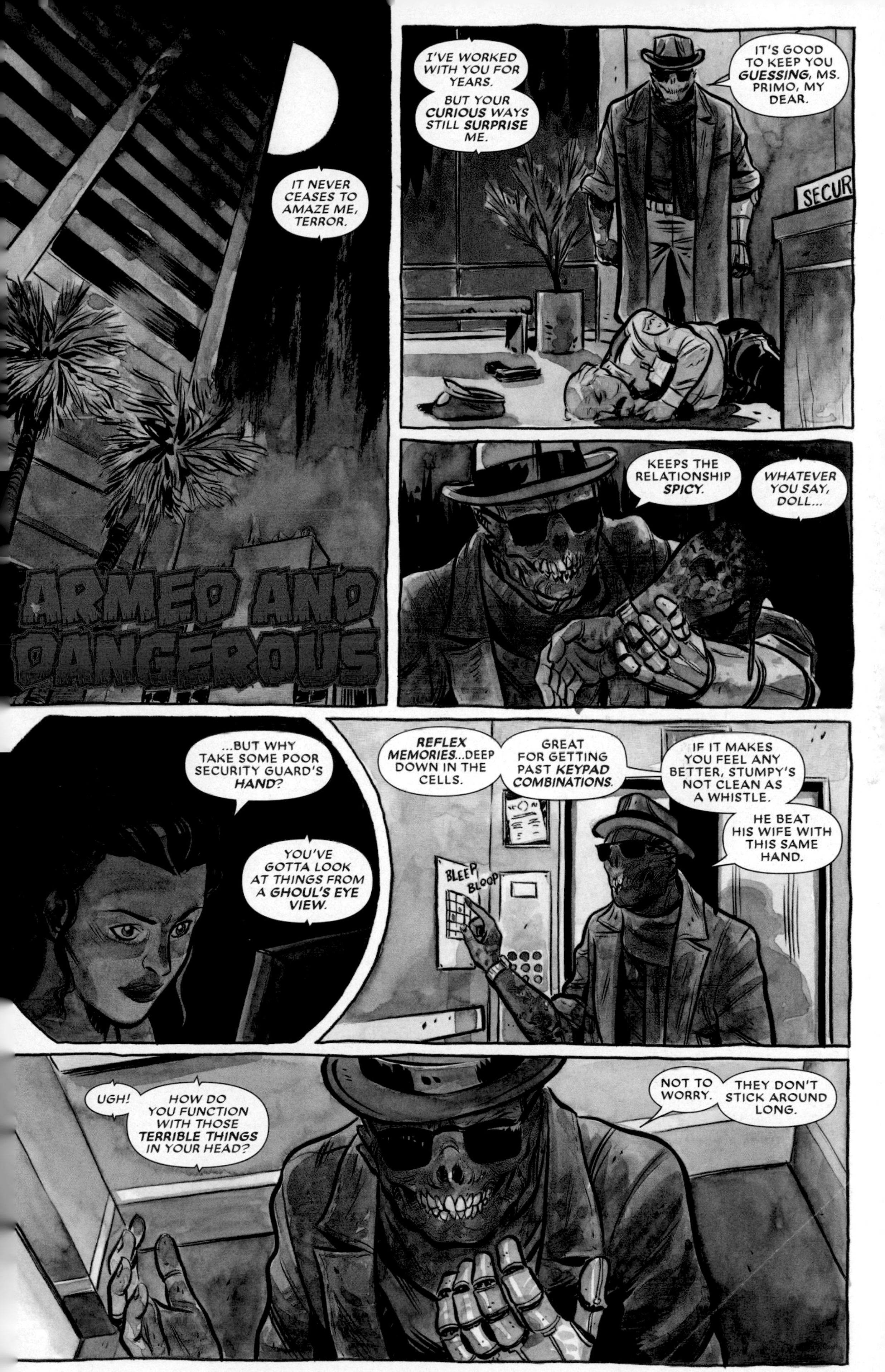

IT NEVER CEASES TO AMAZE ME, TERROR.
ARMED AND DANGEROUS
I'VE WORKED WITH YOU FOR YEARS.
BUT YOUR CURIOUS WAYS STILL SURPRISE ME.
IT'S GOOD TO KEEP YOU GUESSING, MS. PRIMO, MY DEAR.
SECUR
KEEPS THE RELATIONSHIP SPICY.
WHATEVER YOU SAY, DOLL...
...BUT WHY TAKE SOME POOR SECURITY GUARD'S HAND?
YOU'VE GOTTA LOOK AT THINGS FROM A GHOUL'S EYE VIEW.
REFLEX MEMORIES...DEEP DOWN IN THE CELLS.
GREAT FOR GETTING PAST KEYPAD COMBINATIONS.
IF IT MAKES YOU FEEL ANY BETTER, STUMPY'S NOT CLEAN AS A WHISTLE.
HE BEAT HIS WIFE WITH THIS SAME HAND.
BLEEP
BLOOP
UGH!
HOW DO YOU FUNCTION WITH THOSE TERRIBLE THINGS IN YOUR HEAD?
NOT TO WORRY.
THEY DON'T STICK AROUND LONG.

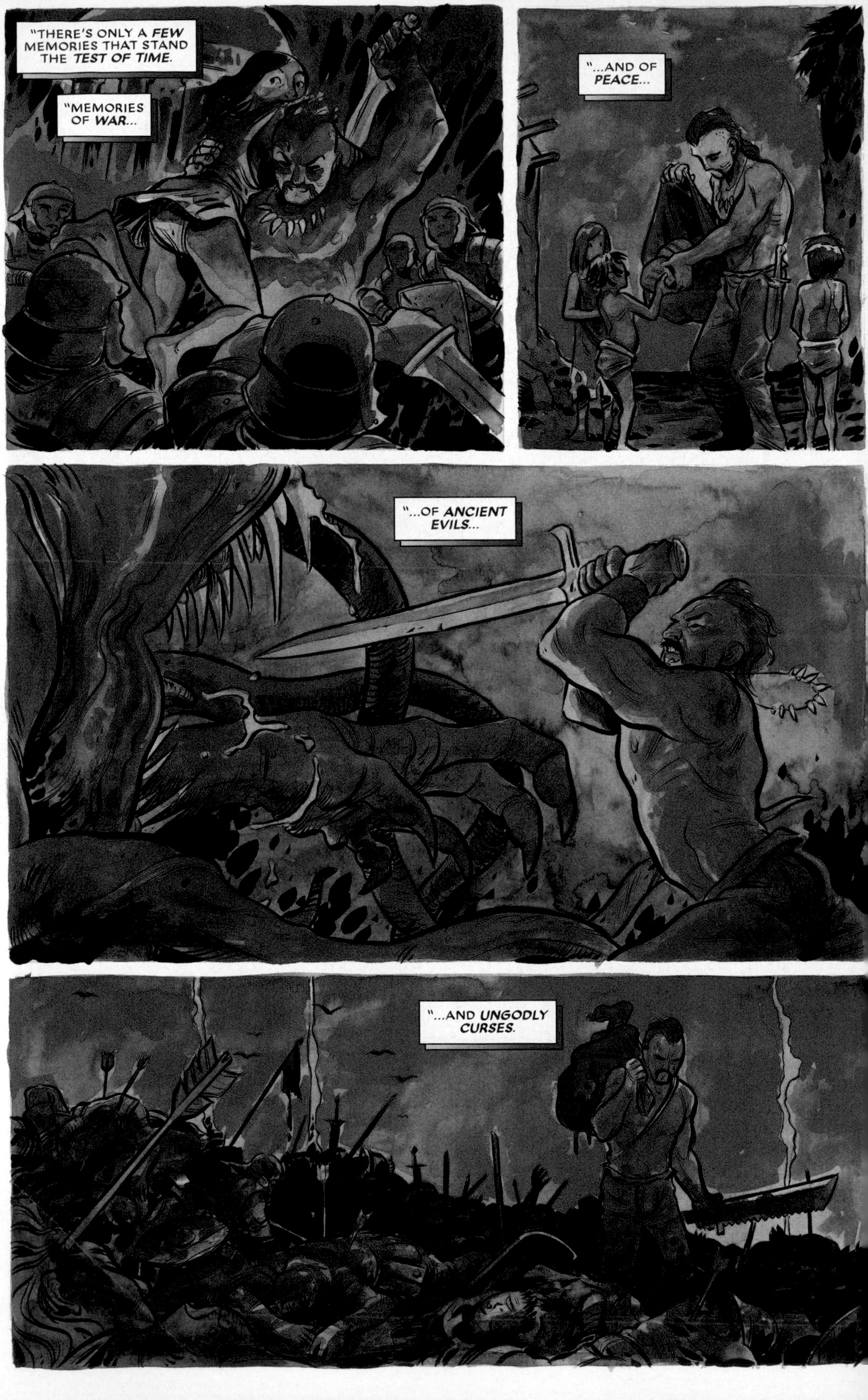
"THERE'S ONLY A FEW MEMORIES THAT STAND THE TEST OF TIME.
"MEMORIES OF WAR...
"...AND OF PEACE...
"...OF ANCIENT EVILS...
"...AND UNGODLY CURSES.

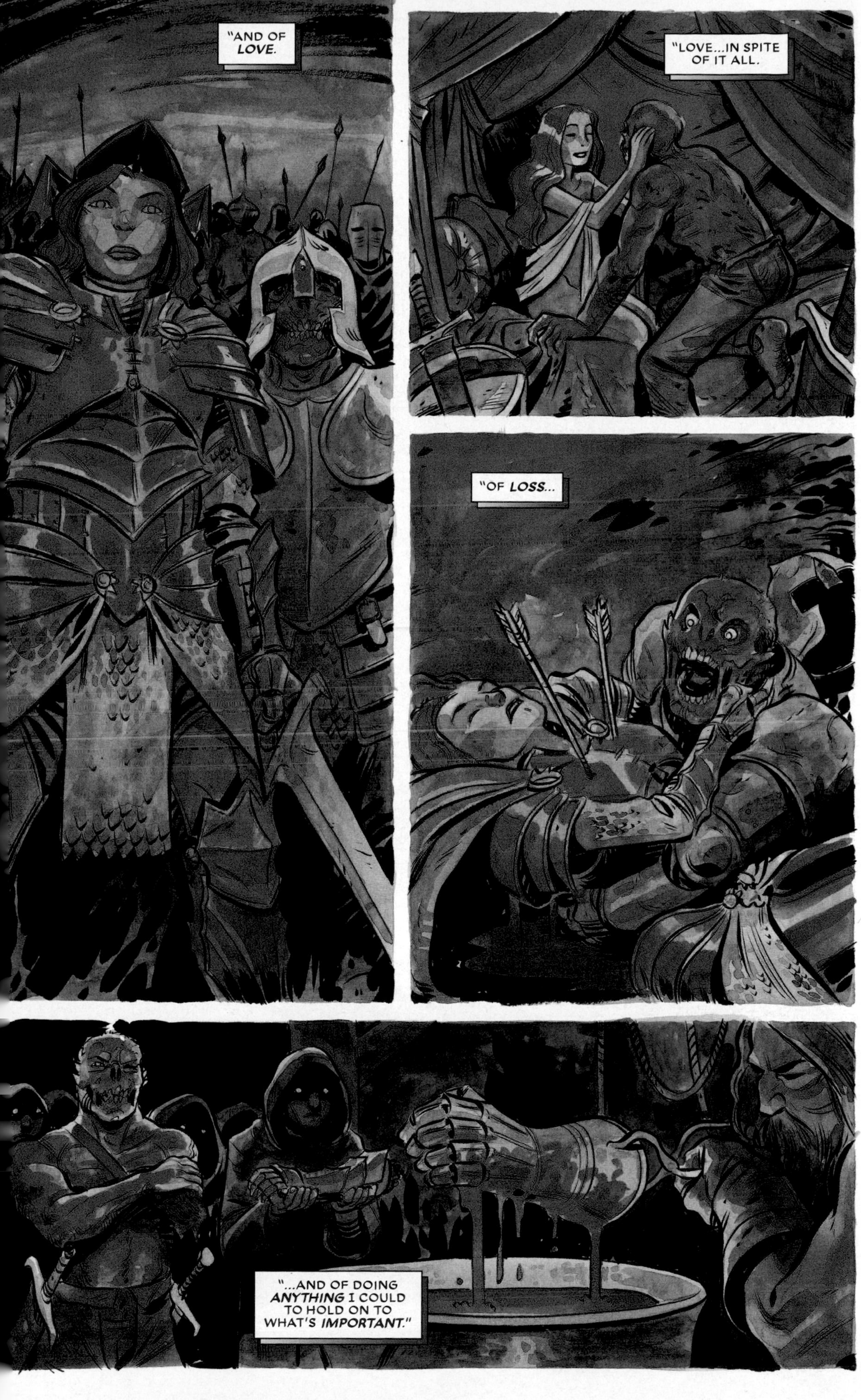
"AND OF LOVE.
"LOVE...IN SPITE OF IT ALL.
"OF LOSS...
"...AND OF DOING ANYTHING I COULD TO HOLD ON TO WHAT'S IMPORTANT."

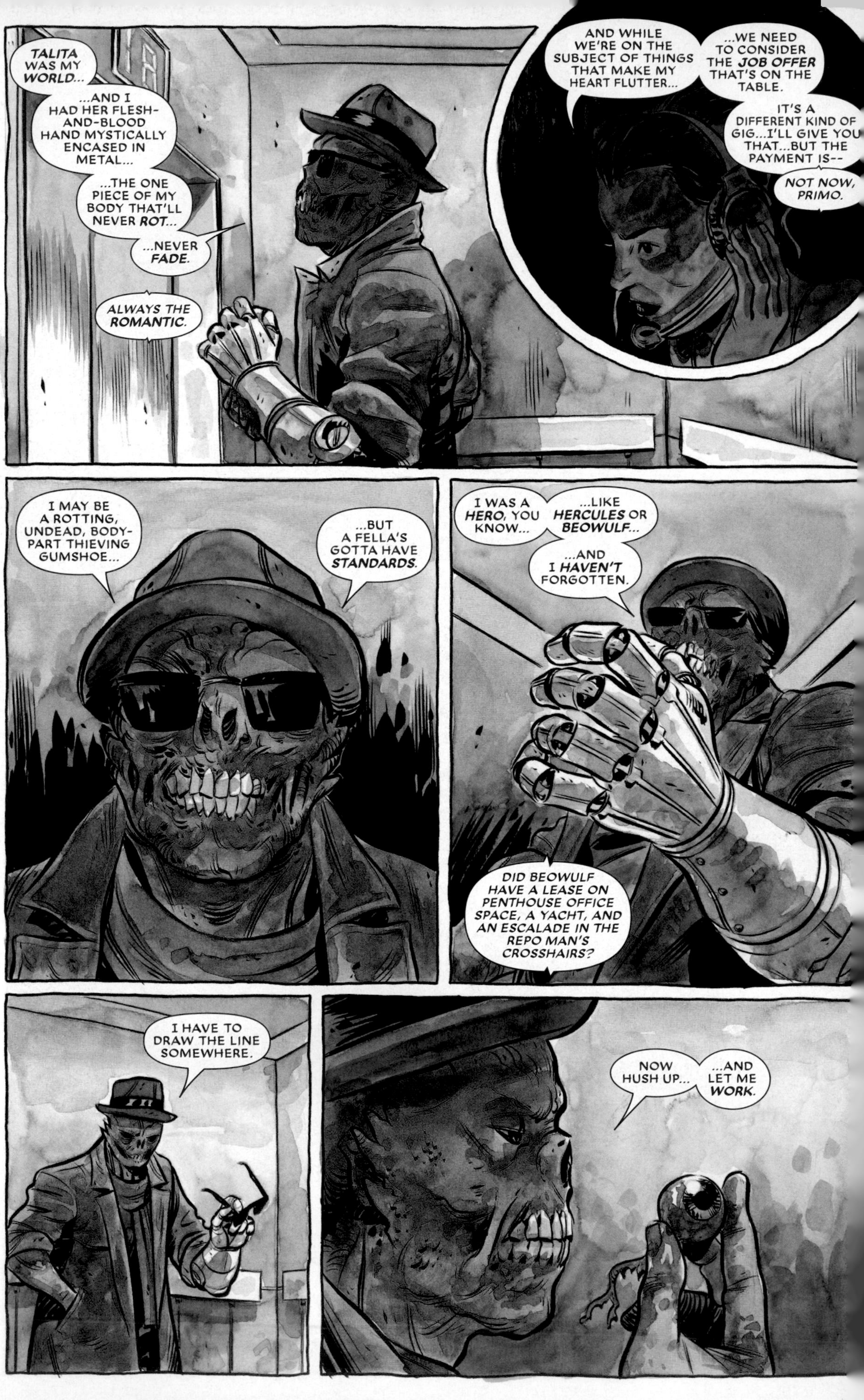
TALITA WAS MY WORLD...
...AND I HAD HER FLESH-AND-BLOOD HAND MYSTICALLY ENCASED IN METAL...
...THE ONE PIECE OF MY BODY THAT'LL NEVER ROT...
...NEVER FADE.
ALWAYS THE ROMANTIC.
AND WHILE WE'RE ON THE SUBJECT OF THINGS THAT MAKE MY HEART FLUTTER...
...WE NEED TO CONSIDER THE JOB OFFER THAT'S ON THE TABLE.
IT'S A DIFFERENT KIND OF GIG...I'LL GIVE YOU THAT...BUT THE PAYMENT IS--
NOT NOW, PRIMO.
I MAY BE A ROTTING, UNDEAD, BODY-PART THIEVING GUMSHOE...
...BUT A FELLA'S GOTTA HAVE STANDARDS.
I WAS A HERO, YOU KNOW...
...LIKE HERCULES OR BEOWULF...
...AND I HAVEN'T FORGOTTEN.
DID BEOWULF HAVE A LEASE ON PENTHOUSE OFFICE SPACE, A YACHT, AND AN ESCALADE IN THE REPO MAN'S CROSSHAIRS?
I HAVE TO DRAW THE LINE SOMEWHERE.
NOW HUSH UP...
...AND LET ME WORK.

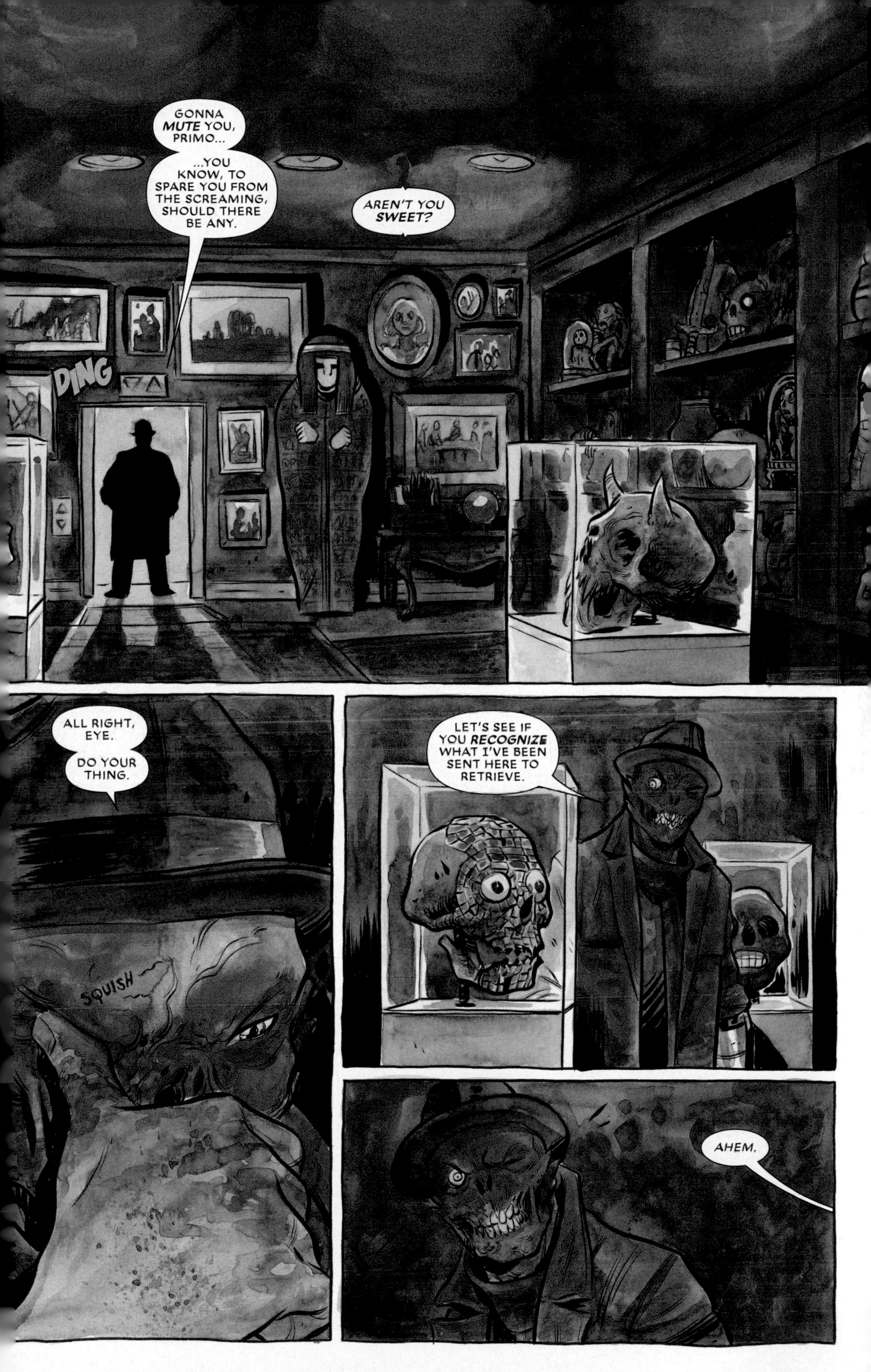
GONNA MUTE YOU, PRIMO...
...YOU KNOW, TO SPARE YOU FROM THE SCREAMING, SHOULD THERE BE ANY.
AREN'T YOU SWEET?
DING
ALL RIGHT, EYE.
DO YOUR THING.
SQUISH
LET'S SEE IF YOU RECOGNIZE WHAT I'VE BEEN SENT HERE TO RETRIEVE.
AHEM.

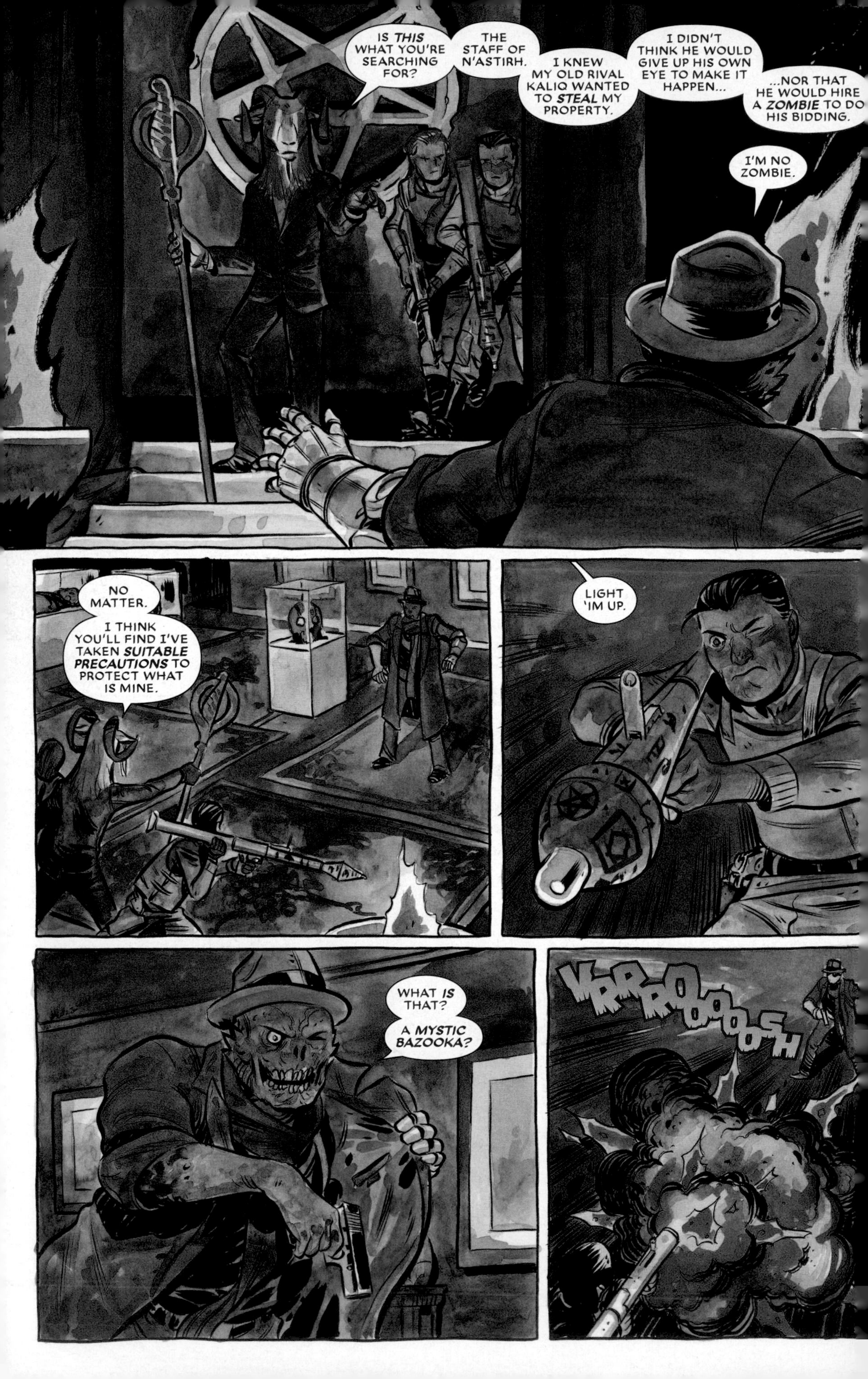

IS THIS WHAT YOU'RE SEARCHING FOR?
THE STAFF OF N'ASTIRH.
I KNEW MY OLD RIVAL KALIQ WANTED TO STEAL MY PROPERTY.
I DIDN'T THINK HE WOULD GIVE UP HIS OWN EYE TO MAKE IT HAPPEN...
...NOR THAT HE WOULD HIRE A ZOMBIE TO DO HIS BIDDING.
I'M NO ZOMBIE.
NO MATTER.
I THINK YOU'LL FIND I'VE TAKEN SUITABLE PRECAUTIONS TO PROTECT WHAT IS MINE.
LIGHT 'IM UP.
WHAT IS THAT?
A MYSTIC BAZOOKA?
VRRROOOOOSH

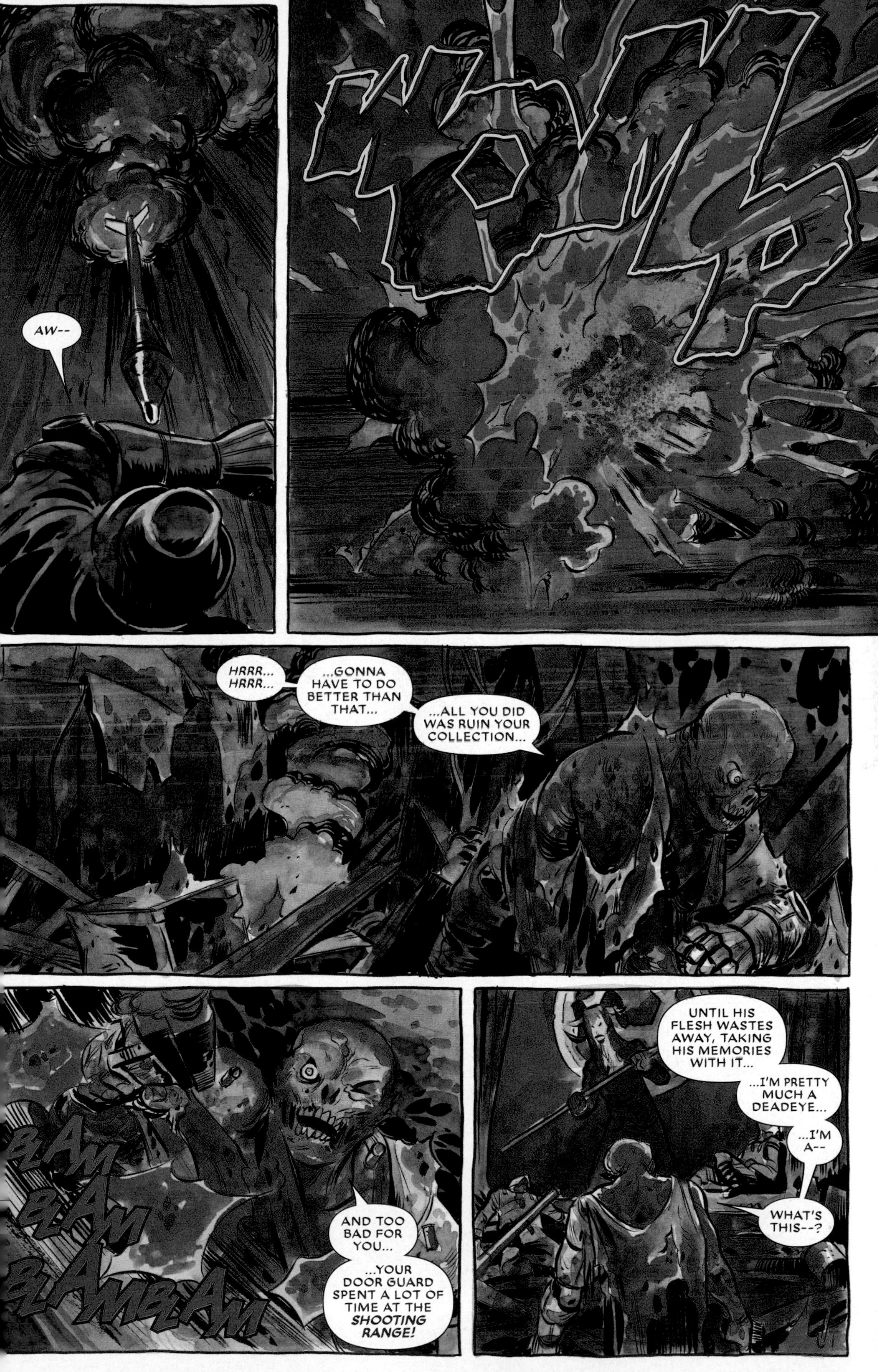
AW--
WHOOOMP
HRRR... HRRR...
...GONNA HAVE TO DO BETTER THAN THAT...
...ALL YOU DID WAS RUIN YOUR COLLECTION...
BLAM BLAM BLAM BLAMBLAM
AND TOO BAD FOR YOU...
...YOUR DOOR GUARD SPENT A LOT OF TIME AT THE SHOOTING RANGE!
UNTIL HIS FLESH WASTES AWAY, TAKING HIS MEMORIES WITH IT...
...I'M PRETTY MUCH A DEADEYE...
...I'M A--
WHAT'S THIS--?

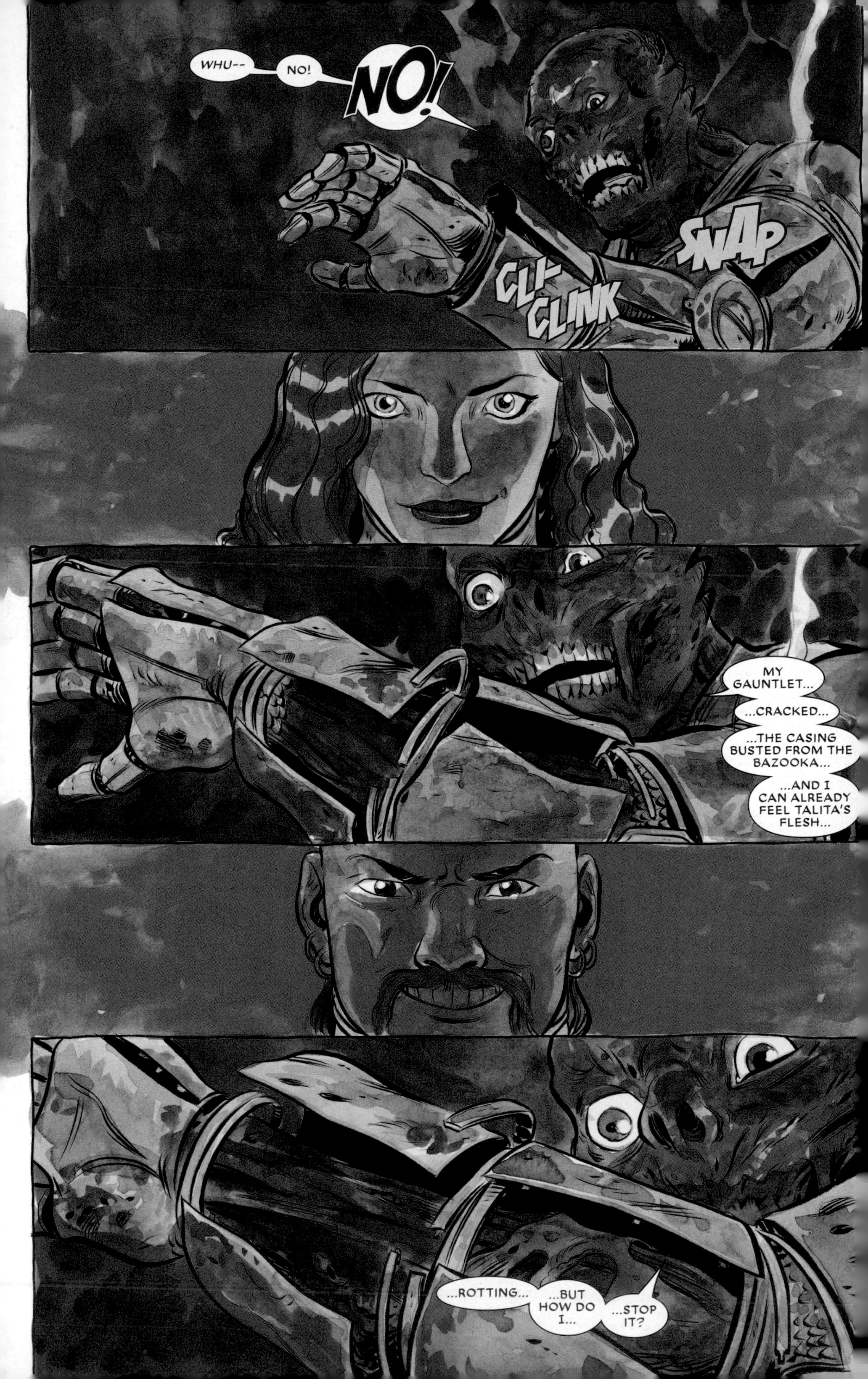
WHU--
NO!
NO!
SNAP
CLI-CLINK
MY GAUNTLET...
...CRACKED...
...THE CASING BUSTED FROM THE BAZOOKA...
...AND I CAN ALREADY FEEL TALITA'S FLESH...
...ROTTING...
...BUT HOW DO I...
...STOP IT?

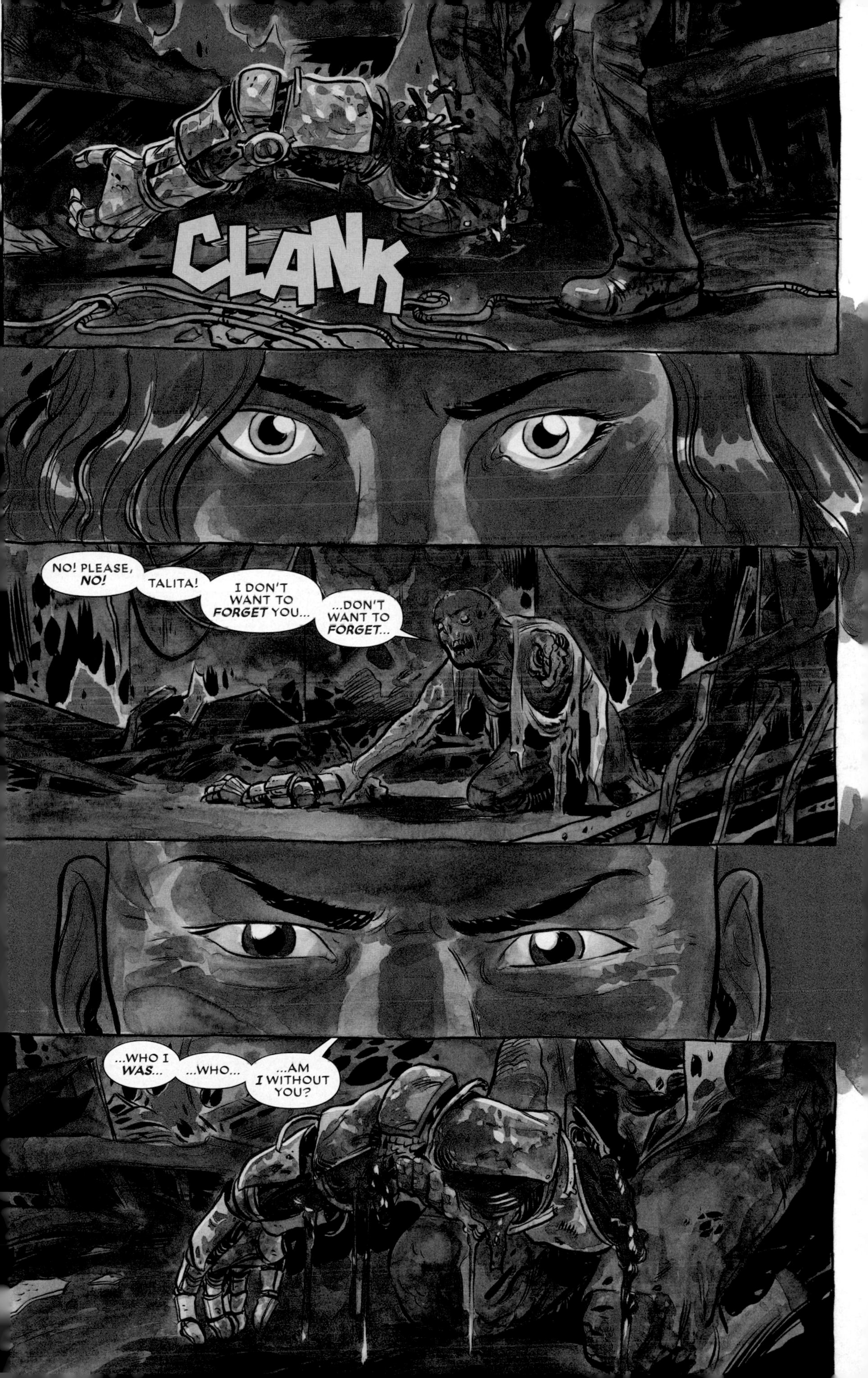
CLANK
NO! PLEASE, NO!
TALITA!
I DON'T WANT TO FORGET YOU...
...DON'T WANT TO FORGET...
...WHO I WAS...
...WHO...
...AM I WITHOUT YOU?

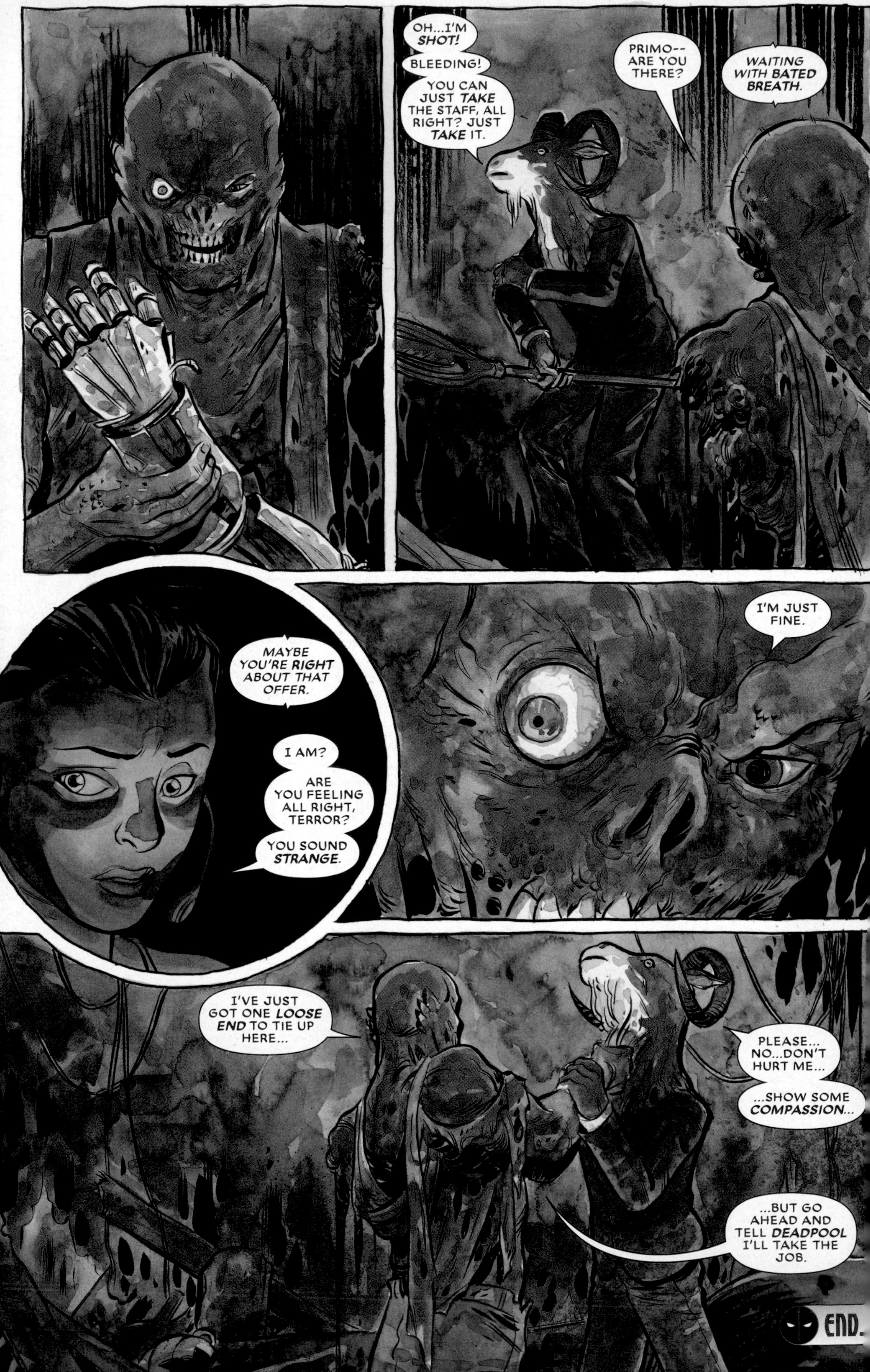
OH...I'M SHOT!
BLEEDING!
YOU CAN JUST TAKE THE STAFF, ALL RIGHT? JUST TAKE IT.
PRIMO--ARE YOU THERE?
WAITING WITH BATED BREATH.
MAYBE YOU'RE RIGHT ABOUT THAT OFFER.
I'M JUST FINE.
I AM?
ARE YOU FEELING ALL RIGHT, TERROR?
YOU SOUND STRANGE.
I'VE JUST GOT ONE LOOSE END TO TIE UP HERE...
PLEASE... NO...DON'T HURT ME...
...SHOW SOME COMPASSION...
...BUT GO AHEAD AND TELL DEADPOOL I'LL TAKE THE JOB.
END.

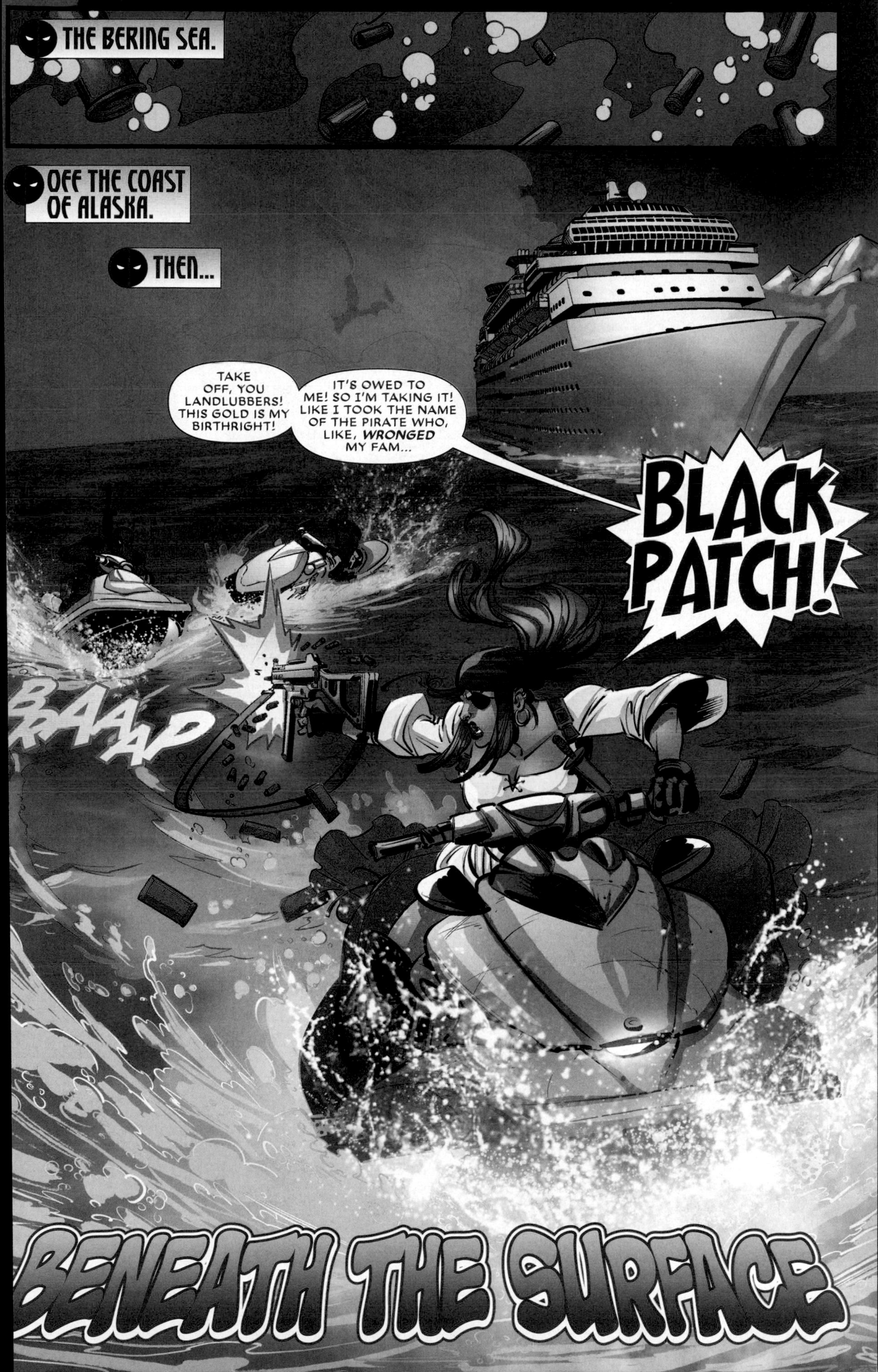

THE BERING SEA.
OFF THE COAST OF ALASKA.
THEN...
TAKE OFF, YOU LANDLUBBERS! THIS GOLD IS MY BIRTHRIGHT!
IT'S OWED TO ME! SO I'M TAKING IT! LIKE I TOOK THE NAME OF THE PIRATE WHO, LIKE, *WRONGED* MY FAM...
BLACK PATCH!
BRAAAAP
BENEATH THE SURFACE

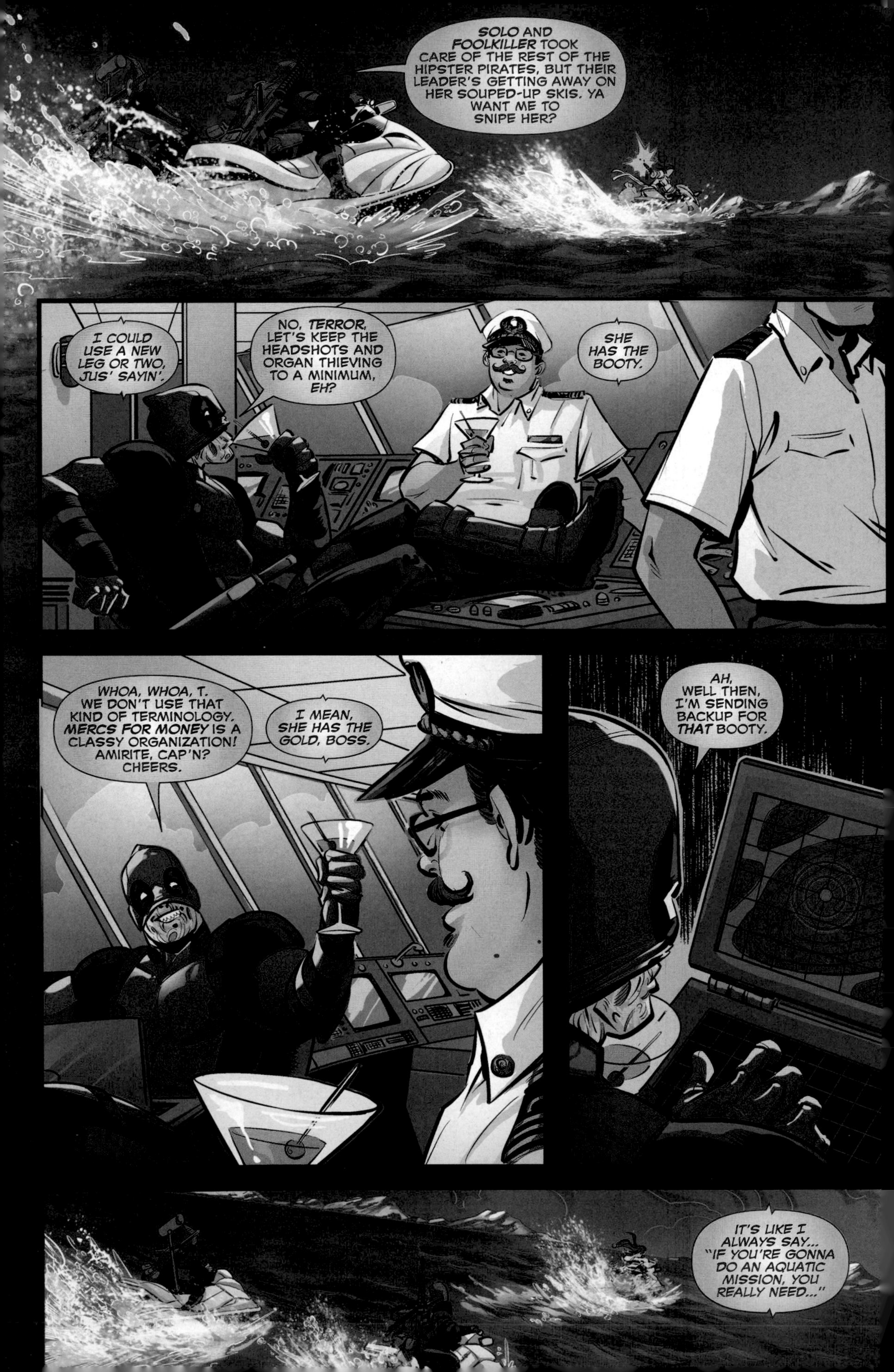
SOLO AND FOOLKILLER TOOK CARE OF THE REST OF THE HIPSTER PIRATES, BUT THEIR LEADER'S GETTING AWAY ON HER SOUPED-UP SKIS. YA WANT ME TO SNIPE HER?
I COULD USE A NEW LEG OR TWO, JUS' SAYIN'.
NO, TERROR, LET'S KEEP THE HEADSHOTS AND ORGAN THIEVING TO A MINIMUM, EH?
SHE HAS THE BOOTY.
WHOA, WHOA, T. WE DON'T USE THAT KIND OF TERMINOLOGY. MERCS FOR MONEY IS A CLASSY ORGANIZATION! AMIRITE, CAP'N? CHEERS.
I MEAN, SHE HAS THE GOLD, BOSS.
AH, WELL THEN, I'M SENDING BACKUP FOR THAT BOOTY.
IT'S LIKE I ALWAYS SAY... "IF YOU'RE GONNA DO AN AQUATIC MISSION, YOU REALLY NEED..."

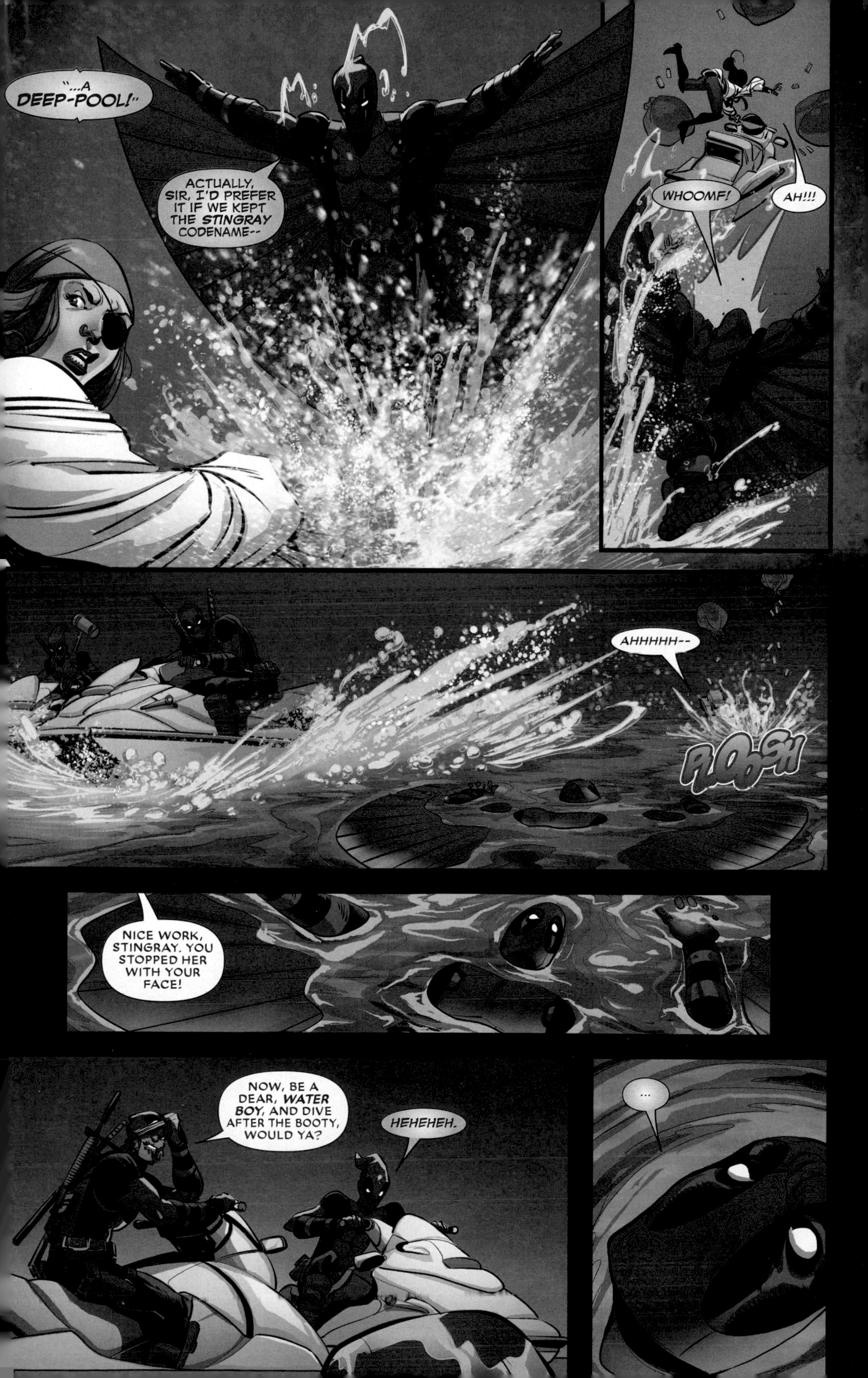
"...A DEEP-POOL!"
ACTUALLY, SIR, I'D PREFER IT IF WE KEPT THE STINGRAY CODENAME--
WHOOMF!
AH!!!
AHHHHH--
PLOOSH
NICE WORK, STINGRAY. YOU STOPPED HER WITH YOUR FACE!
NOW, BE A DEAR, WATER BOY, AND DIVE AFTER THE BOOTY, WOULD YA?
HEHEHEH.
...

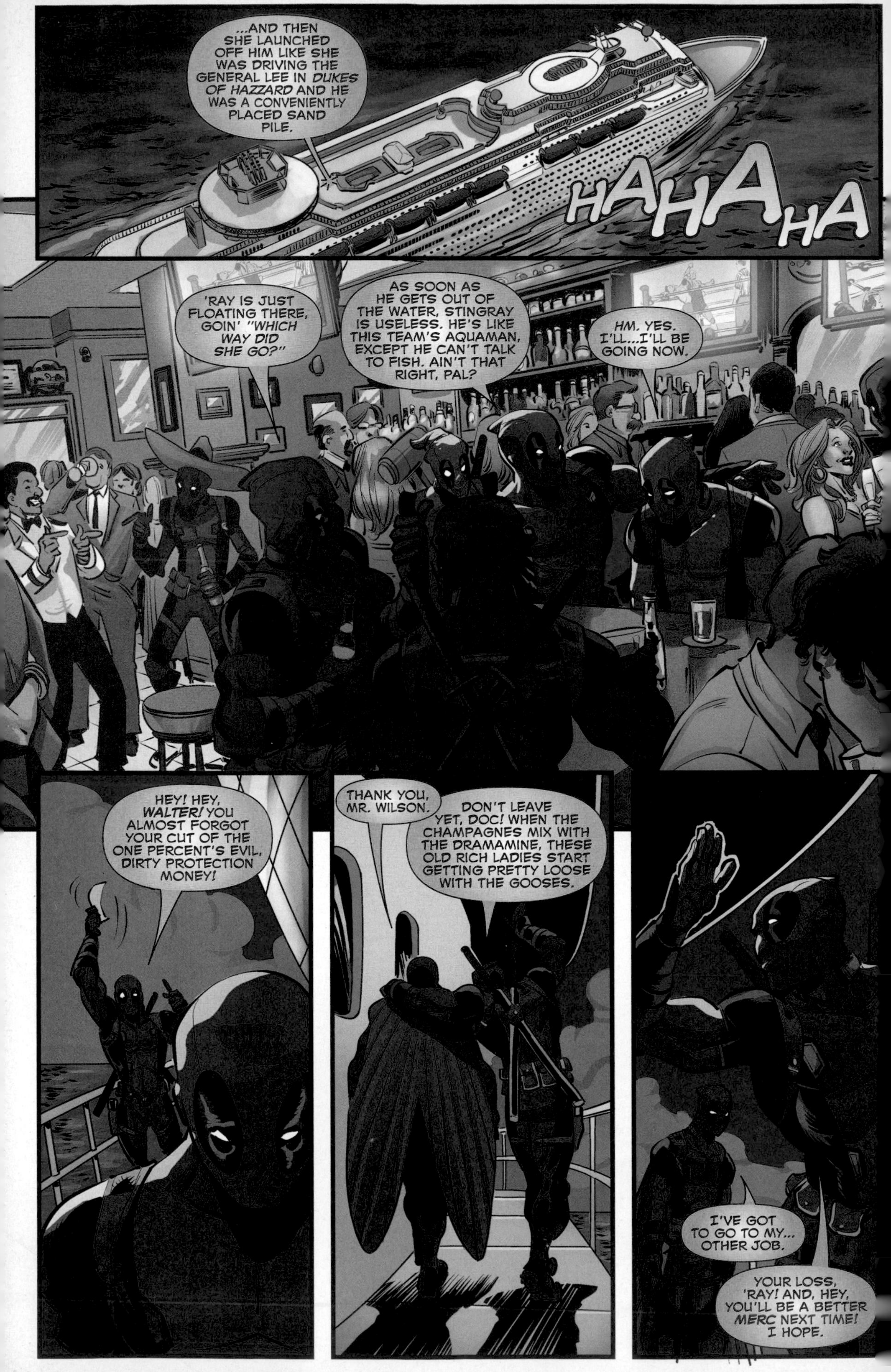

...AND THEN SHE LAUNCHED OFF HIM LIKE SHE WAS DRIVING THE GENERAL LEE IN DUKES OF HAZZARD AND HE WAS A CONVENIENTLY PLACED SAND PILE.
HAHAHAHA
'RAY IS JUST FLOATING THERE, GOIN' "WHICH WAY DID SHE GO?"
AS SOON AS HE GETS OUT OF THE WATER, STINGRAY IS USELESS. HE'S LIKE THIS TEAM'S AQUAMAN, EXCEPT HE CAN'T TALK TO FISH. AIN'T THAT RIGHT, PAL?
HM. YES. I'LL...I'LL BE GOING NOW.
HEY! HEY, WALTER! YOU ALMOST FORGOT YOUR CUT OF THE ONE PERCENT'S EVIL, DIRTY PROTECTION MONEY!
THANK YOU, MR. WILSON.
DON'T LEAVE YET, DOC! WHEN THE CHAMPAGNES MIX WITH THE DRAMAMINE, THESE OLD RICH LADIES START GETTING PRETTY LOOSE WITH THE GOOSES.
I'VE GOT TO GO TO MY... OTHER JOB.
YOUR LOSS, 'RAY! AND, HEY, YOU'LL BE A BETTER MERC NEXT TIME! I HOPE.

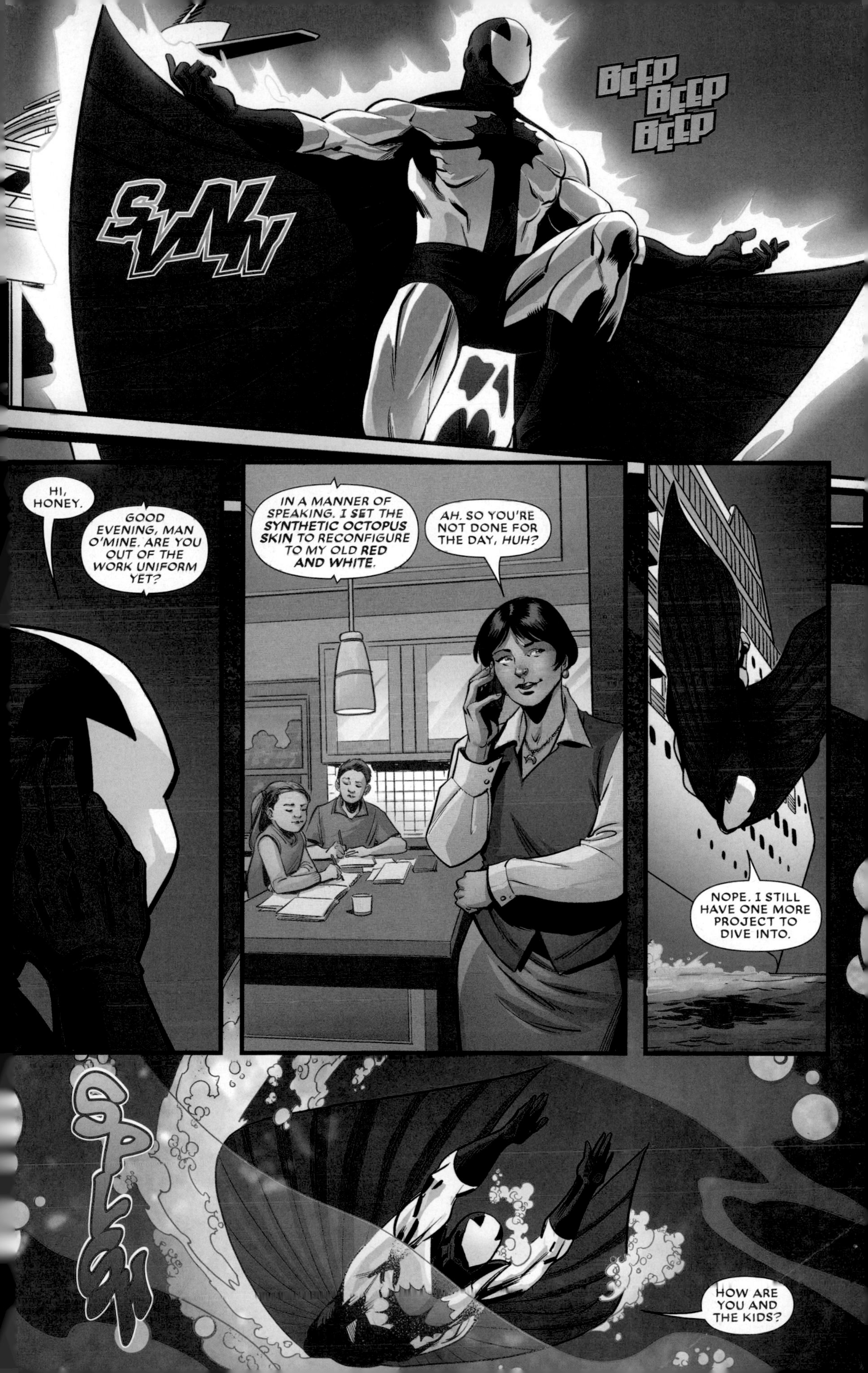
BEEP BEEP BEEP
SWNK
HI, HONEY.
GOOD EVENING, MAN O'MINE. ARE YOU OUT OF THE WORK UNIFORM YET?
IN A MANNER OF SPEAKING. I SET THE SYNTHETIC OCTOPUS SKIN TO RECONFIGURE TO MY OLD RED AND WHITE.
AH. SO YOU'RE NOT DONE FOR THE DAY, HUH?
NOPE. I STILL HAVE ONE MORE PROJECT TO DIVE INTO.
SPLOOSH
HOW ARE YOU AND THE KIDS?

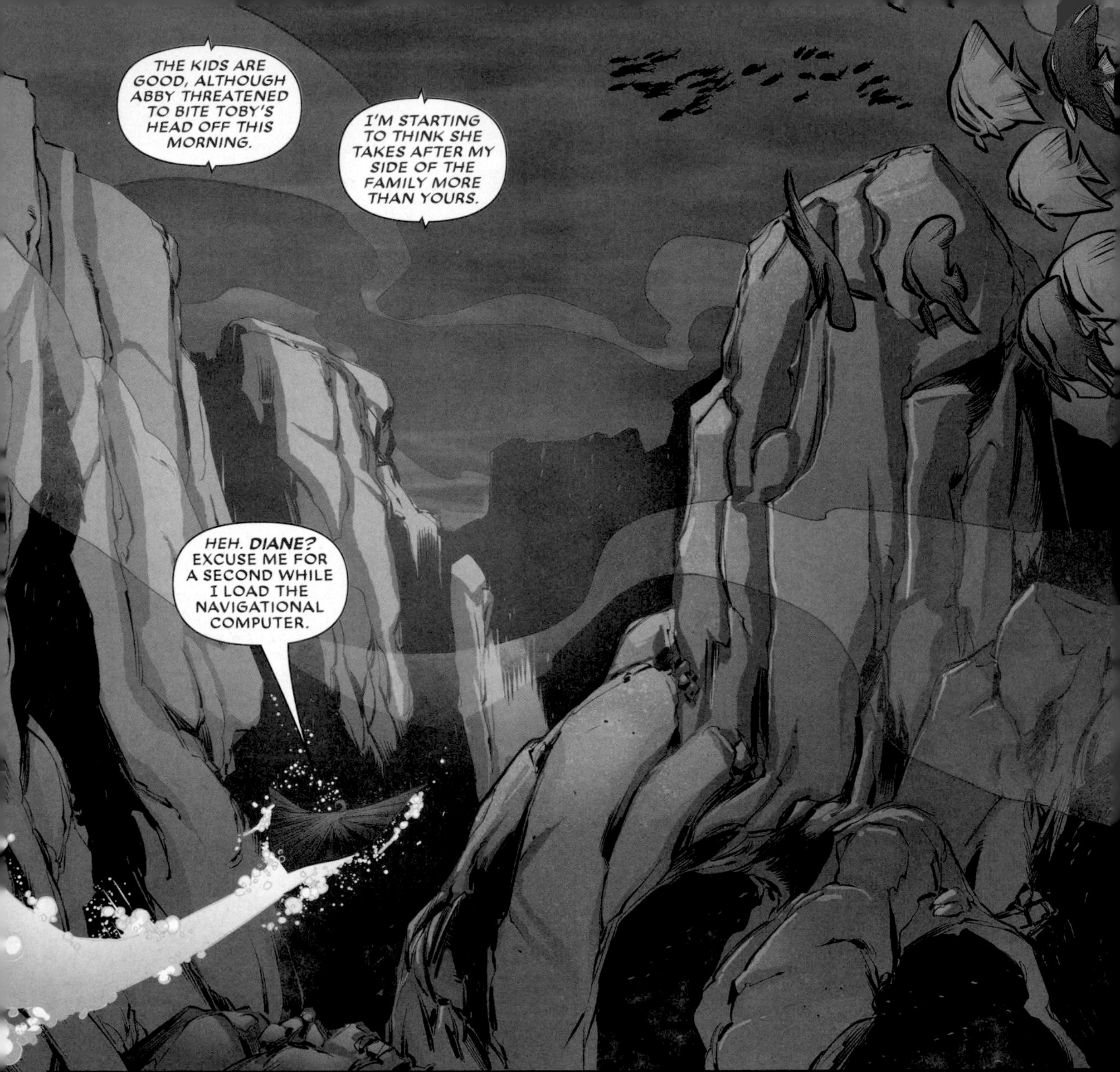
THE KIDS ARE GOOD, ALTHOUGH ABBY THREATENED TO BITE TOBY'S HEAD OFF THIS MORNING.
I'M STARTING TO THINK SHE TAKES AFTER MY SIDE OF THE FAMILY MORE THAN YOURS.
HEH. DIANE? EXCUSE ME FOR A SECOND WHILE I LOAD THE NAVIGATIONAL COMPUTER.

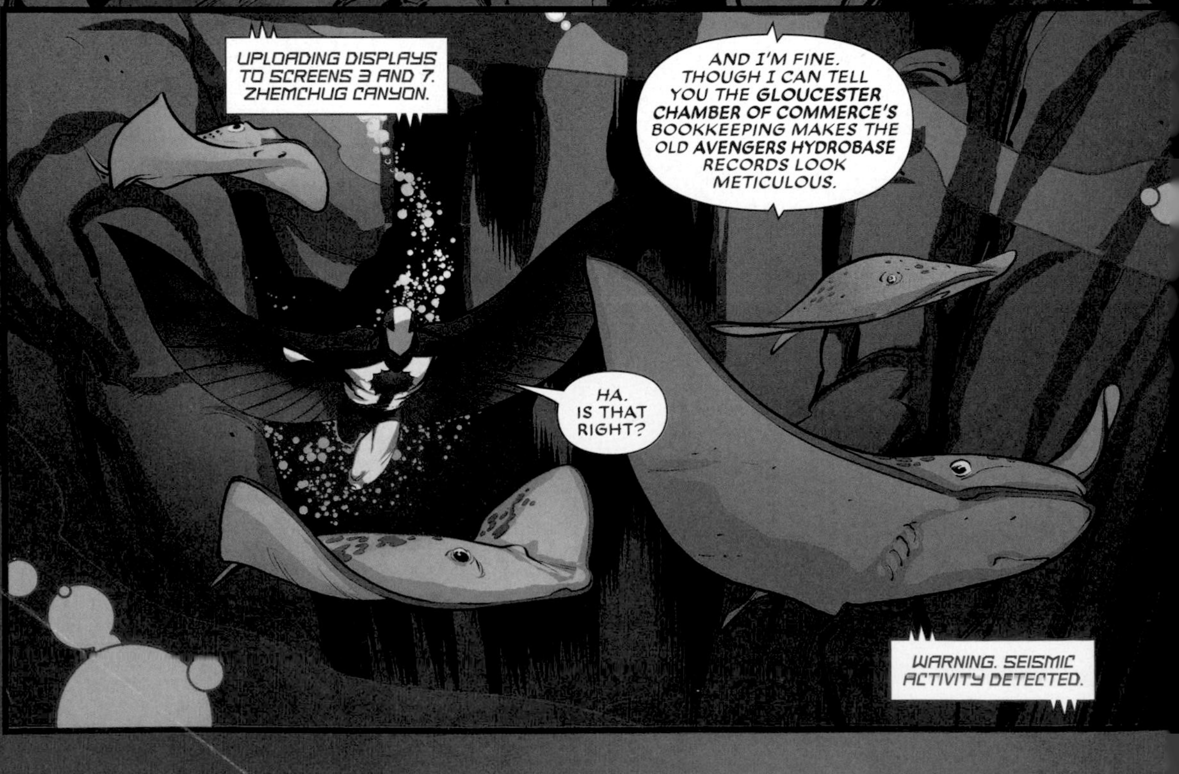
UPLOADING DISPLAYS TO SCREENS 3 AND 7. ZHEMCHUG CANYON.
AND I'M FINE. THOUGH I CAN TELL YOU THE GLOUCESTER CHAMBER OF COMMERCE'S BOOKKEEPING MAKES THE OLD AVENGERS HYDROBASE RECORDS LOOK METICULOUS.
HA. IS THAT RIGHT?
WARNING. SEISMIC ACTIVITY DETECTED.

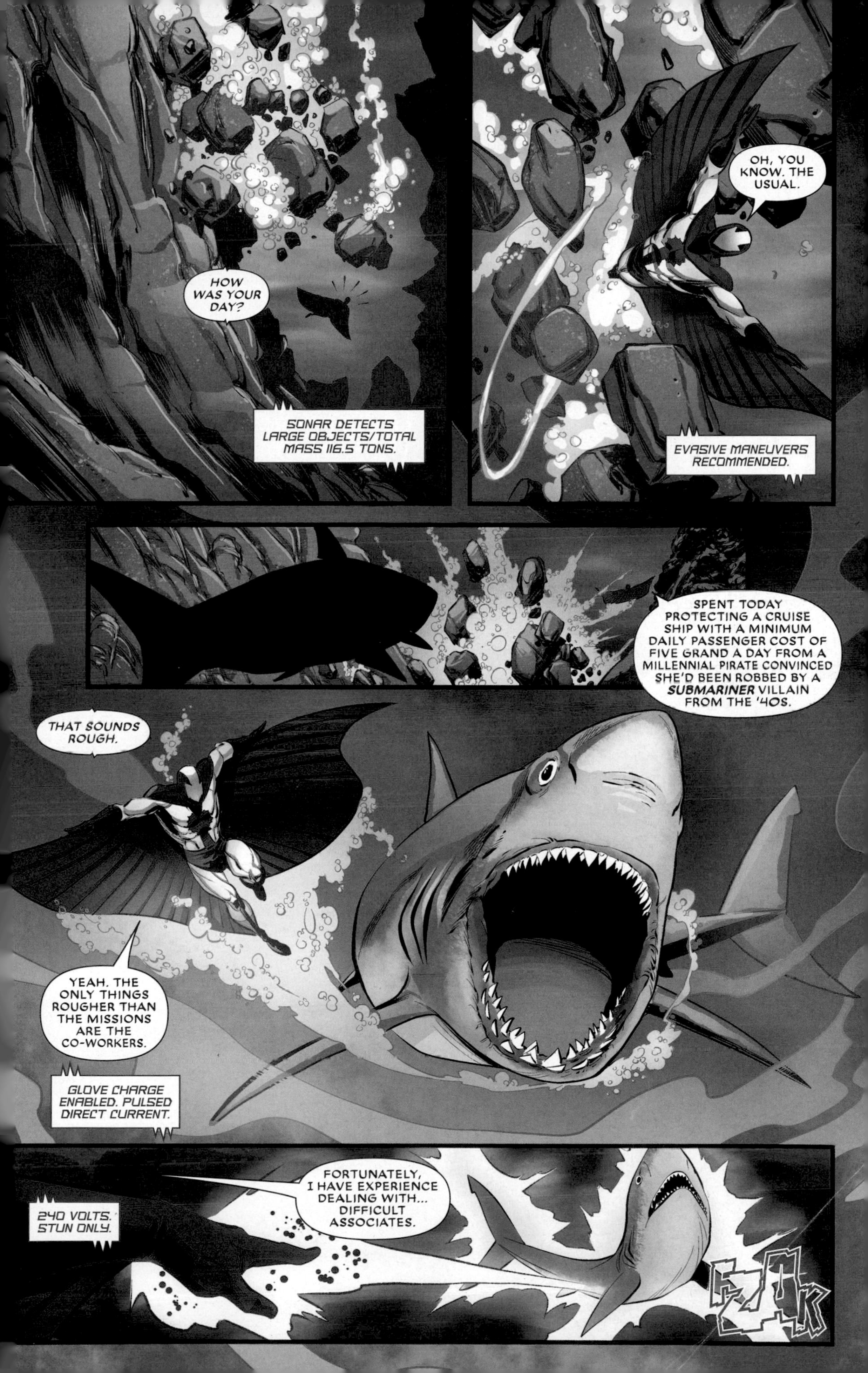
HOW WAS YOUR DAY?
SONAR DETECTS LARGE OBJECTS/TOTAL MASS 116.5 TONS.
OH, YOU KNOW. THE USUAL.
EVASIVE MANEUVERS RECOMMENDED.
SPENT TODAY PROTECTING A CRUISE SHIP WITH A MINIMUM DAILY PASSENGER COST OF FIVE GRAND A DAY FROM A MILLENNIAL PIRATE CONVINCED SHE'D BEEN ROBBED BY A SUBMARINER VILLAIN FROM THE '40S.
THAT SOUNDS ROUGH.
YEAH. THE ONLY THINGS ROUGHER THAN THE MISSIONS ARE THE CO-WORKERS.
GLOVE CHARGE ENABLED. PULSED DIRECT CURRENT.
240 VOLTS. STUN ONLY.
FORTUNATELY, I HAVE EXPERIENCE DEALING WITH... DIFFICULT ASSOCIATES.

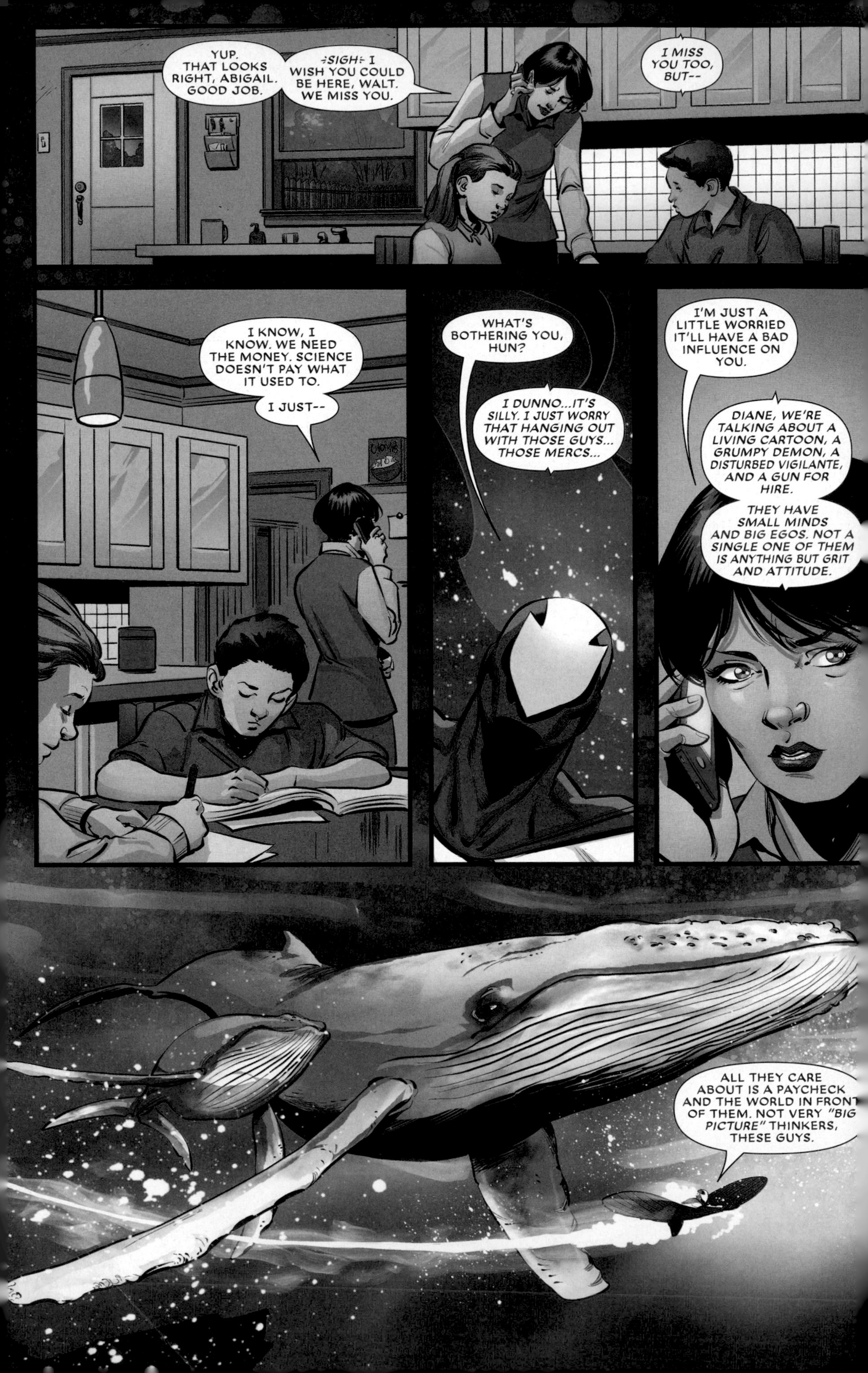
YUP. THAT LOOKS RIGHT, ABIGAIL. GOOD JOB.
=SIGH= I WISH YOU COULD BE HERE, WALT. WE MISS YOU.
I MISS YOU TOO, BUT--
I KNOW, I KNOW. WE NEED THE MONEY. SCIENCE DOESN'T PAY WHAT IT USED TO.
I JUST--
WHAT'S BOTHERING YOU, HUN?
I DUNNO...IT'S SILLY. I JUST WORRY THAT HANGING OUT WITH THOSE GUYS... THOSE MERCS...
I'M JUST A LITTLE WORRIED IT'LL HAVE A BAD INFLUENCE ON YOU.
DIANE, WE'RE TALKING ABOUT A LIVING CARTOON, A GRUMPY DEMON, A DISTURBED VIGILANTE, AND A GUN FOR HIRE.
THEY HAVE SMALL MINDS AND BIG EGOS. NOT A SINGLE ONE OF THEM IS ANYTHING BUT GRIT AND ATTITUDE.
ALL THEY CARE ABOUT IS A PAYCHECK AND THE WORLD IN FRONT OF THEM. NOT VERY "BIG PICTURE" THINKERS, THESE GUYS.

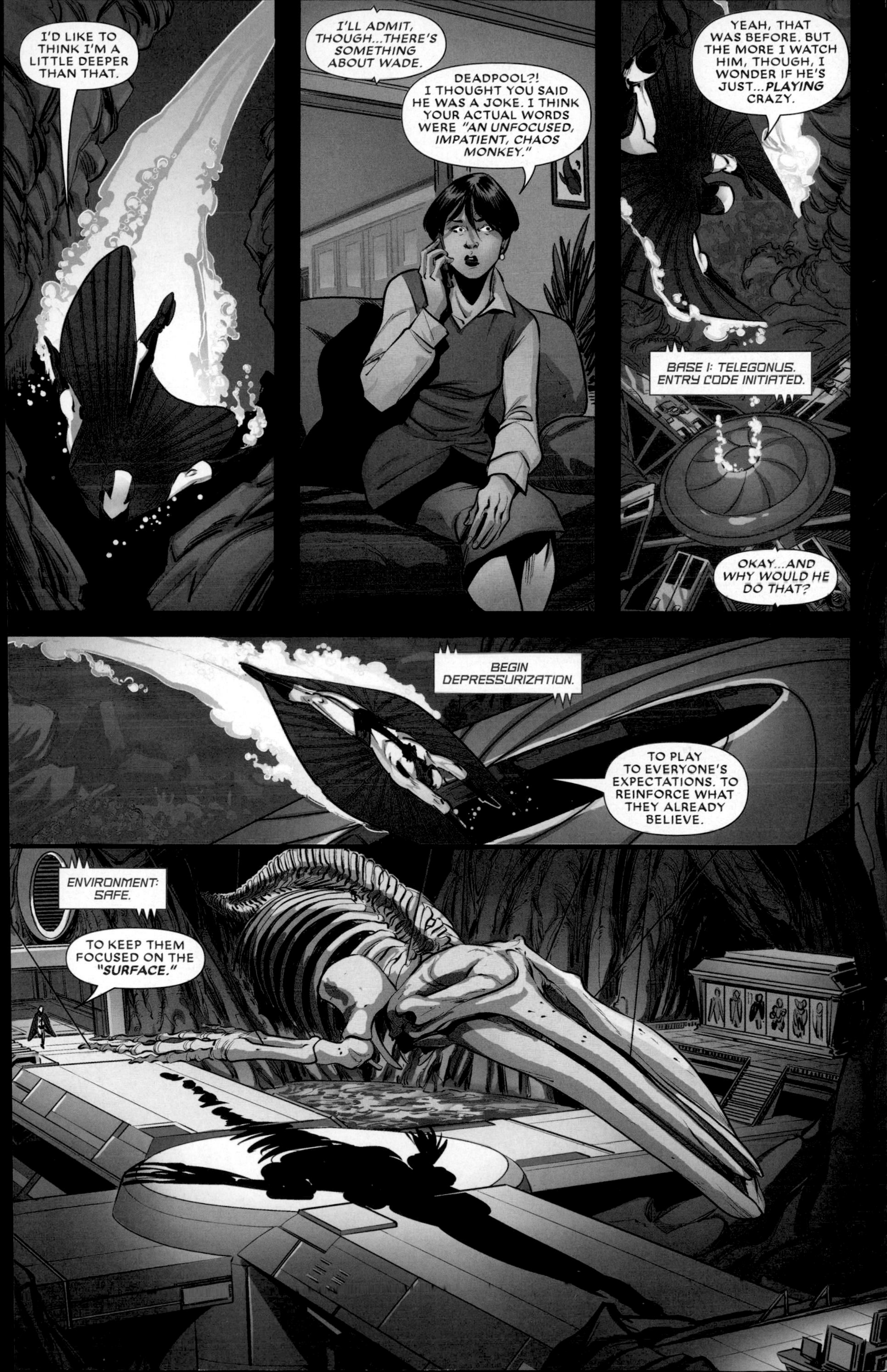
I'D LIKE TO THINK I'M A LITTLE DEEPER THAN THAT.
I'LL ADMIT, THOUGH...THERE'S SOMETHING ABOUT WADE.
DEADPOOL?! I THOUGHT YOU SAID HE WAS A JOKE. I THINK YOUR ACTUAL WORDS WERE "AN UNFOCUSED, IMPATIENT, CHAOS MONKEY."
YEAH, THAT WAS BEFORE. BUT THE MORE I WATCH HIM, THOUGH, I WONDER IF HE'S JUST...PLAYING CRAZY.
BASE I: TELEGONUS. ENTRY CODE INITIATED.
OKAY...AND WHY WOULD HE DO THAT?
BEGIN DEPRESSURIZATION.
TO PLAY TO EVERYONE'S EXPECTATIONS. TO REINFORCE WHAT THEY ALREADY BELIEVE.
ENVIRONMENT: SAFE.
TO KEEP THEM FOCUSED ON THE "SURFACE."

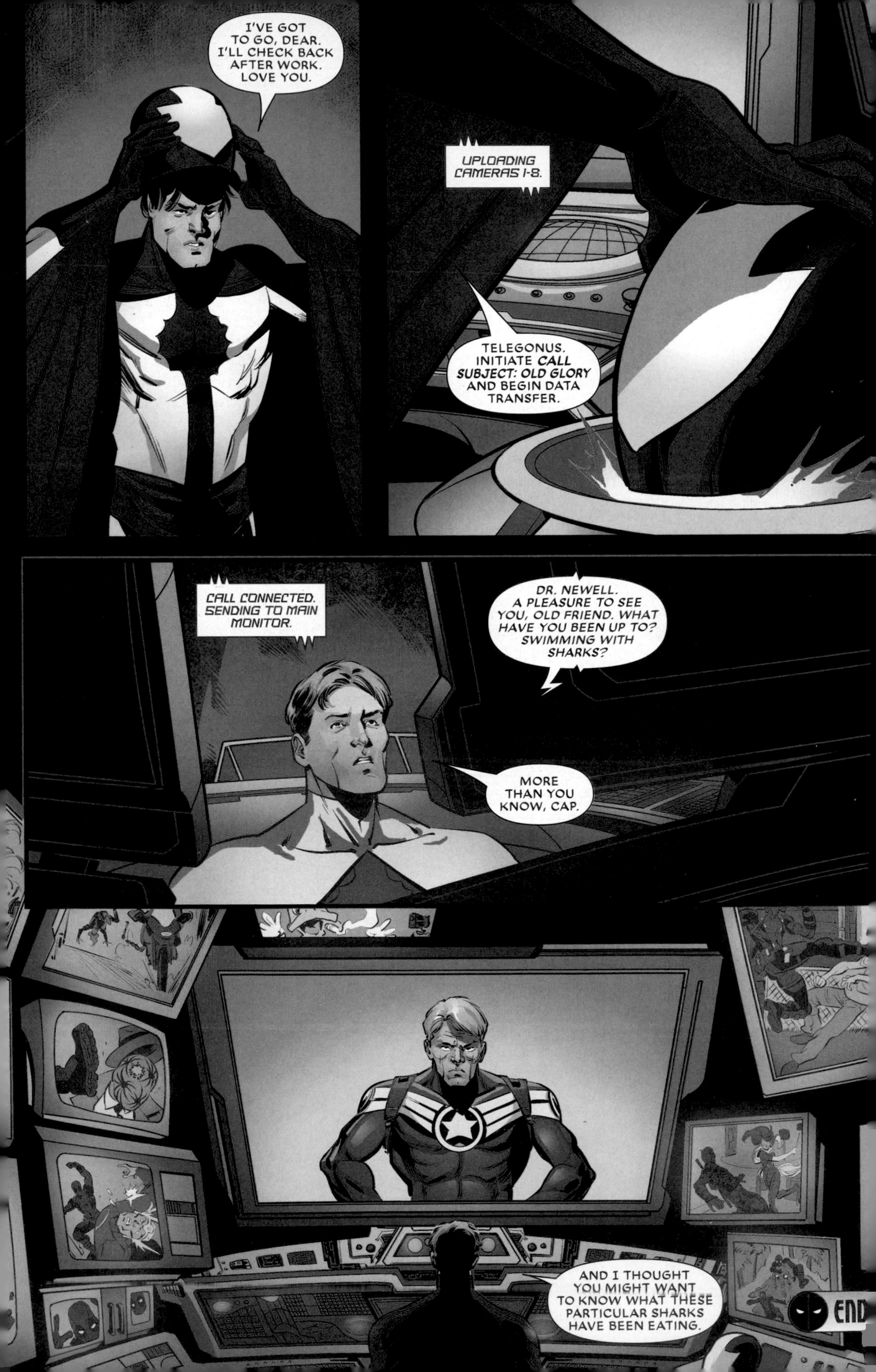
I'VE GOT TO GO, DEAR. I'LL CHECK BACK AFTER WORK. LOVE YOU.
UPLOADING CAMERAS 1-8.
TELEGONUS. INITIATE CALL SUBJECT: OLD GLORY AND BEGIN DATA TRANSFER.
CALL CONNECTED. SENDING TO MAIN MONITOR.
DR. NEWELL. A PLEASURE TO SEE YOU, OLD FRIEND. WHAT HAVE YOU BEEN UP TO? SWIMMING WITH SHARKS?
MORE THAN YOU KNOW, CAP.
AND I THOUGHT YOU MIGHT WANT TO KNOW WHAT THESE PARTICULAR SHARKS HAVE BEEN EATING.
END

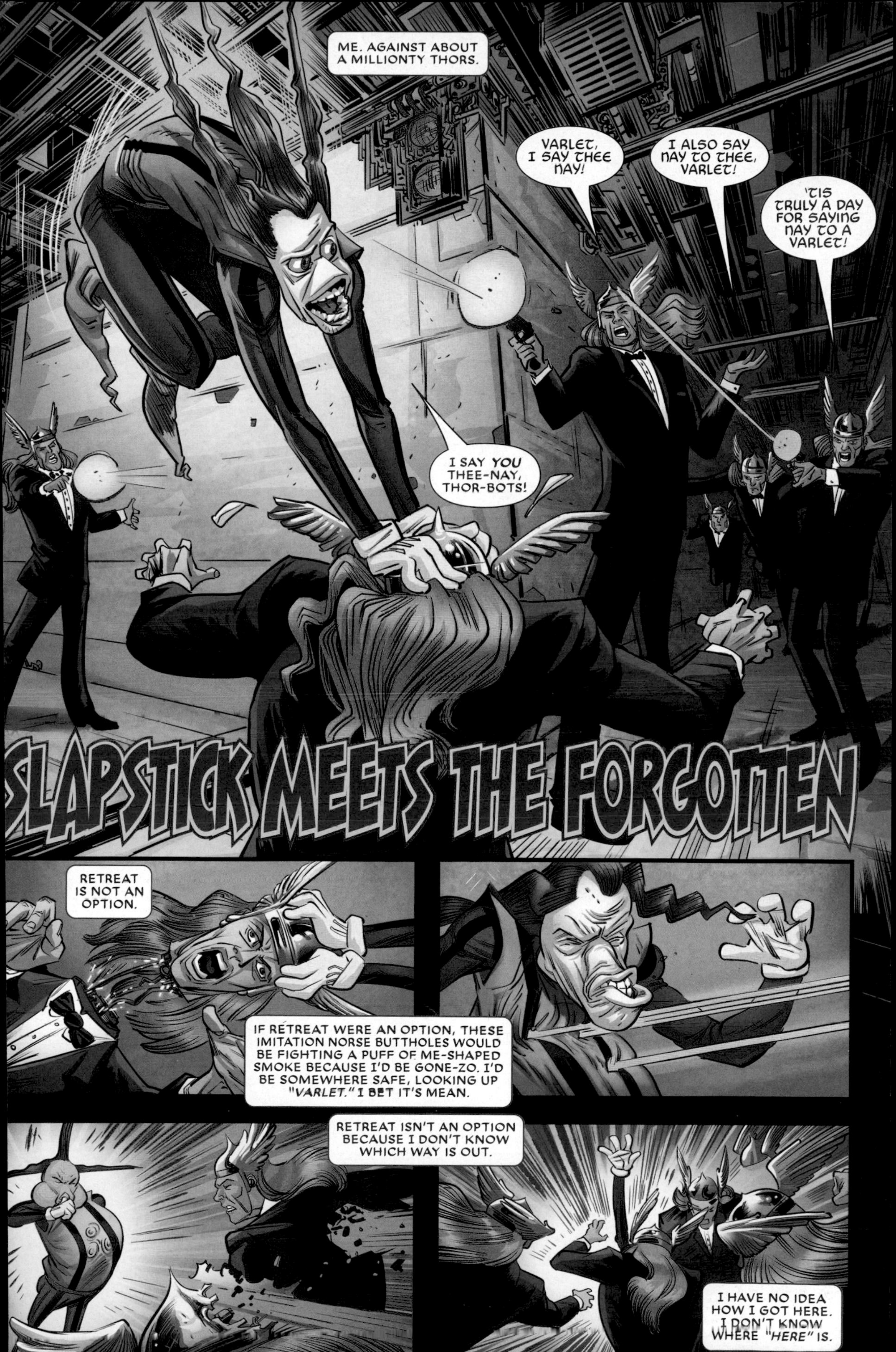
ME. AGAINST ABOUT A MILLIONTY THORS.
VARLET, I SAY THEE NAY!
I ALSO SAY NAY TO THEE, VARLET!
'TIS TRULY A DAY FOR SAYING NAY TO A VARLET!
I SAY *YOU* THEE-NAY, THOR-BOTS!
SLAPSTICK MEETS THE FORGOTTEN
RETREAT IS NOT AN OPTION.
IF RETREAT WERE AN OPTION, THESE IMITATION NORSE BUTTHOLES WOULD BE FIGHTING A PUFF OF ME-SHAPED SMOKE BECAUSE I'D BE GONE-ZO. I'D BE SOMEWHERE SAFE, LOOKING UP "*VARLET.*" I BET IT'S MEAN.
RETREAT ISN'T AN OPTION BECAUSE I DON'T KNOW WHICH WAY IS OUT.
I HAVE NO IDEA HOW I GOT HERE. I DON'T KNOW WHERE "*HERE*" IS.

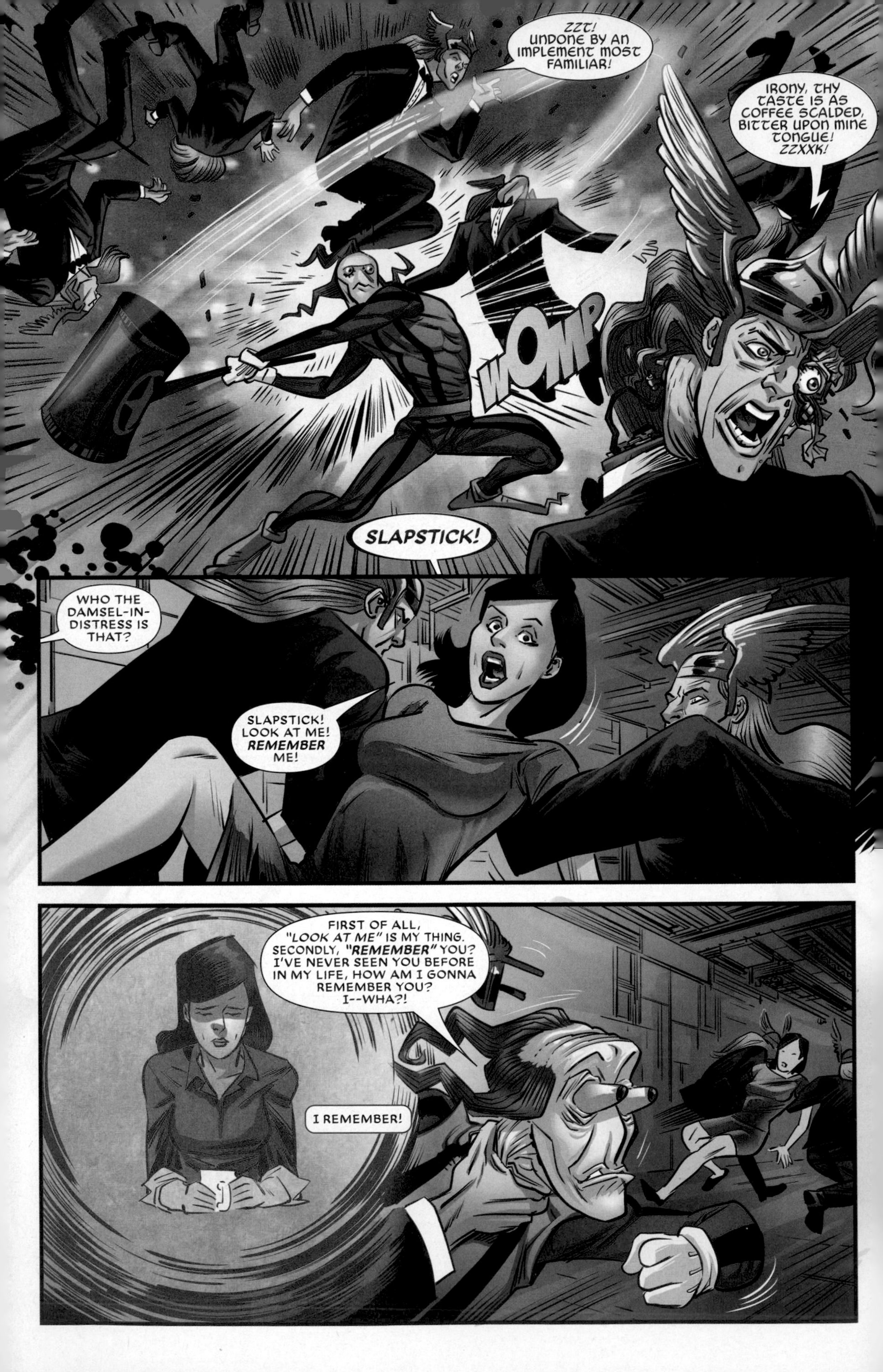

ZZT! UNDONE BY AN IMPLEMENT MOST FAMILIAR!
IRONY, THY TASTE IS AS COFFEE SCALDED, BITTER UPON MINE TONGUE! ZZXXK!
WOMP
SLAPSTICK!
WHO THE DAMSEL-IN-DISTRESS IS THAT?
SLAPSTICK! LOOK AT ME! REMEMBER ME!
FIRST OF ALL, "LOOK AT ME" IS MY THING. SECONDLY, "REMEMBER" YOU? I'VE NEVER SEEN YOU BEFORE IN MY LIFE, HOW AM I GONNA REMEMBER YOU? I--WHA?!
I REMEMBER!

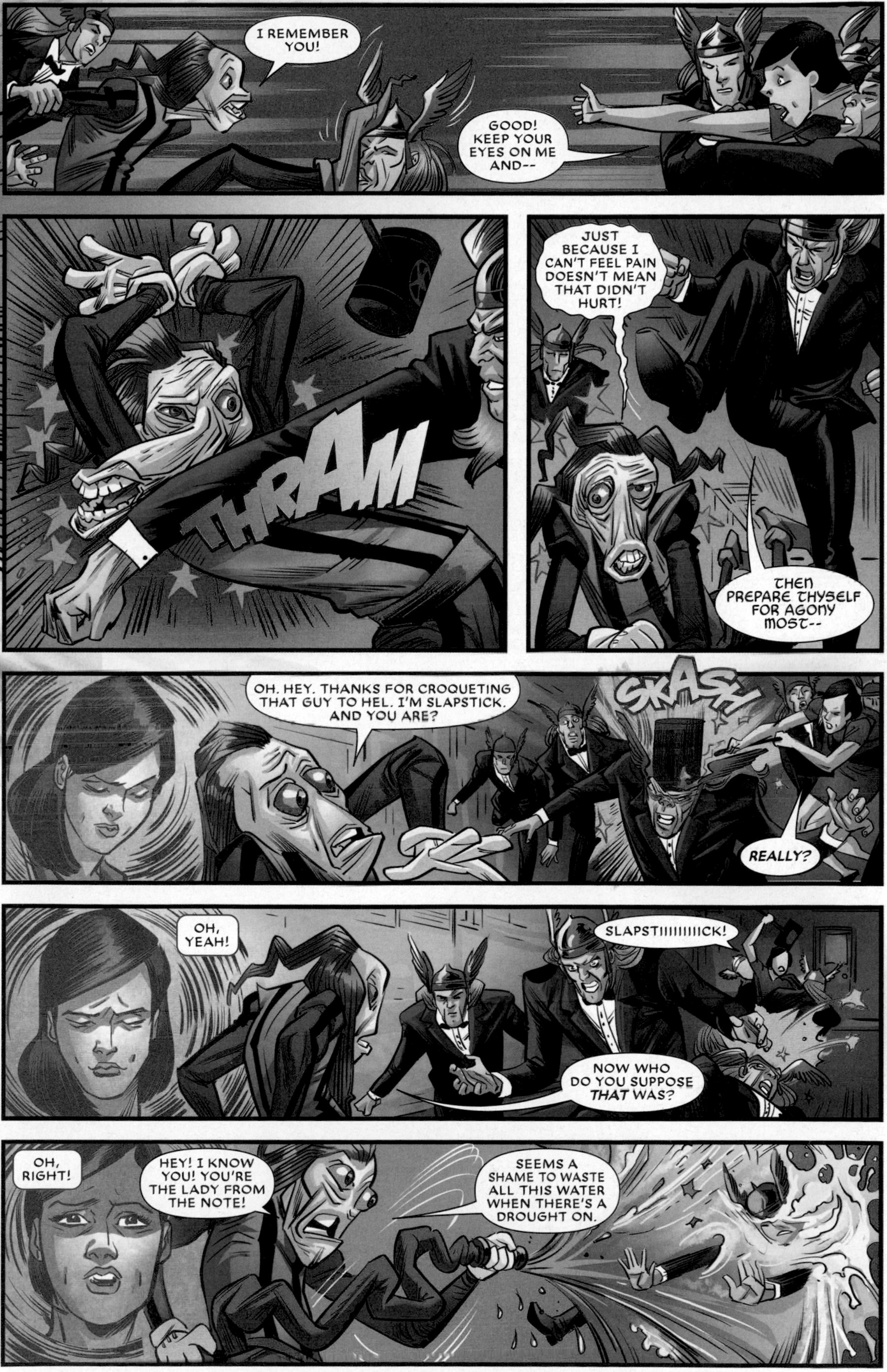
I REMEMBER YOU!
GOOD! KEEP YOUR EYES ON ME AND--
THRAM
JUST BECAUSE I CAN'T FEEL PAIN DOESN'T MEAN THAT DIDN'T HURT!
THEN PREPARE THYSELF FOR AGONY MOST--
OH. HEY. THANKS FOR CROQUETING THAT GUY TO HEL. I'M SLAPSTICK. AND YOU ARE?
SKASH
REALLY?
OH, YEAH!
SLAPSTIIIIIIIIIICK!
NOW WHO DO YOU SUPPOSE *THAT* WAS?
OH, RIGHT!
HEY! I KNOW YOU! YOU'RE THE LADY FROM THE NOTE!
SEEMS A SHAME TO WASTE ALL THIS WATER WHEN THERE'S A DROUGHT ON.

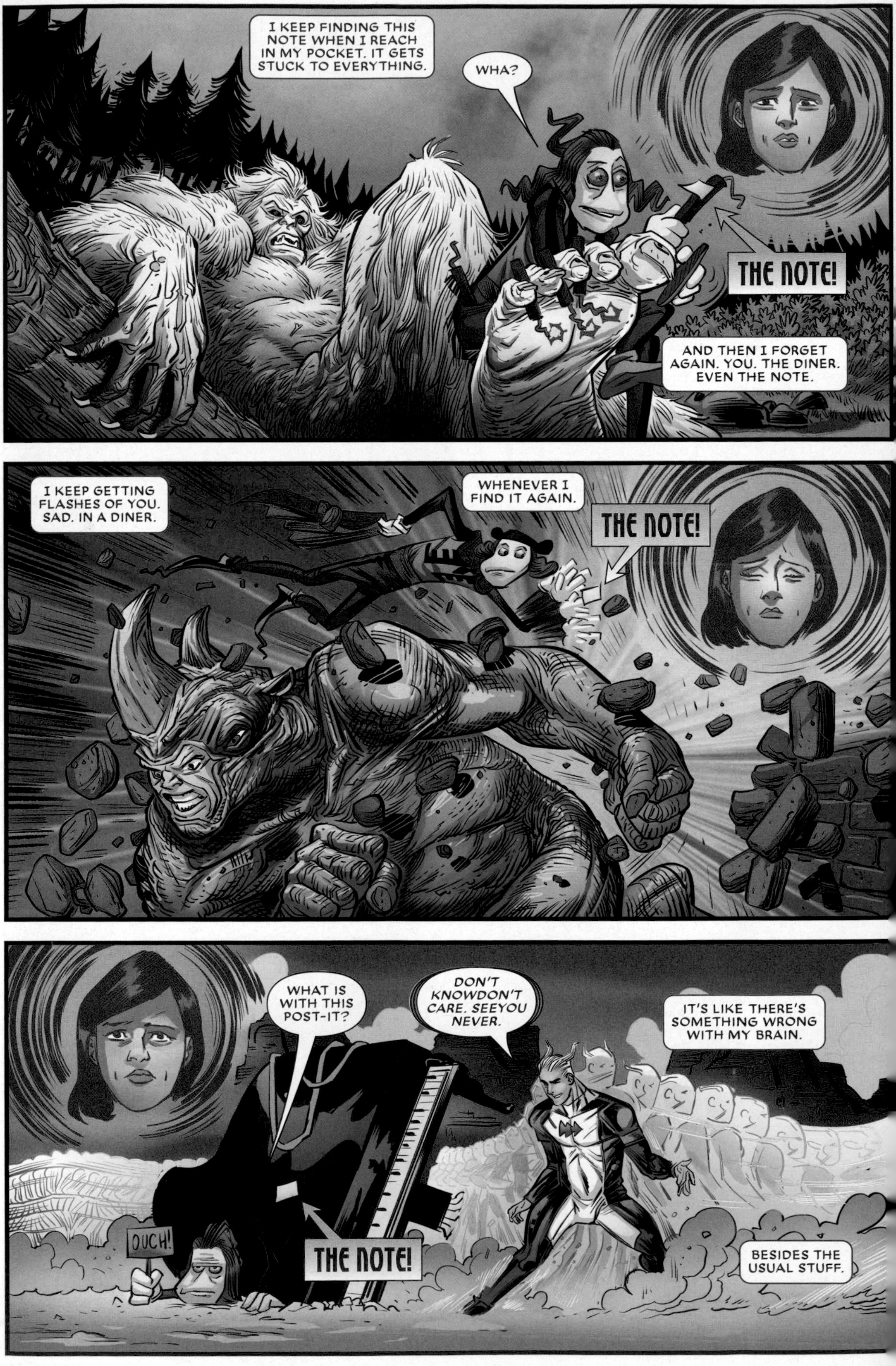
I KEEP FINDING THIS NOTE WHEN I REACH IN MY POCKET. IT GETS STUCK TO EVERYTHING.
WHA?
THE NOTE!
AND THEN I FORGET AGAIN. YOU. THE DINER. EVEN THE NOTE.
I KEEP GETTING FLASHES OF YOU. SAD. IN A DINER.
WHENEVER I FIND IT AGAIN.
THE NOTE!
WHAT IS WITH THIS POST-IT?
DON'T KNOWDON'T CARE. SEEYOU NEVER.
IT'S LIKE THERE'S SOMETHING WRONG WITH MY BRAIN.
OUCH!
THE NOTE!
BESIDES THE USUAL STUFF.

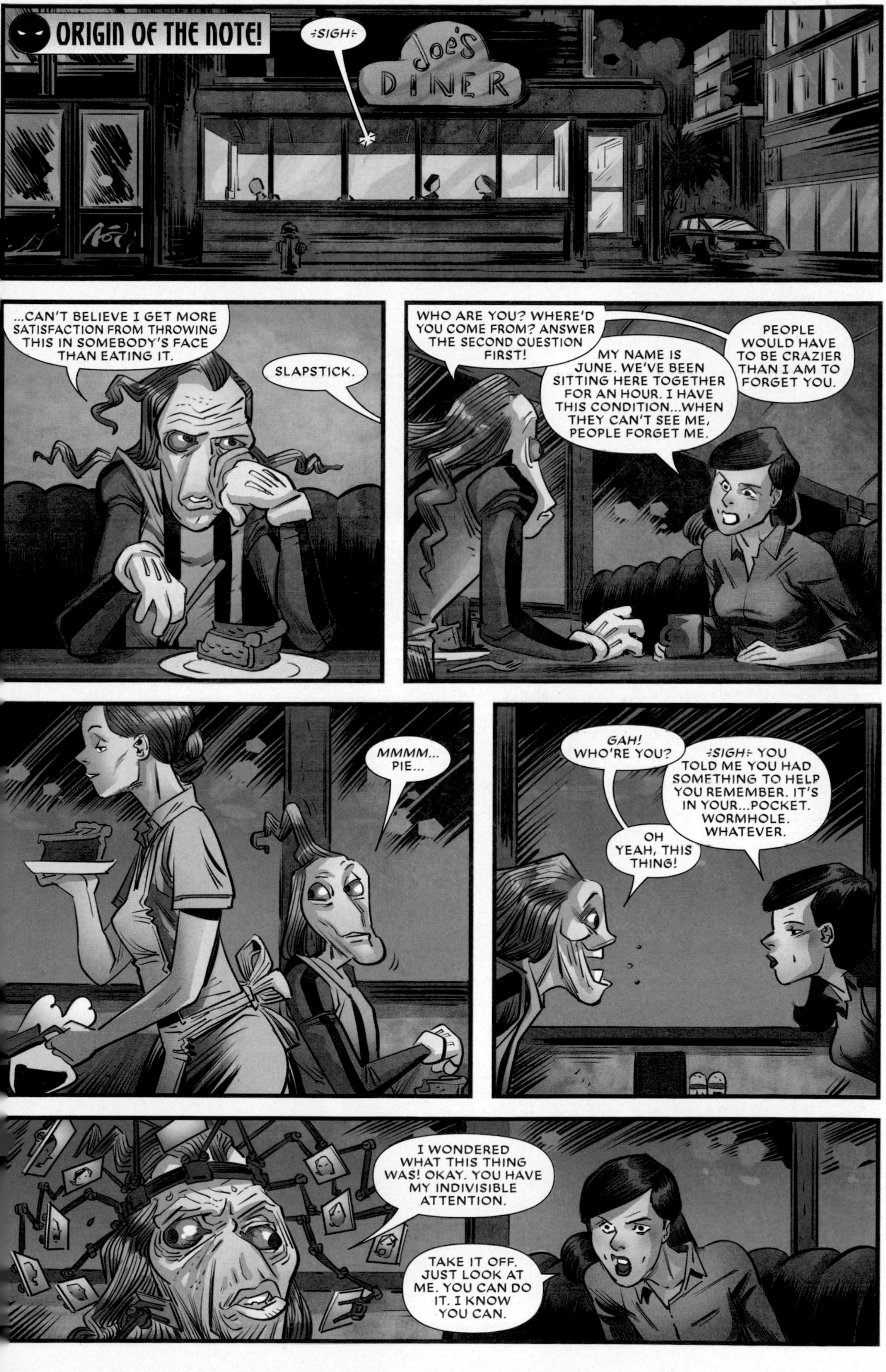
ORIGIN OF THE NOTE!
SIGH
JOE'S DINER
...CAN'T BELIEVE I GET MORE SATISFACTION FROM THROWING THIS IN SOMEBODY'S FACE THAN EATING IT.
SLAPSTICK.
WHO ARE YOU? WHERE'D YOU COME FROM? ANSWER THE SECOND QUESTION FIRST!
MY NAME IS JUNE. WE'VE BEEN SITTING HERE TOGETHER FOR AN HOUR. I HAVE THIS CONDITION...WHEN THEY CAN'T SEE ME, PEOPLE FORGET ME.
PEOPLE WOULD HAVE TO BE CRAZIER THAN I AM TO FORGET YOU.
MMMM... PIE...
GAH! WHO'RE YOU?
SIGH YOU TOLD ME YOU HAD SOMETHING TO HELP YOU REMEMBER. IT'S IN YOUR...POCKET. WORMHOLE. WHATEVER.
OH YEAH, THIS THING!
I WONDERED WHAT THIS THING WAS! OKAY. YOU HAVE MY INDIVISIBLE ATTENTION.
TAKE IT OFF. JUST LOOK AT ME. YOU CAN DO IT. I KNOW YOU CAN.

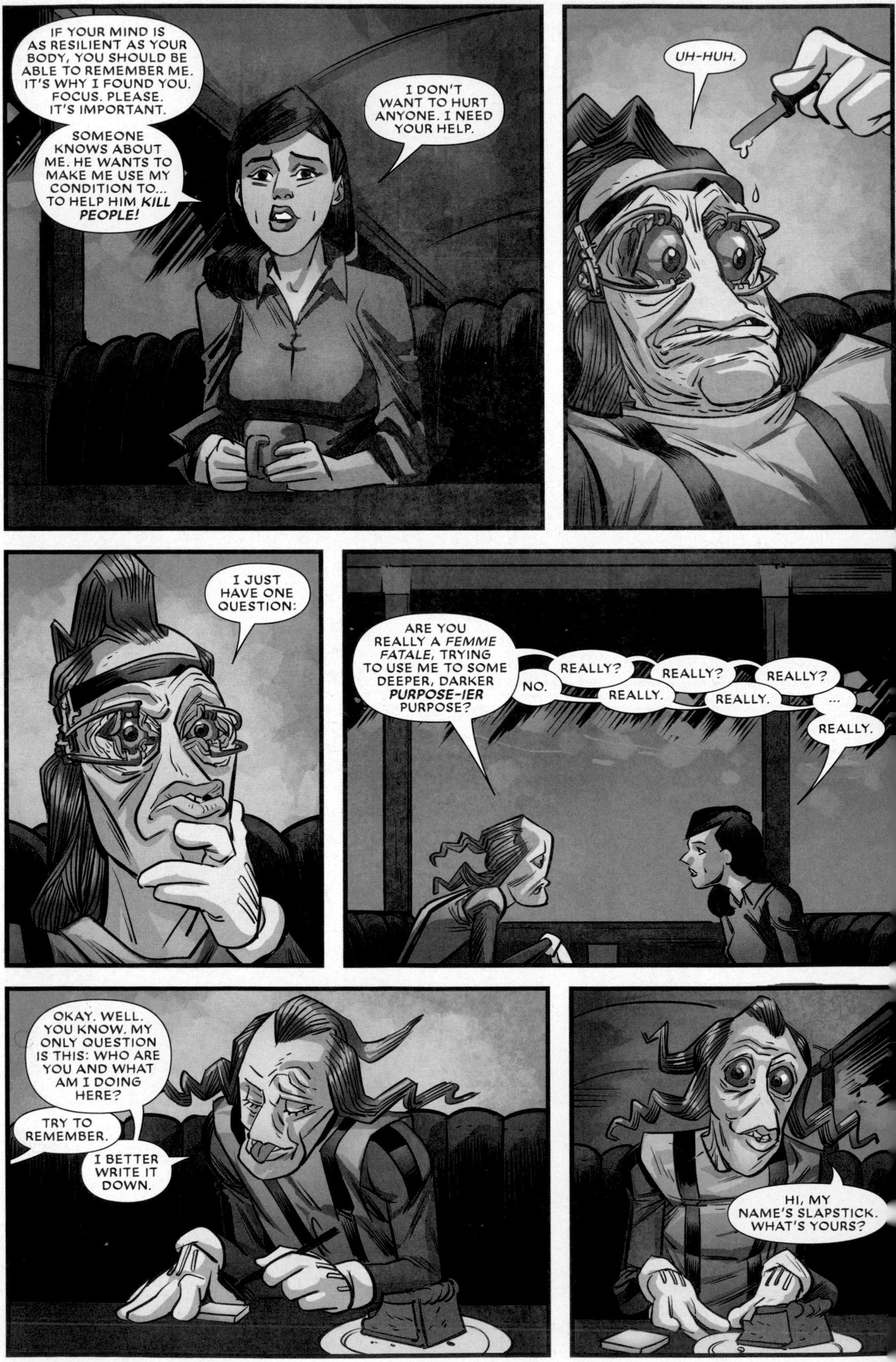
IF YOUR MIND IS AS RESILIENT AS YOUR BODY, YOU SHOULD BE ABLE TO REMEMBER ME. IT'S WHY I FOUND YOU. FOCUS. PLEASE. IT'S IMPORTANT.
SOMEONE KNOWS ABOUT ME. HE WANTS TO MAKE ME USE MY CONDITION TO... TO HELP HIM *KILL PEOPLE!*
I DON'T WANT TO HURT ANYONE. I NEED YOUR HELP.
UH-HUH.
I JUST HAVE ONE QUESTION:
ARE YOU REALLY A *FEMME FATALE*, TRYING TO USE ME TO SOME DEEPER, DARKER ***PURPOSE-IER*** PURPOSE?
NO.
REALLY?
REALLY.
REALLY?
REALLY.
REALLY?
...
REALLY.
OKAY. WELL. YOU KNOW. MY ONLY QUESTION IS THIS: WHO ARE YOU AND WHAT AM I DOING HERE?
TRY TO REMEMBER.
I BETTER WRITE IT DOWN.
HI, MY NAME'S SLAPSTICK. WHAT'S YOURS?

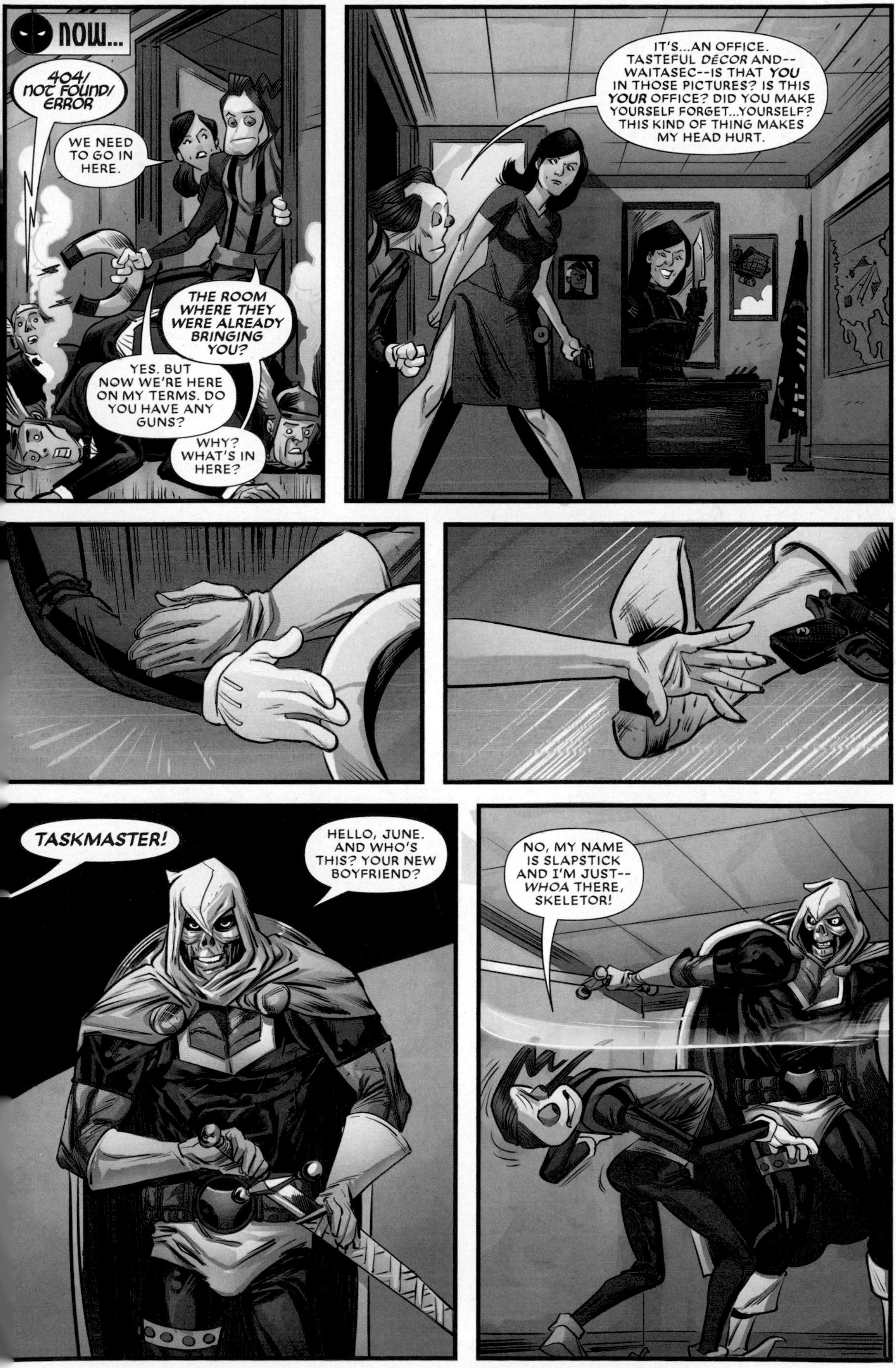
NOW...
404/ NOT FOUND/ ERROR
WE NEED TO GO IN HERE.
THE ROOM WHERE THEY WERE ALREADY BRINGING YOU?
YES. BUT NOW WE'RE HERE ON MY TERMS. DO YOU HAVE ANY GUNS?
WHY? WHAT'S IN HERE?
IT'S...AN OFFICE. TASTEFUL DÉCOR AND-- WAITASEC--IS THAT YOU IN THOSE PICTURES? IS THIS YOUR OFFICE? DID YOU MAKE YOURSELF FORGET...YOURSELF? THIS KIND OF THING MAKES MY HEAD HURT.
TASKMASTER!
HELLO, JUNE. AND WHO'S THIS? YOUR NEW BOYFRIEND?
NO, MY NAME IS SLAPSTICK AND I'M JUST-- WHOA THERE, SKELETOR!

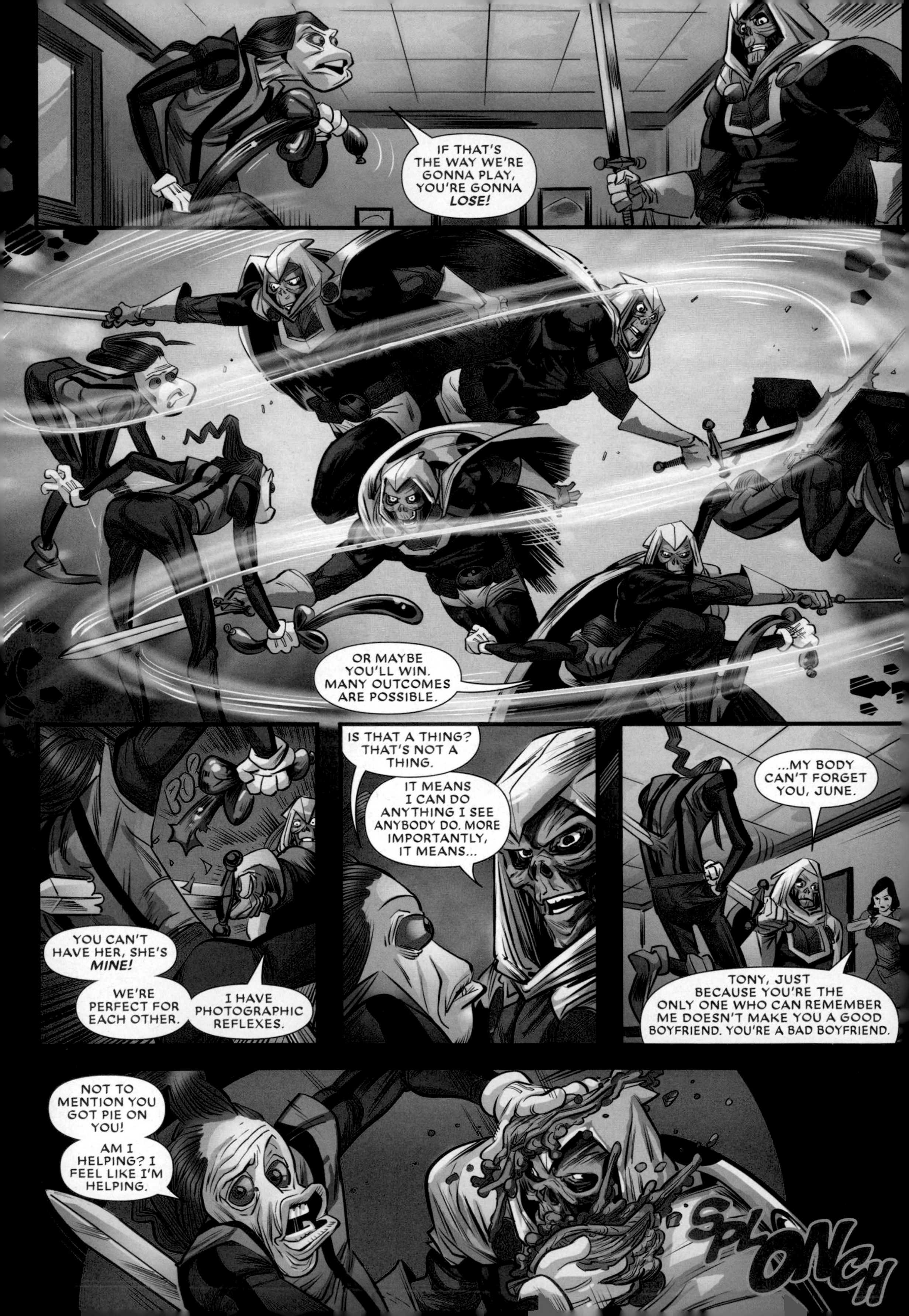

IF THAT'S THE WAY WE'RE GONNA PLAY, YOU'RE GONNA *LOSE!*
OR MAYBE YOU'LL WIN. MANY OUTCOMES ARE POSSIBLE.
POP
YOU CAN'T HAVE HER, SHE'S *MINE!*
WE'RE PERFECT FOR EACH OTHER.
I HAVE PHOTOGRAPHIC REFLEXES.
IS THAT A THING? THAT'S NOT A THING.
IT MEANS I CAN DO ANYTHING I SEE ANYBODY DO. MORE IMPORTANTLY, IT MEANS...
...MY BODY CAN'T FORGET YOU, JUNE.
TONY, JUST BECAUSE YOU'RE THE ONLY ONE WHO CAN REMEMBER ME DOESN'T MAKE YOU A GOOD BOYFRIEND. YOU'RE A BAD BOYFRIEND.
NOT TO MENTION YOU GOT PIE ON YOU!
AM I HELPING? I FEEL LIKE I'M HELPING.
SPLONCH

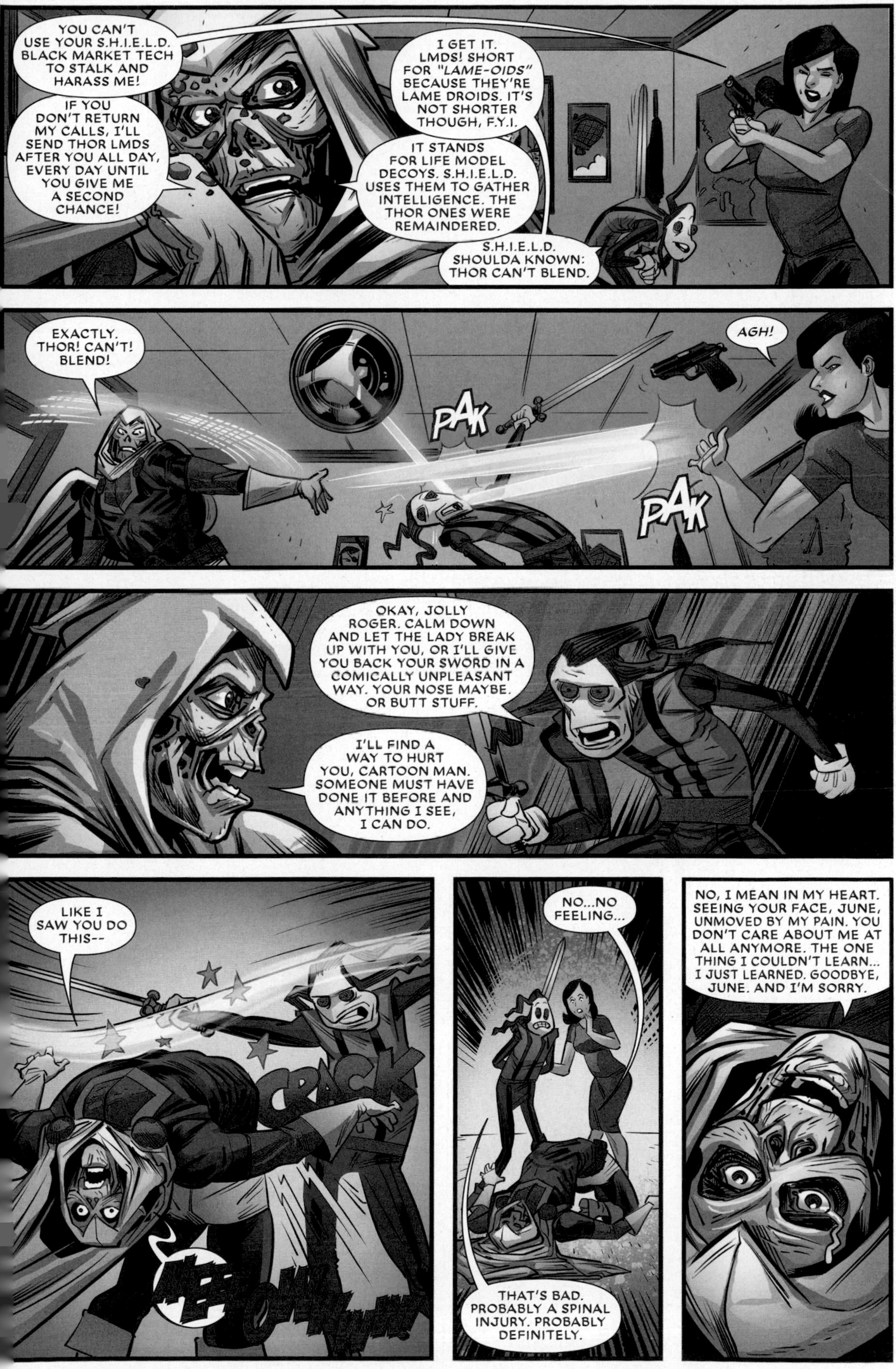
YOU CAN'T USE YOUR S.H.I.E.L.D. BLACK MARKET TECH TO STALK AND HARASS ME!
IF YOU DON'T RETURN MY CALLS, I'LL SEND THOR LMDS AFTER YOU ALL DAY, EVERY DAY UNTIL YOU GIVE ME A SECOND CHANCE!
I GET IT. LMDS! SHORT FOR "LAME-OIDS" BECAUSE THEY'RE LAME DROIDS. IT'S NOT SHORTER THOUGH, F.Y.I.
IT STANDS FOR LIFE MODEL DECOYS. S.H.I.E.L.D. USES THEM TO GATHER INTELLIGENCE. THE THOR ONES WERE REMAINDERED.
S.H.I.E.L.D. SHOULDA KNOWN: THOR CAN'T BLEND.
EXACTLY. THOR! CAN'T! BLEND!
AGH!
PAK
PAK
OKAY, JOLLY ROGER. CALM DOWN AND LET THE LADY BREAK UP WITH YOU, OR I'LL GIVE YOU BACK YOUR SWORD IN A COMICALLY UNPLEASANT WAY. YOUR NOSE MAYBE. OR BUTT STUFF.
I'LL FIND A WAY TO HURT YOU, CARTOON MAN. SOMEONE MUST HAVE DONE IT BEFORE AND ANYTHING I SEE, I CAN DO.
LIKE I SAW YOU DO THIS--
CRACK
NO...NO FEELING...
THAT'S BAD. PROBABLY A SPINAL INJURY. PROBABLY DEFINITELY.
NO, I MEAN IN MY HEART. SEEING YOUR FACE, JUNE, UNMOVED BY MY PAIN. YOU DON'T CARE ABOUT ME AT ALL ANYMORE. THE ONE THING I COULDN'T LEARN... I JUST LEARNED. GOODBYE, JUNE. AND I'M SORRY.

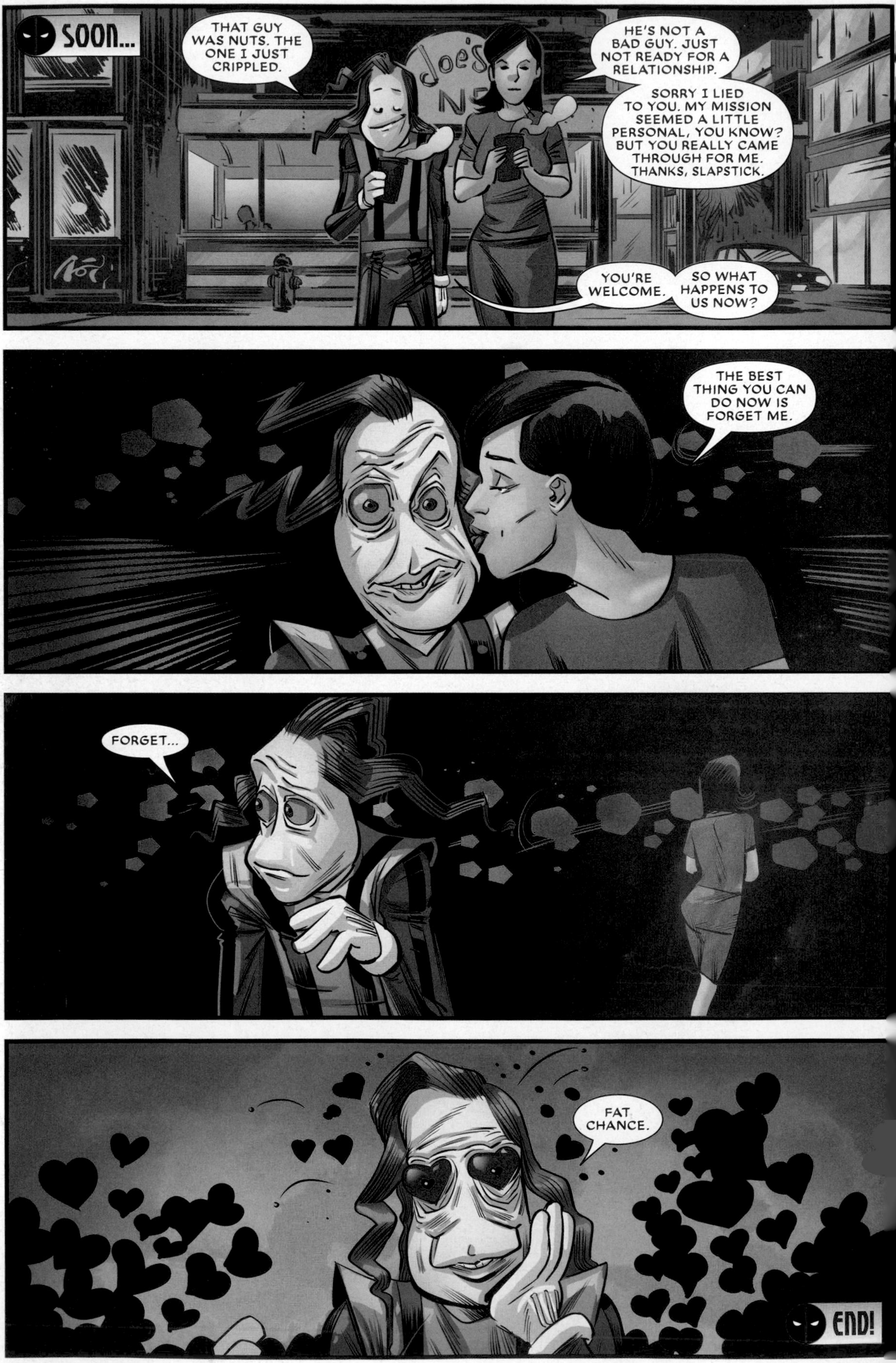
SOON...
THAT GUY WAS NUTS. THE ONE I JUST CRIPPLED.
HE'S NOT A BAD GUY. JUST NOT READY FOR A RELATIONSHIP.
SORRY I LIED TO YOU. MY MISSION SEEMED A LITTLE PERSONAL, YOU KNOW? BUT YOU REALLY CAME THROUGH FOR ME. THANKS, SLAPSTICK.
YOU'RE WELCOME.
SO WHAT HAPPENS TO US NOW?
THE BEST THING YOU CAN DO NOW IS FORGET ME.
FORGET...
FAT CHANCE.
END!

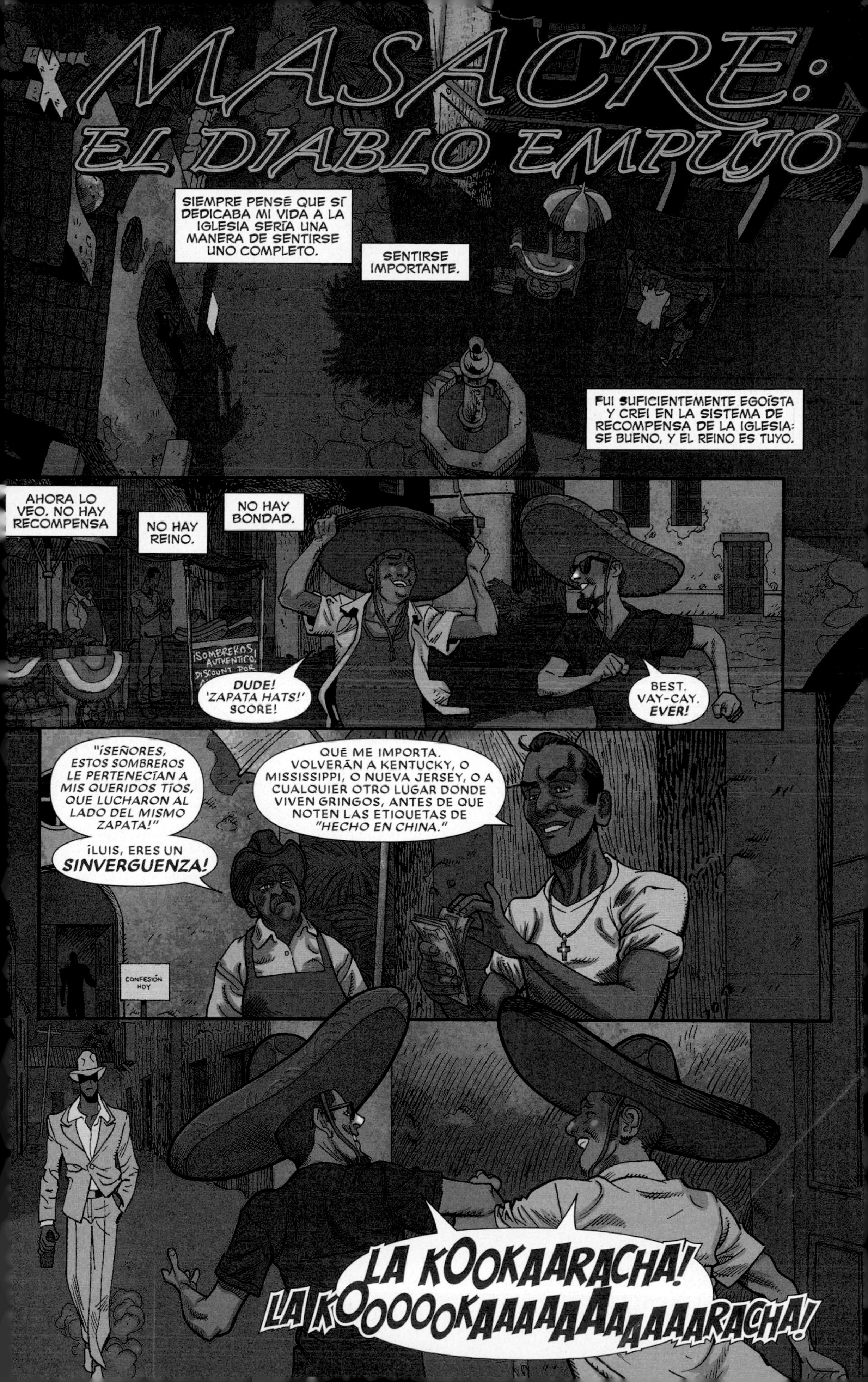
MASACRE: EL DIABLO EMPUJÓ
SIEMPRE PENSÉ QUE SÍ DEDICABA MI VIDA A LA IGLESIA SERÍA UNA MANERA DE SENTIRSE UNO COMPLETO.
SENTIRSE IMPORTANTE.
FUI SUFICIENTEMENTE EGOÍSTA Y CREI EN LA SISTEMA DE RECOMPENSA DE LA IGLESIA: SE BUENO, Y EL REINO ES TUYO.
AHORA LO VEO. NO HAY RECOMPENSA
NO HAY REINO.
NO HAY BONDAD.
¡SOMBREROS AUTENTICO!
DUDE! 'ZAPATA HATS!' SCORE!
BEST. VAY-CAY. EVER!
"¡SEÑORES, ESTOS SOMBREROS LE PERTENECÍAN A MIS QUERIDOS TÍOS, QUE LUCHARON AL LADO DEL MISMO ZAPATA!"
¡LUIS, ERES UN SINVERGUENZA!
QUÉ ME IMPORTA. VOLVERÁN A KENTUCKY, O MISSISSIPPI, O NUEVA JERSEY, O A CUALQUIER OTRO LUGAR DONDE VIVEN GRINGOS, ANTES DE QUE NOTEN LAS ETIQUETAS DE "HECHO EN CHINA."
CONFESIÓN HOY
LA KOOKAARACHA! LA KOOOOOKAAAAAAAAAAAARACHA!

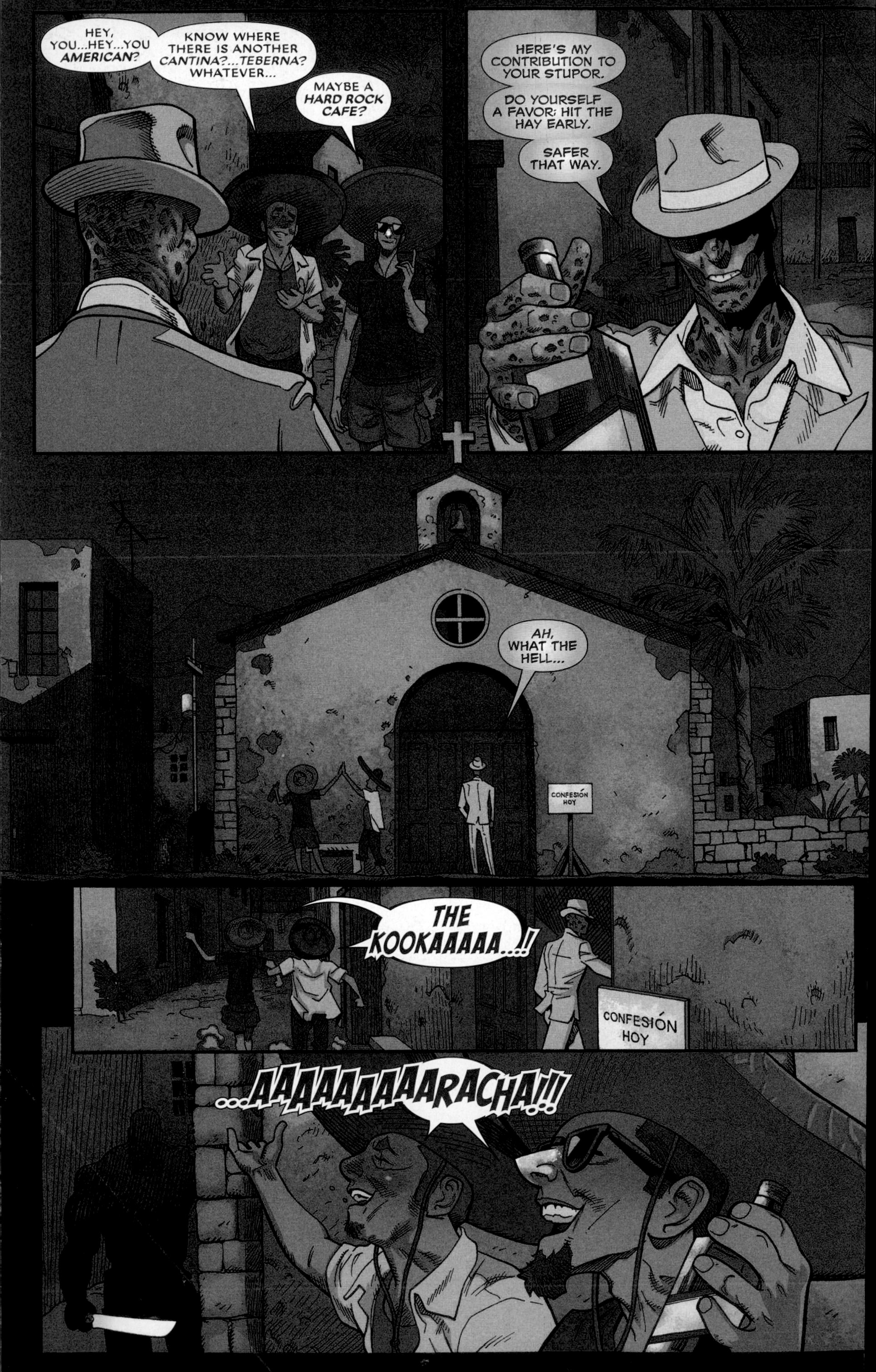
HEY, YOU...HEY...YOU *AMERICAN*?
KNOW WHERE THERE IS ANOTHER *CANTINA*?...*TEBERNA*? WHATEVER...
MAYBE A *HARD ROCK CAFE*?
HERE'S MY CONTRIBUTION TO YOUR STUPOR.
DO YOURSELF A FAVOR; HIT THE HAY EARLY.
SAFER THAT WAY.
AH, WHAT THE HELL...
CONFESIÓN HOY
THE KOOKAAAAA...!!
CONFESIÓN HOY
...AAAAAAAAARACHA!!!

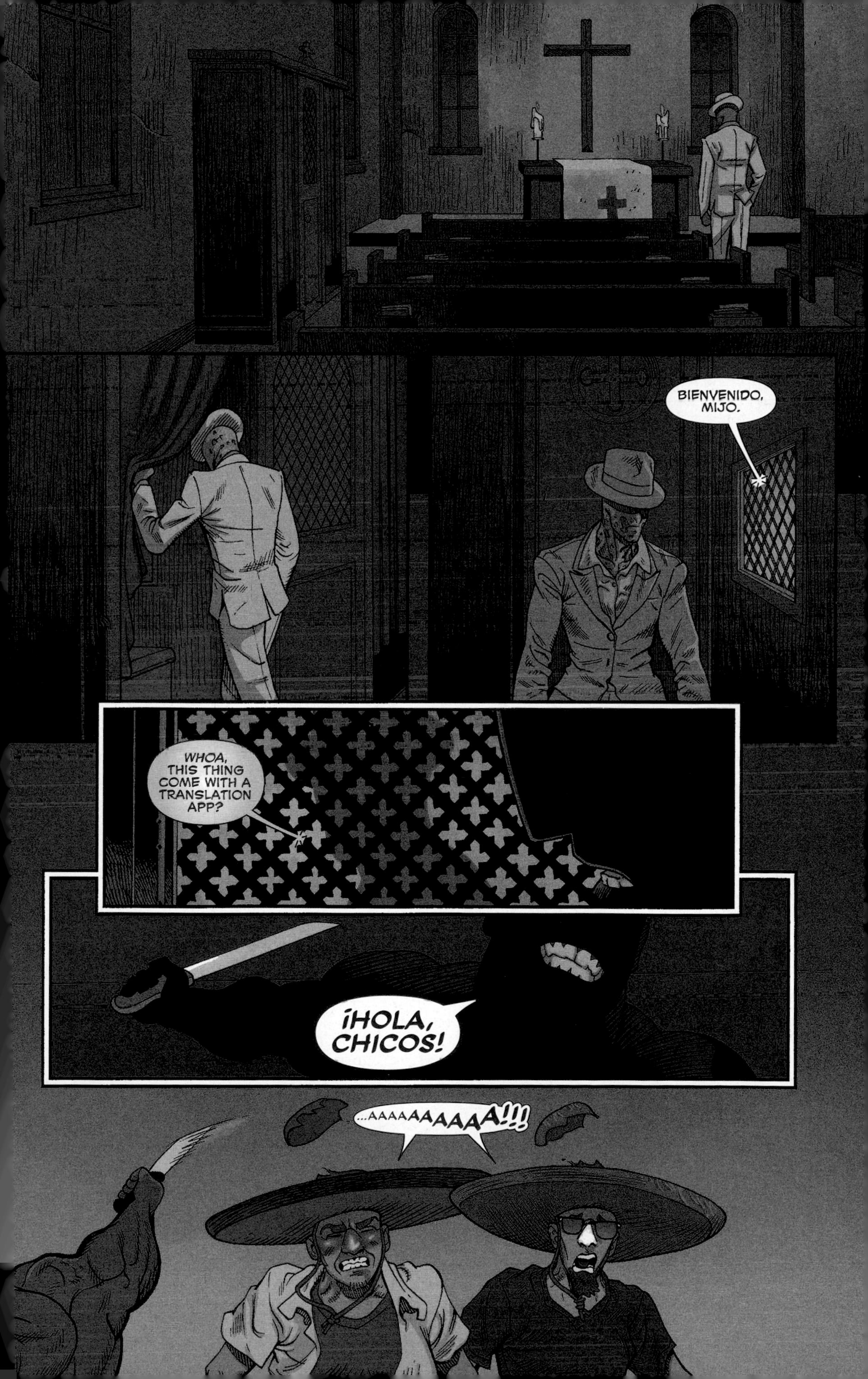
BIENVENIDO, MIJO.
WHOA, THIS THING COME WITH A TRANSLATION APP?
¡HOLA, CHICOS!
...AAAAAAAAAA!!!

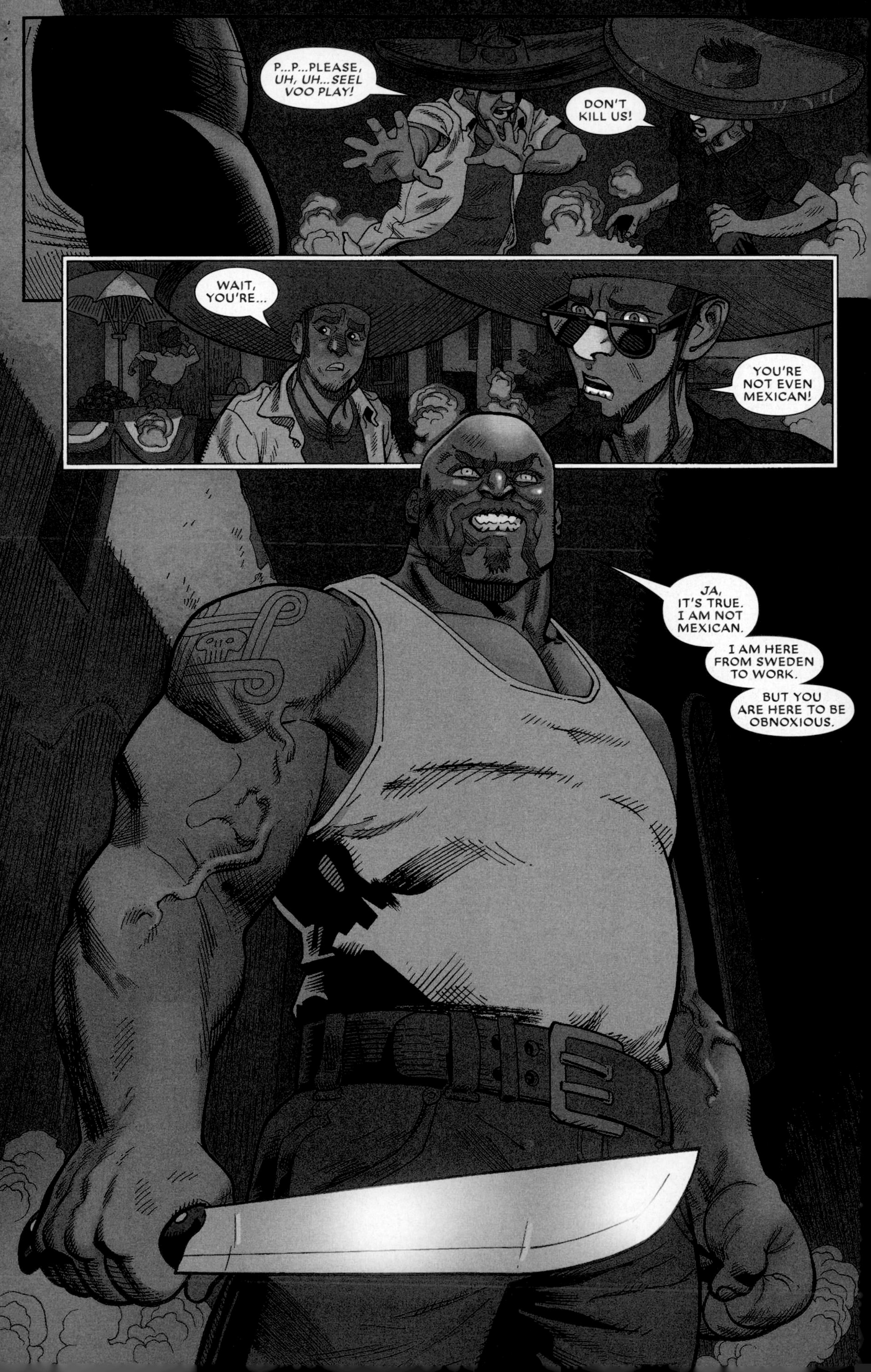
P...P...PLEASE, UH, UH...SEEL VOO PLAY!
DON'T KILL US!
WAIT, YOU'RE...
YOU'RE NOT EVEN MEXICAN!
JA, IT'S TRUE. I AM NOT MEXICAN.
I AM HERE FROM SWEDEN TO WORK.
BUT YOU ARE HERE TO BE OBNOXIOUS.

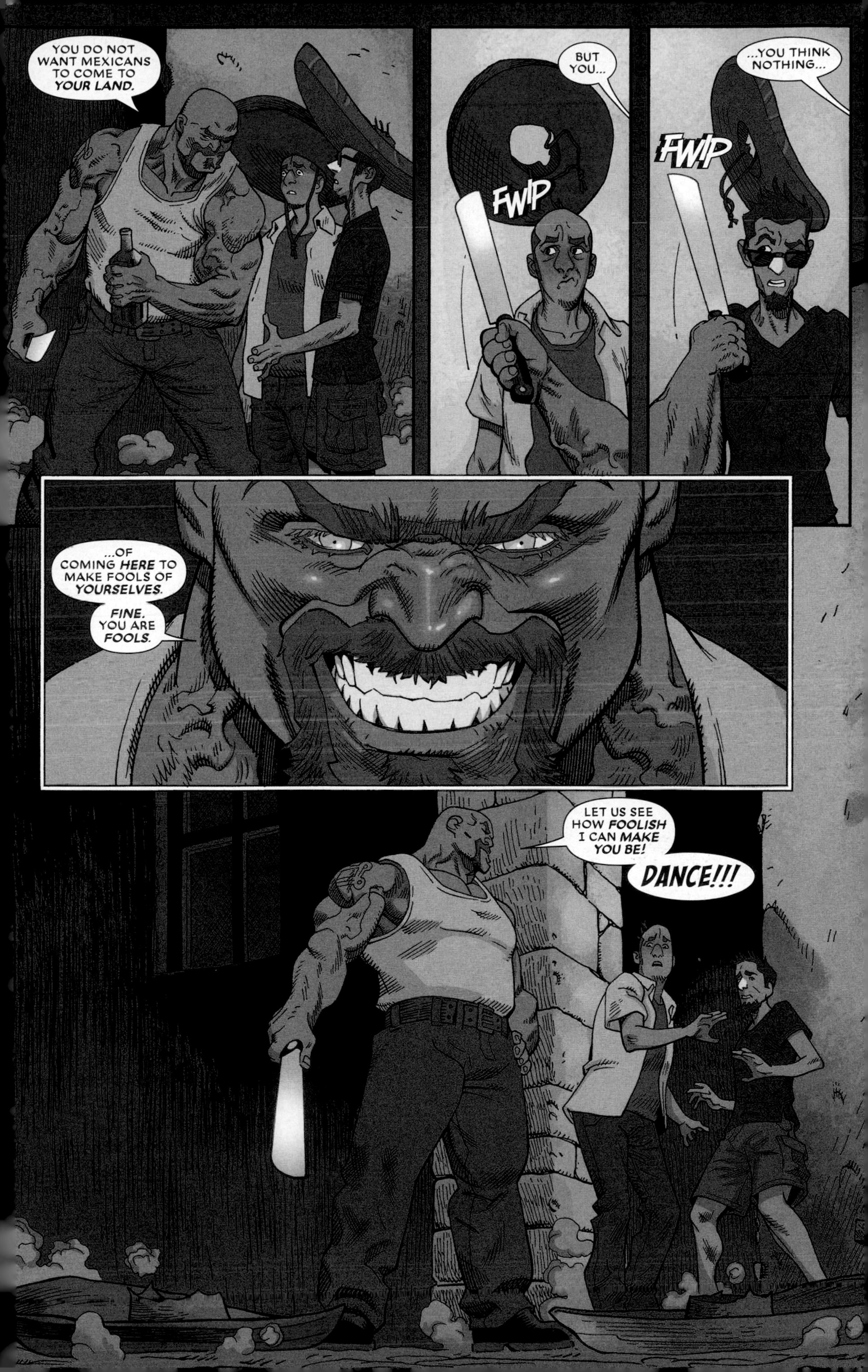
YOU DO NOT WANT MEXICANS TO COME TO YOUR LAND.
BUT YOU...
FWIP
...YOU THINK NOTHING...
FWIP
...OF COMING HERE TO MAKE FOOLS OF YOURSELVES.
FINE. YOU ARE FOOLS.
LET US SEE HOW FOOLISH I CAN MAKE YOU BE!
DANCE!!!

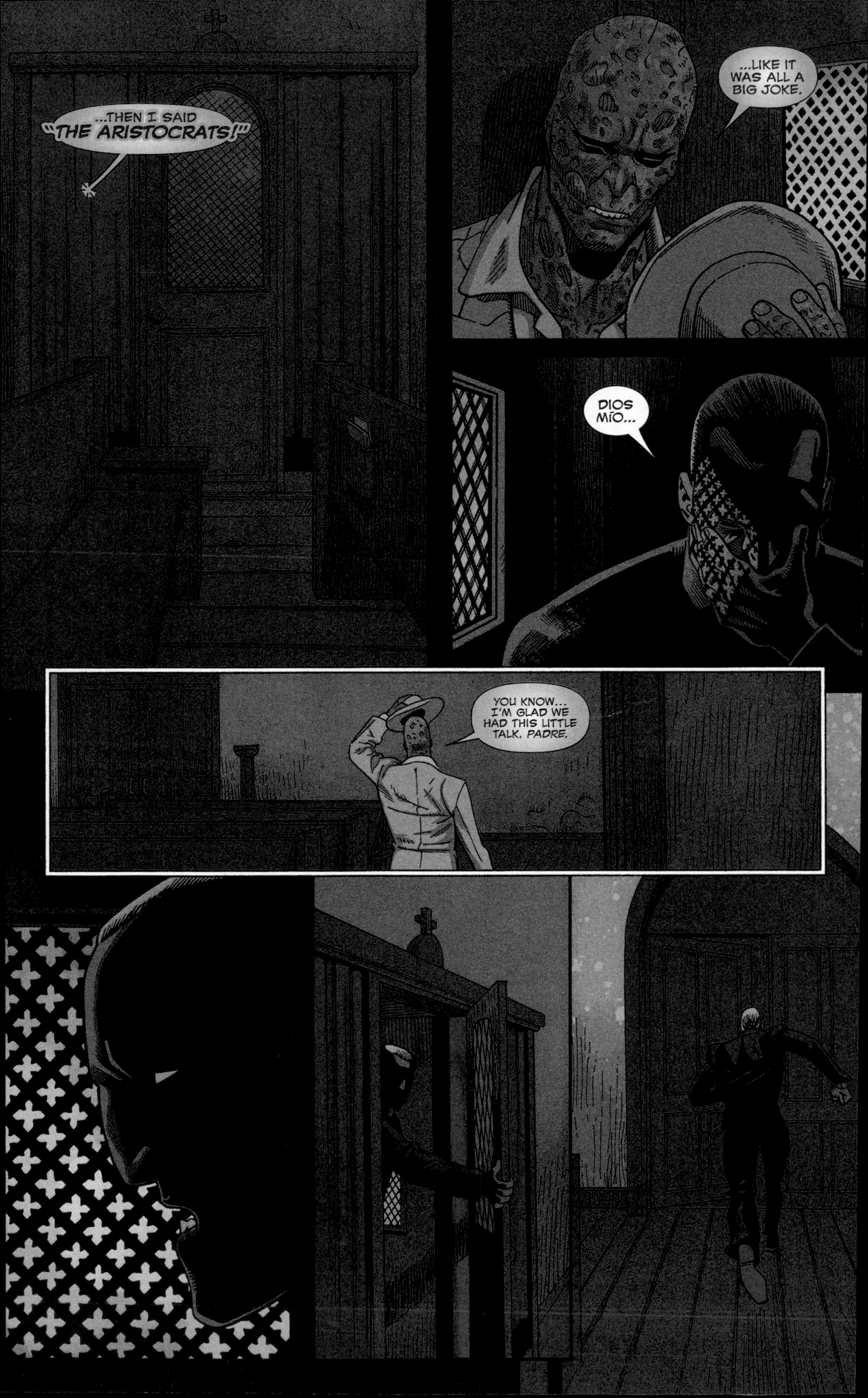
...THEN I SAID "THE ARISTOCRATS!"
...LIKE IT WAS ALL A BIG JOKE.
DIOS MÍO...
YOU KNOW... I'M GLAD WE HAD THIS LITTLE TALK, PADRE.

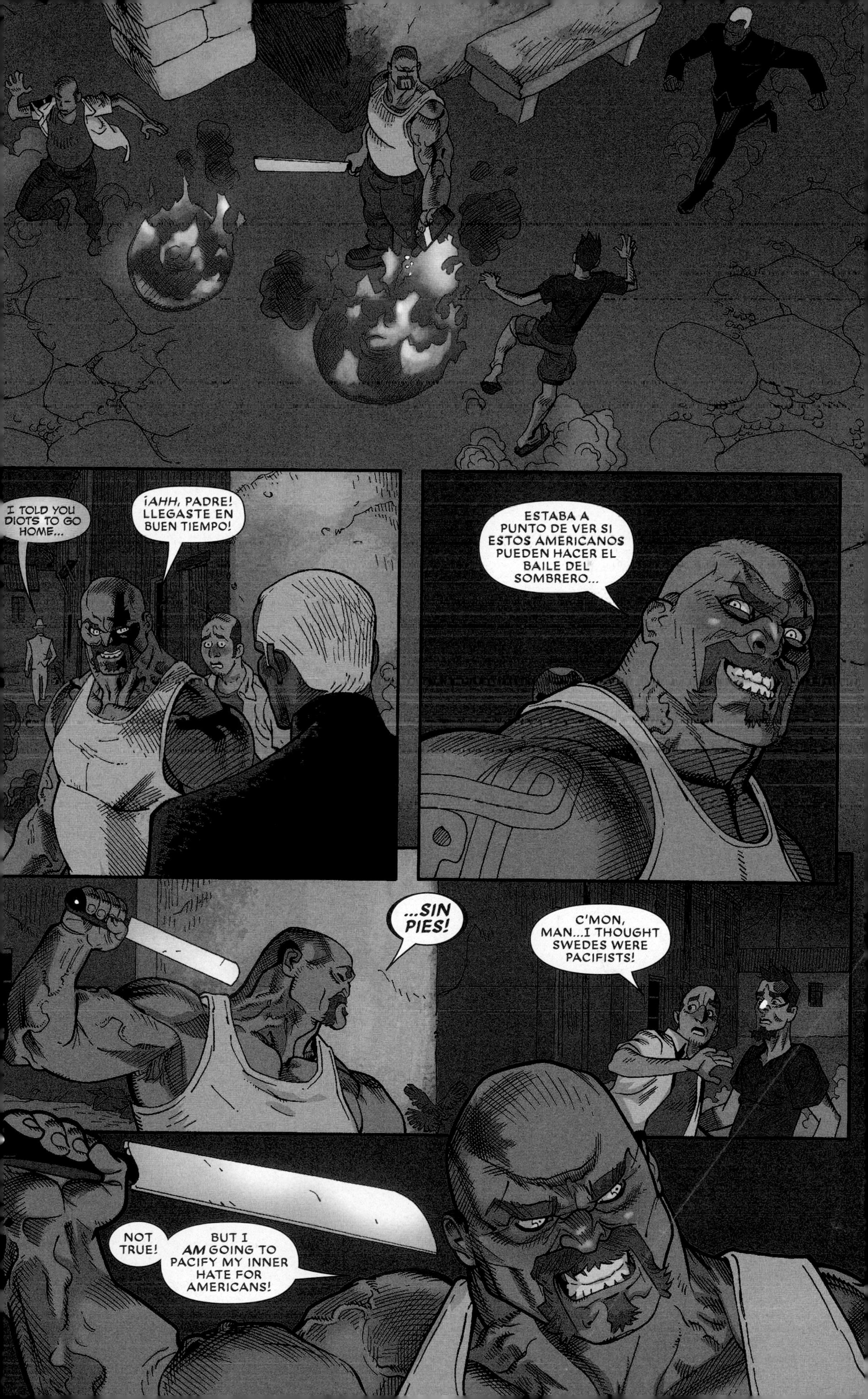
I TOLD YOU IDIOTS TO GO HOME...
¡AHH, PADRE! LLEGASTE EN BUEN TIEMPO!
ESTABA A PUNTO DE VER SI ESTOS AMERICANOS PUEDEN HACER EL BAILE DEL SOMBRERO...
...SIN PIES!
C'MON, MAN...I THOUGHT SWEDES WERE PACIFISTS!
NOT TRUE!
BUT I AM GOING TO PACIFY MY INNER HATE FOR AMERICANS!

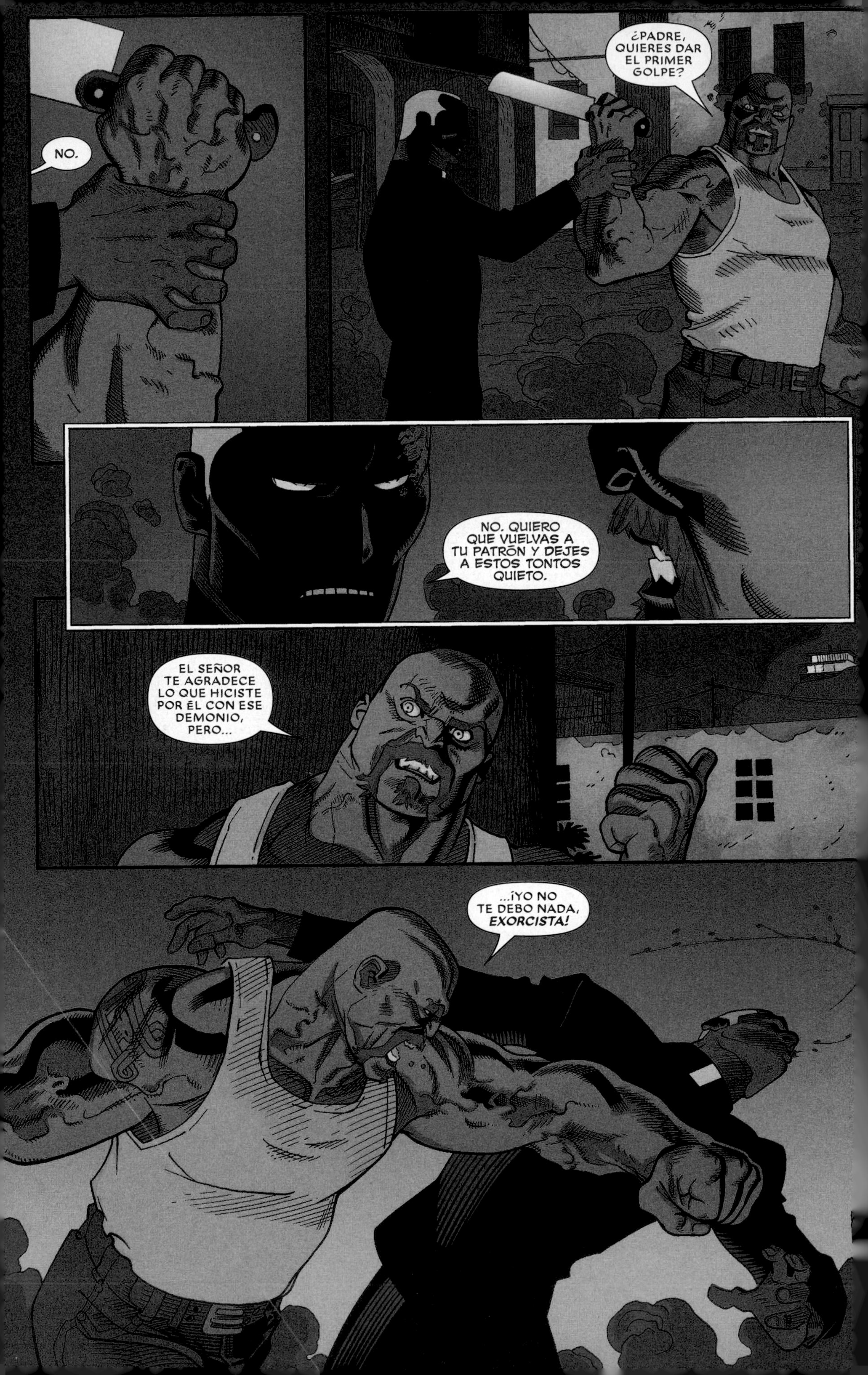
NO.
¿PADRE, QUIERES DAR EL PRIMER GOLPE?
NO. QUIERO QUE VUELVAS A TU PATRÓN Y DEJES A ESTOS TONTOS QUIETO.
EL SEÑOR TE AGRADECE LO QUE HICISTE POR ÉL CON ESE DEMONIO, PERO...
...¡YO NO TE DEBO NADA, *EXORCISTA!*

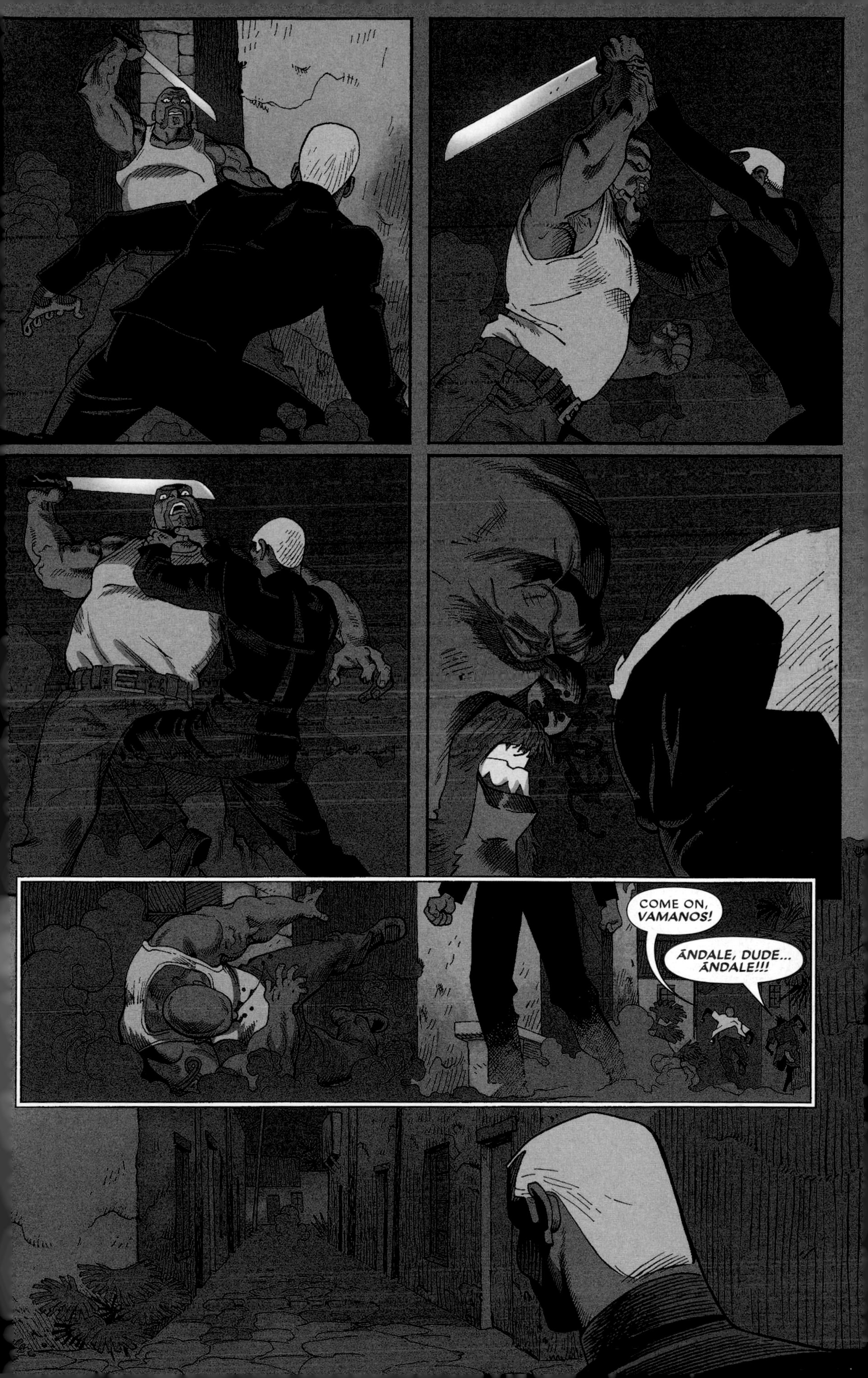
COME ON, VAMANOS!
ÁNDALE, DUDE... ÁNDALE!!!

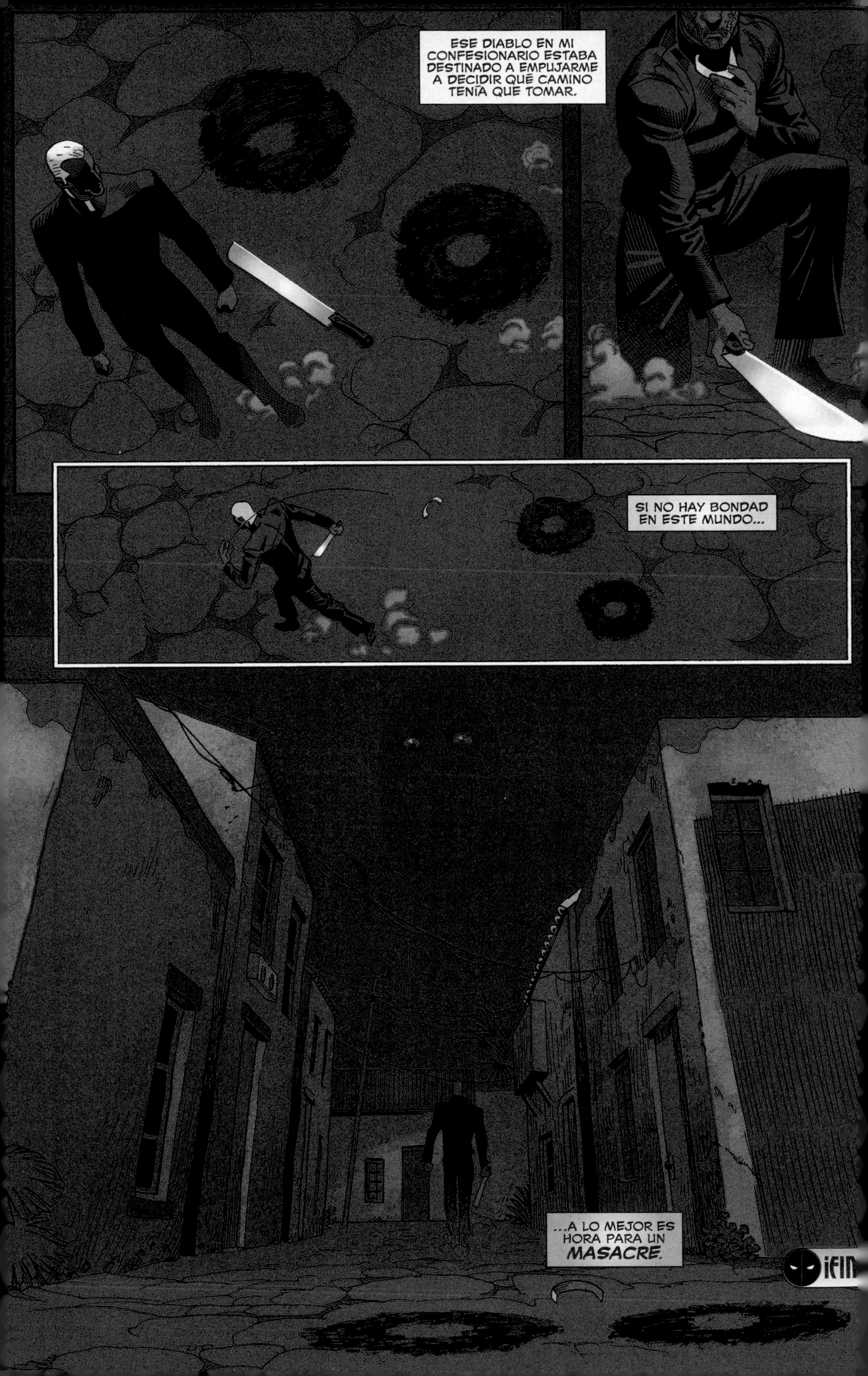
ESE DIABLO EN MI CONFESIONARIO ESTABA DESTINADO A EMPUJARME A DECIDIR QUÉ CAMINO TENÍA QUE TOMAR.
SI NO HAY BONDAD EN ESTE MUNDO...
...A LO MEJOR ES HORA PARA UN MASACRE.
¡FIN

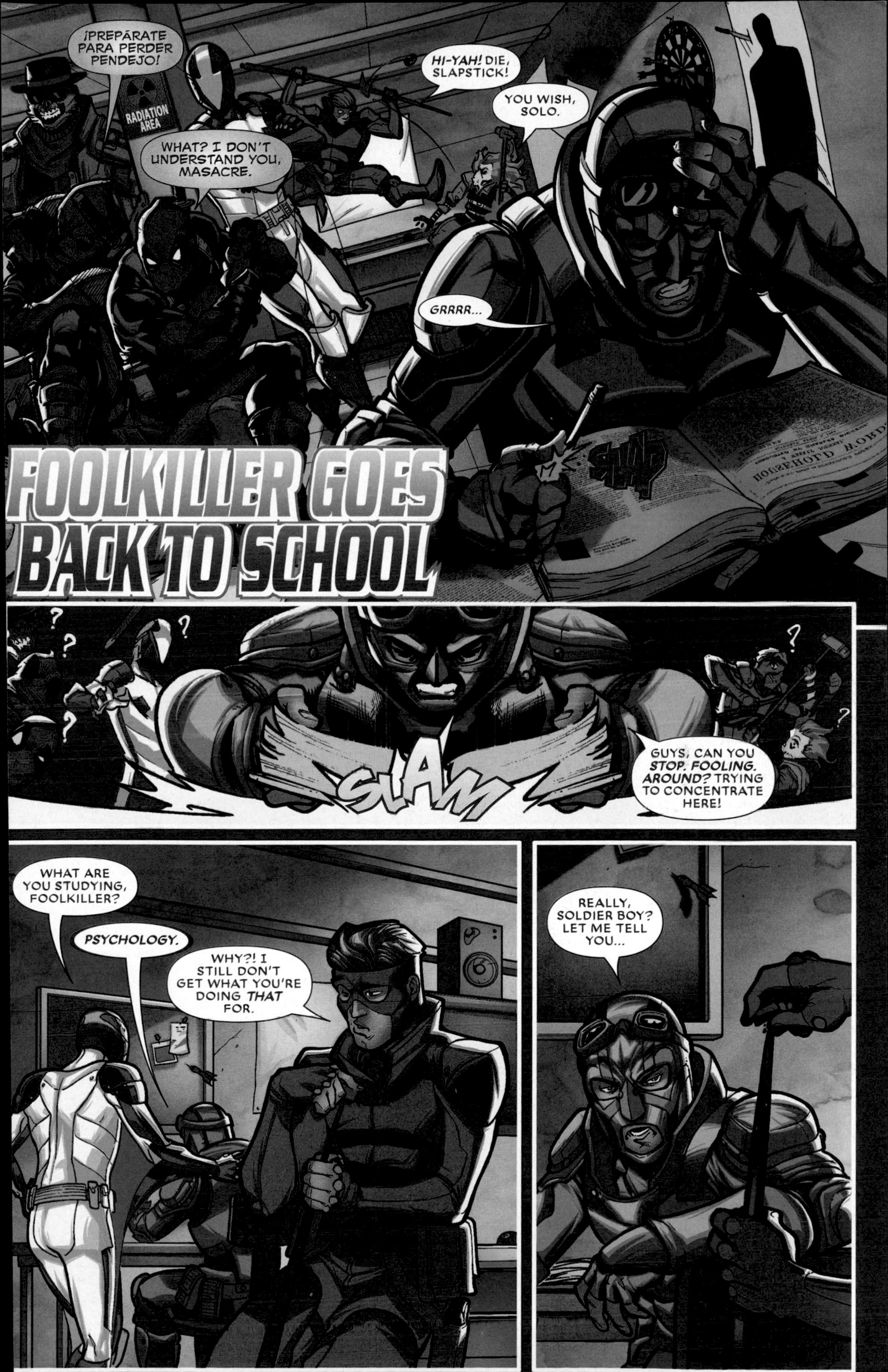
¡PREPÁRATE PARA PERDER PENDEJO!
RADIATION AREA
WHAT? I DON'T UNDERSTAND YOU, MASACRE.
HI-YAH! DIE, SLAPSTICK!
YOU WISH, SOLO.
GRRRR...
FOOLKILLER GOES BACK TO SCHOOL
SLAM
GUYS, CAN YOU STOP. FOOLING. AROUND? TRYING TO CONCENTRATE HERE!
WHAT ARE YOU STUDYING, FOOLKILLER?
PSYCHOLOGY.
WHY?! I STILL DON'T GET WHAT YOU'RE DOING THAT FOR.
REALLY, SOLDIER BOY? LET ME TELL YOU...

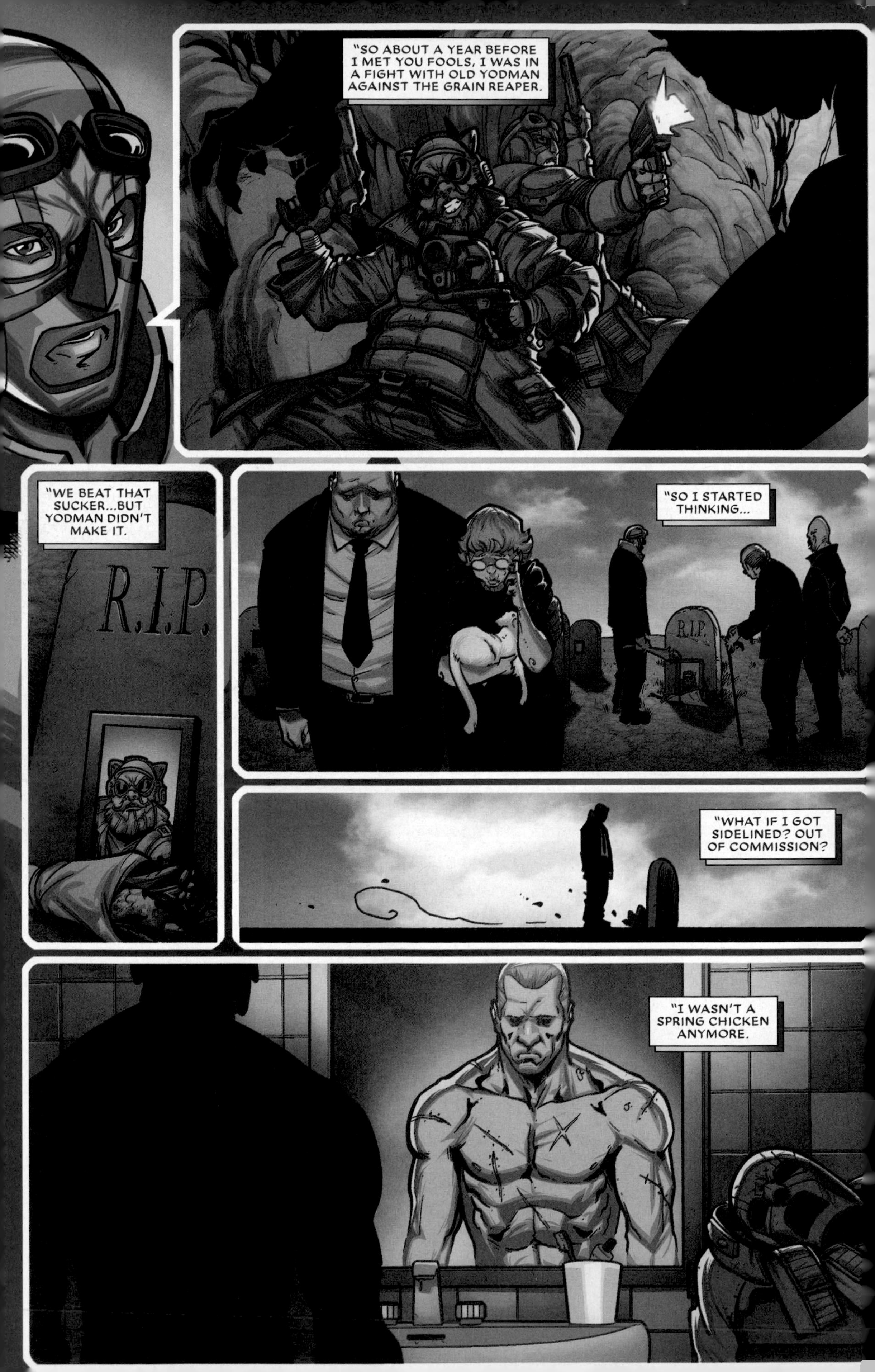
"SO ABOUT A YEAR BEFORE I MET YOU FOOLS, I WAS IN A FIGHT WITH OLD YODMAN AGAINST THE GRAIN REAPER.
"WE BEAT THAT SUCKER...BUT YODMAN DIDN'T MAKE IT.
R.I.P.
"SO I STARTED THINKING...
"WHAT IF I GOT SIDELINED? OUT OF COMMISSION?
"I WASN'T A SPRING CHICKEN ANYMORE.

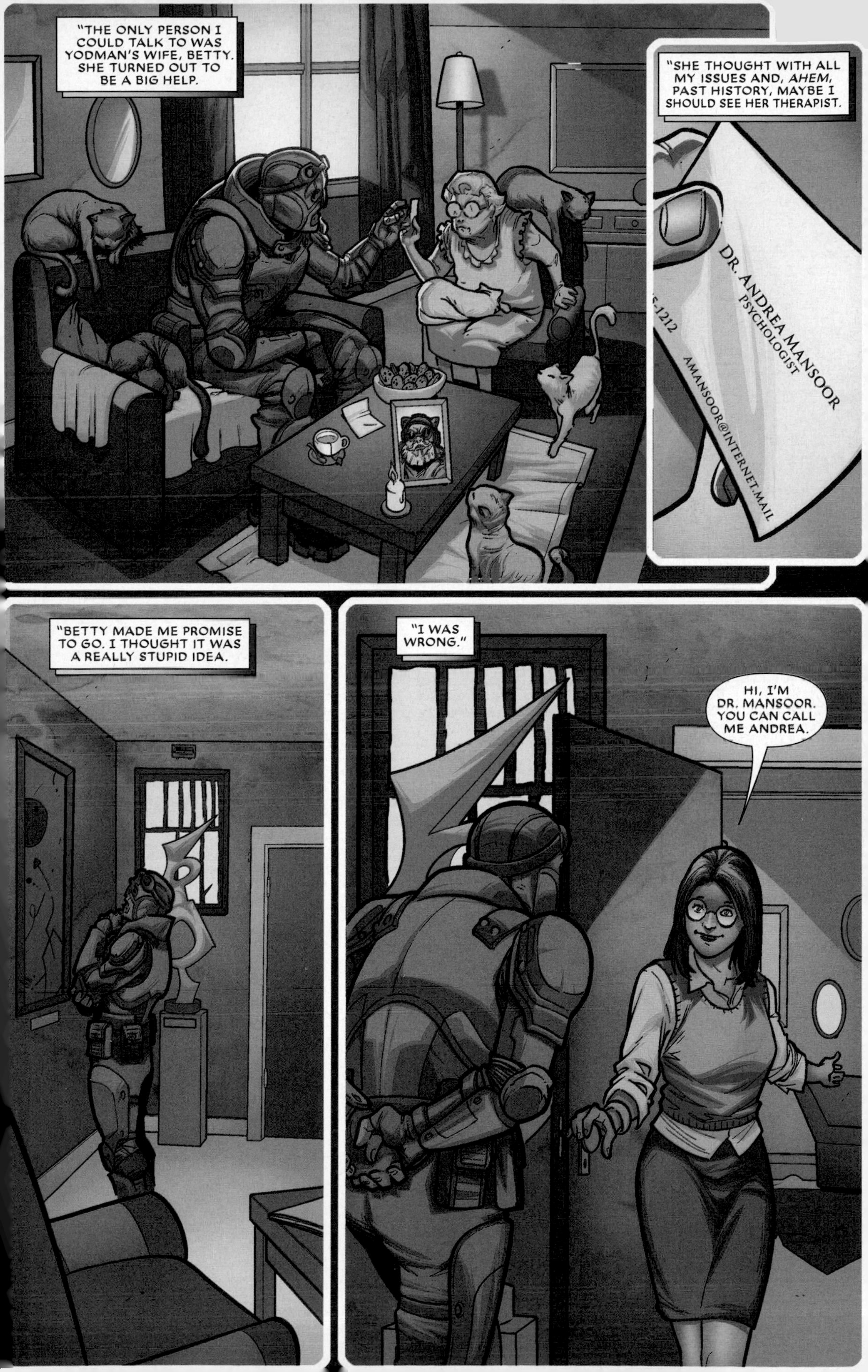
"THE ONLY PERSON I COULD TALK TO WAS YODMAN'S WIFE, BETTY. SHE TURNED OUT TO BE A BIG HELP.
"SHE THOUGHT WITH ALL MY ISSUES AND, *AHEM*, PAST HISTORY, MAYBE I SHOULD SEE HER THERAPIST.
DR. ANDREA MANSOOR
PSYCHOLOGIST
AMANSOOR@INTERNET.MAIL
"BETTY MADE ME PROMISE TO GO. I THOUGHT IT WAS A REALLY STUPID IDEA.
"I WAS WRONG."
HI, I'M DR. MANSOOR. YOU CAN CALL ME ANDREA.

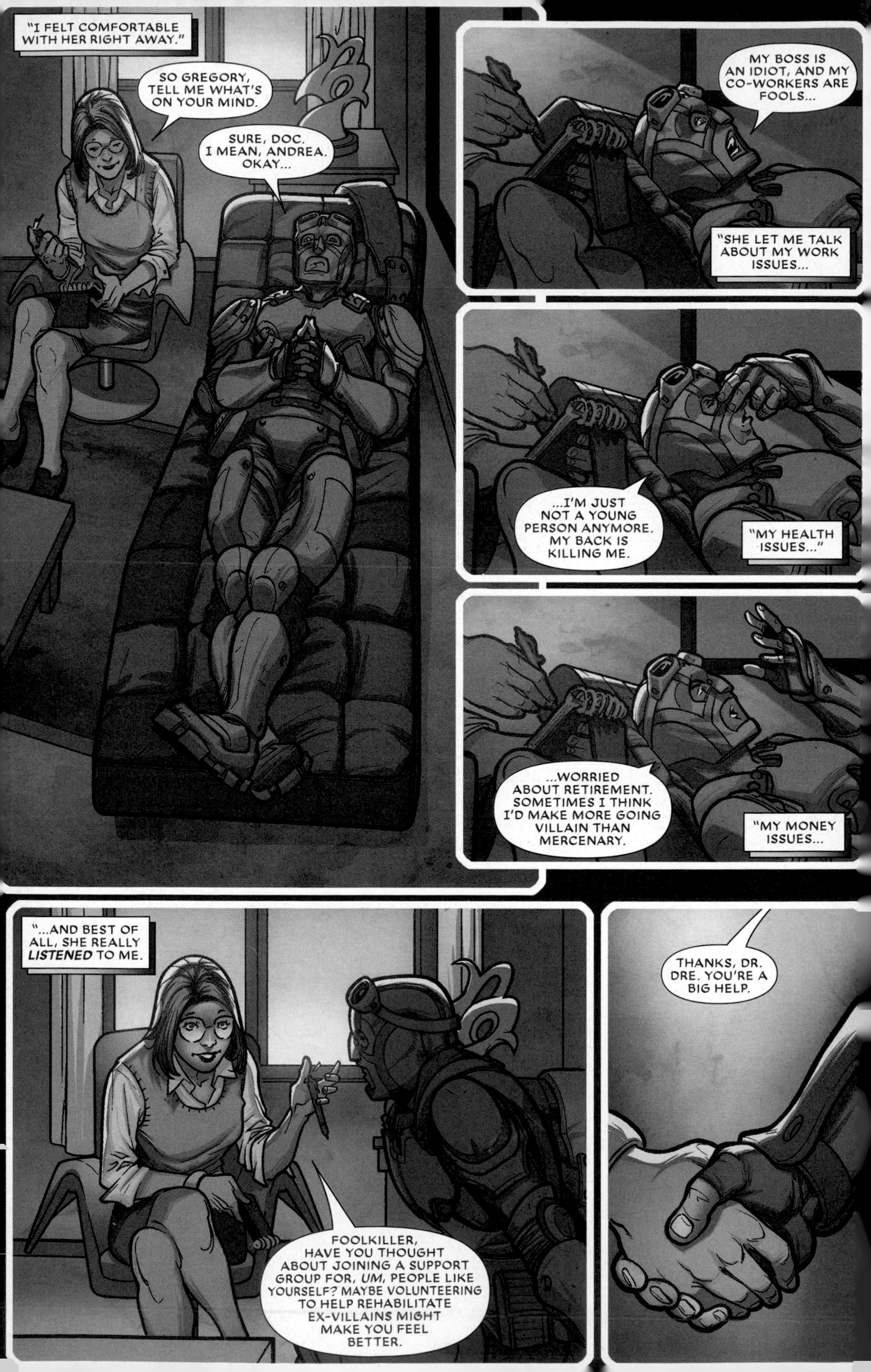
"I FELT COMFORTABLE WITH HER RIGHT AWAY."
SO GREGORY, TELL ME WHAT'S ON YOUR MIND.
SURE, DOC. I MEAN, ANDREA. OKAY...
MY BOSS IS AN IDIOT, AND MY CO-WORKERS ARE FOOLS...
"SHE LET ME TALK ABOUT MY WORK ISSUES...
...I'M JUST NOT A YOUNG PERSON ANYMORE. MY BACK IS KILLING ME.
"MY HEALTH ISSUES..."
...WORRIED ABOUT RETIREMENT. SOMETIMES I THINK I'D MAKE MORE GOING VILLAIN THAN MERCENARY.
"MY MONEY ISSUES...
"...AND BEST OF ALL, SHE REALLY *LISTENED* TO ME.
FOOLKILLER, HAVE YOU THOUGHT ABOUT JOINING A SUPPORT GROUP FOR, *UM,* PEOPLE LIKE YOURSELF? MAYBE VOLUNTEERING TO HELP REHABILITATE EX-VILLAINS MIGHT MAKE YOU FEEL BETTER.
THANKS, DR. DRE. YOU'RE A BIG HELP.

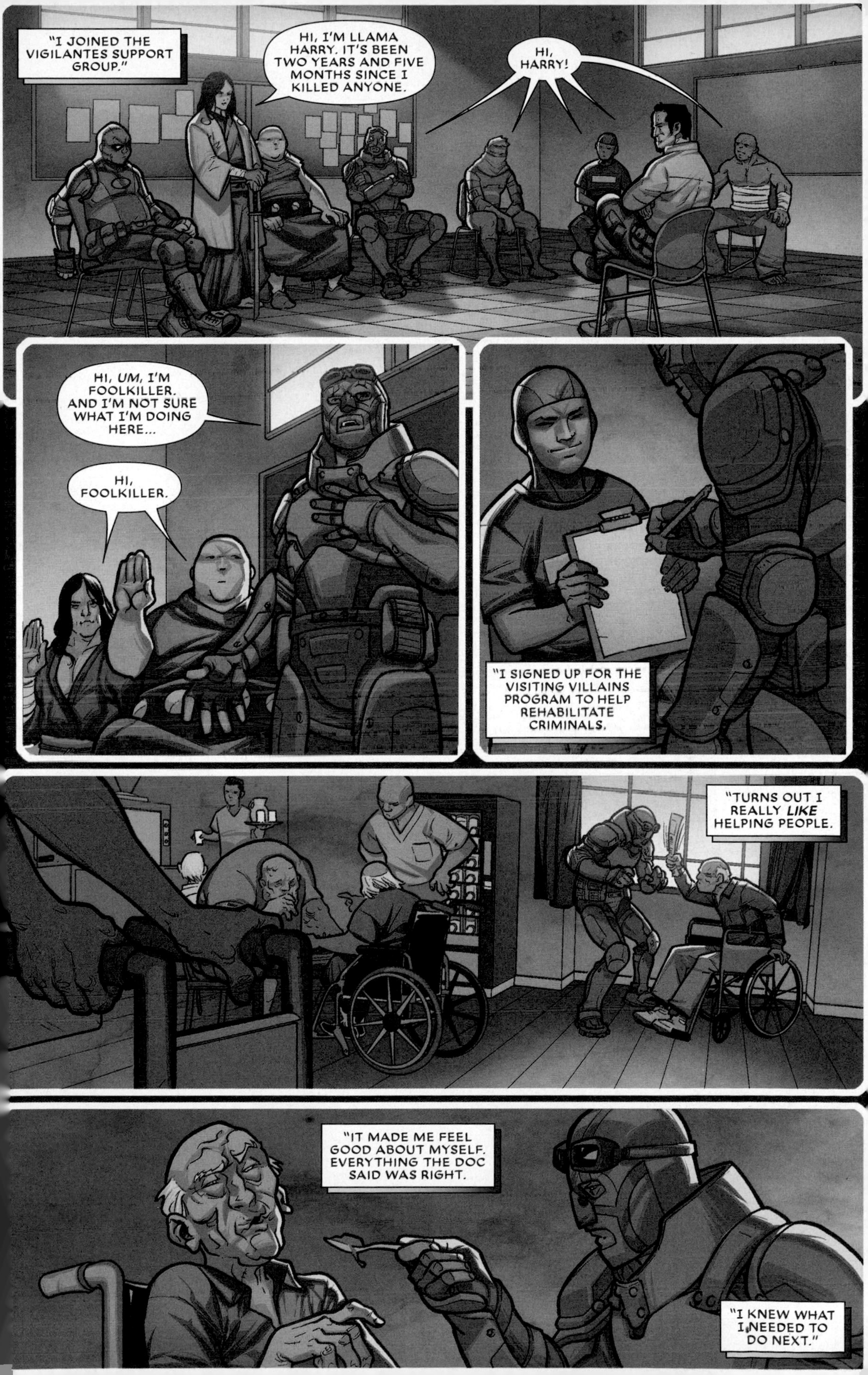
"I JOINED THE VIGILANTES SUPPORT GROUP."
HI, I'M LLAMA HARRY. IT'S BEEN TWO YEARS AND FIVE MONTHS SINCE I KILLED ANYONE.
HI, HARRY!
HI, *UM*, I'M FOOLKILLER. AND I'M NOT SURE WHAT I'M DOING HERE...
HI, FOOLKILLER.
"I SIGNED UP FOR THE VISITING VILLAINS PROGRAM TO HELP REHABILITATE CRIMINALS.
"TURNS OUT I REALLY ***LIKE*** HELPING PEOPLE.
"IT MADE ME FEEL GOOD ABOUT MYSELF. EVERYTHING THE DOC SAID WAS RIGHT.
"I KNEW WHAT I NEEDED TO DO NEXT."

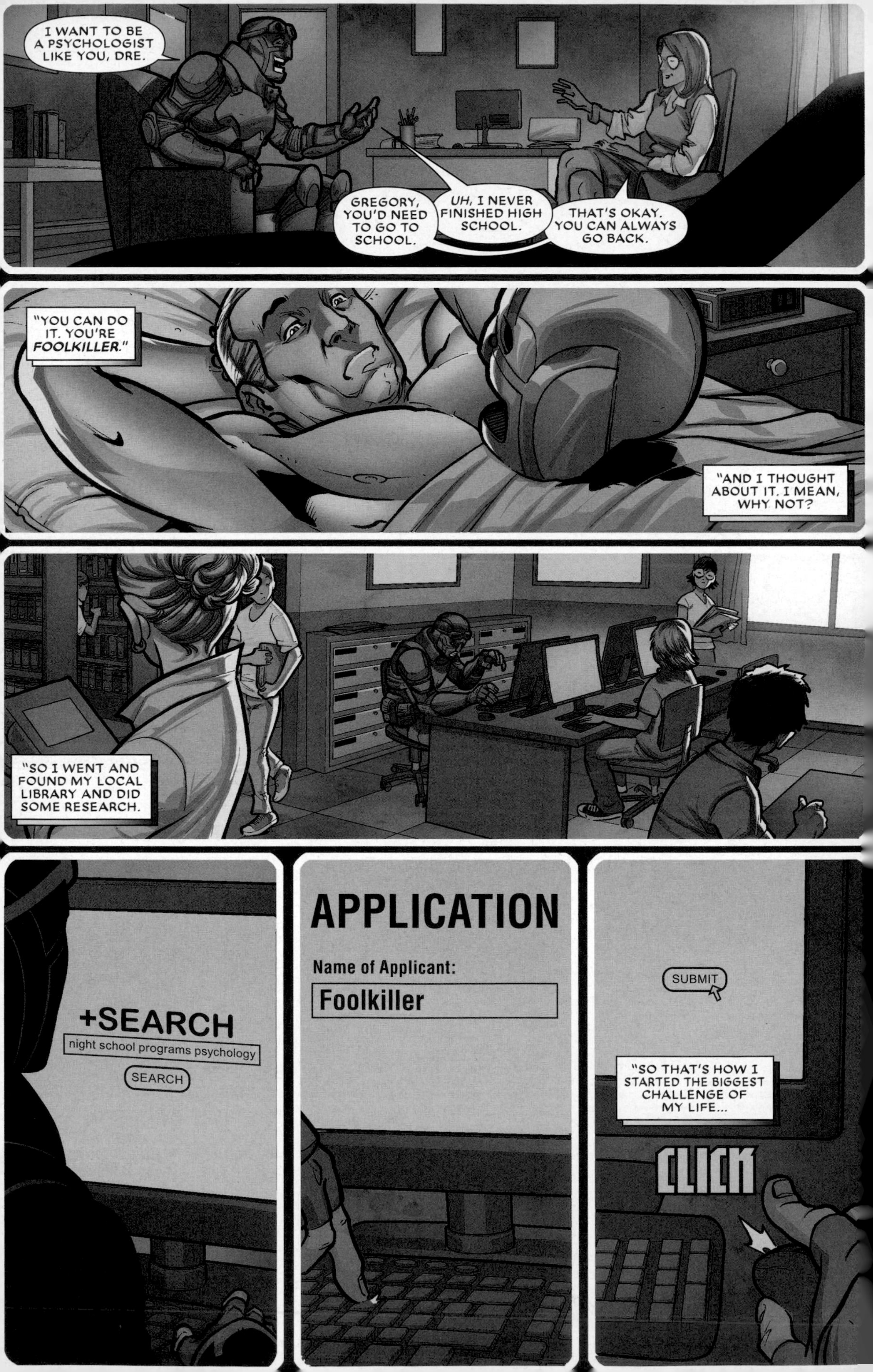
I WANT TO BE A PSYCHOLOGIST LIKE YOU, DRE.
GREGORY, YOU'D NEED TO GO TO SCHOOL.
UH, I NEVER FINISHED HIGH SCHOOL.
THAT'S OKAY. YOU CAN ALWAYS GO BACK.
"YOU CAN DO IT. YOU'RE FOOLKILLER."
"AND I THOUGHT ABOUT IT. I MEAN, WHY NOT?
"SO I WENT AND FOUND MY LOCAL LIBRARY AND DID SOME RESEARCH.
+SEARCH
night school programs psychology
SEARCH
APPLICATION
Name of Applicant:
Foolkiller
SUBMIT
"SO THAT'S HOW I STARTED THE BIGGEST CHALLENGE OF MY LIFE...
CLICK

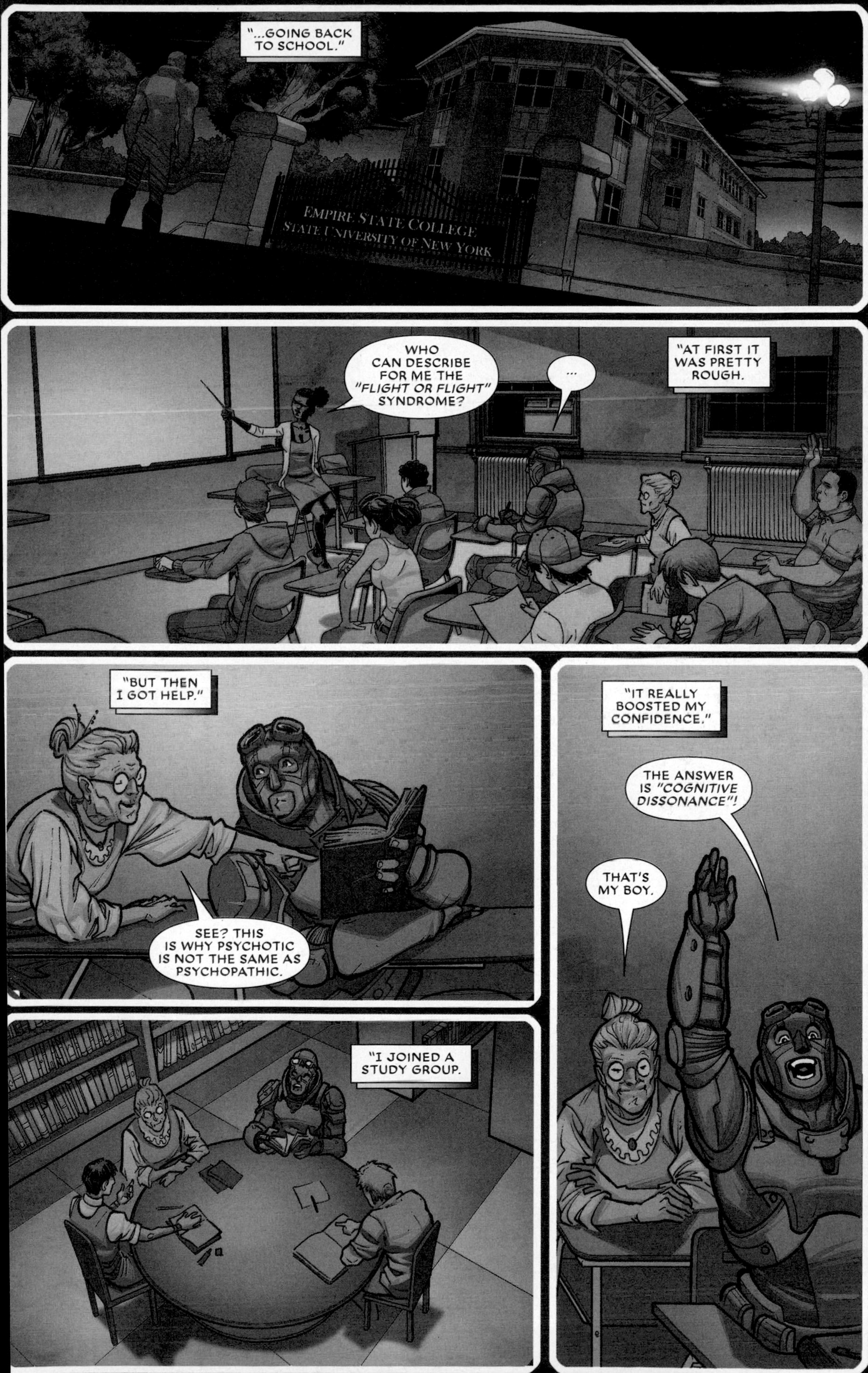
"...GOING BACK TO SCHOOL."
EMPIRE STATE COLLEGE
STATE UNIVERSITY OF NEW YORK
WHO CAN DESCRIBE FOR ME THE "FLIGHT OR FLIGHT" SYNDROME?
...
"AT FIRST IT WAS PRETTY ROUGH.
"BUT THEN I GOT HELP."
SEE? THIS IS WHY PSYCHOTIC IS NOT THE SAME AS PSYCHOPATHIC.
"I JOINED A STUDY GROUP.
"IT REALLY BOOSTED MY CONFIDENCE."
THE ANSWER IS "COGNITIVE DISSONANCE"!
THAT'S MY BOY.

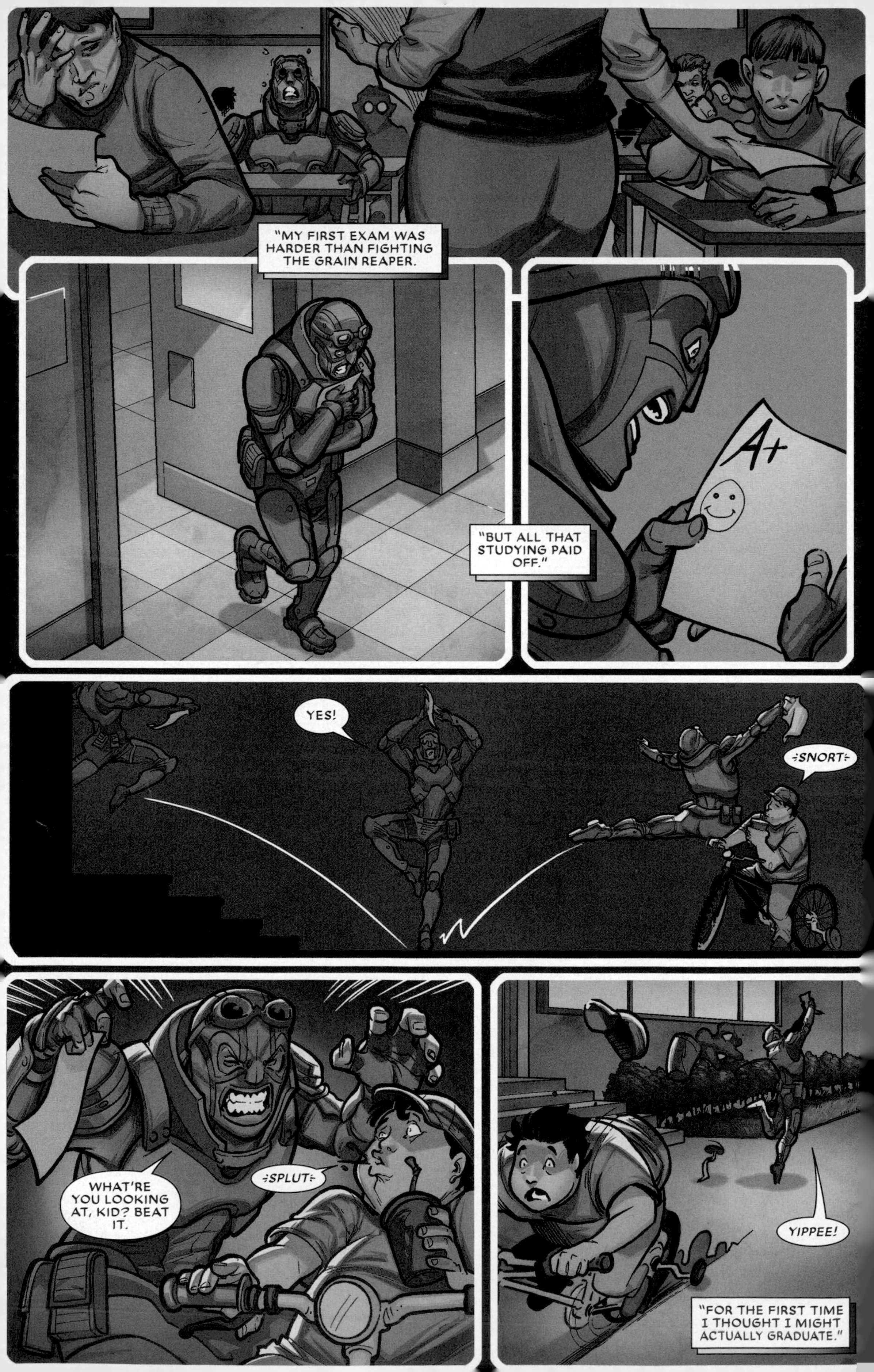
"MY FIRST EXAM WAS HARDER THAN FIGHTING THE GRAIN REAPER.
"BUT ALL THAT STUDYING PAID OFF."
A+
YES!
SNORT
WHAT'RE YOU LOOKING AT, KID? BEAT IT.
SPLUT
YIPPEE!
"FOR THE FIRST TIME I THOUGHT I MIGHT ACTUALLY GRADUATE."

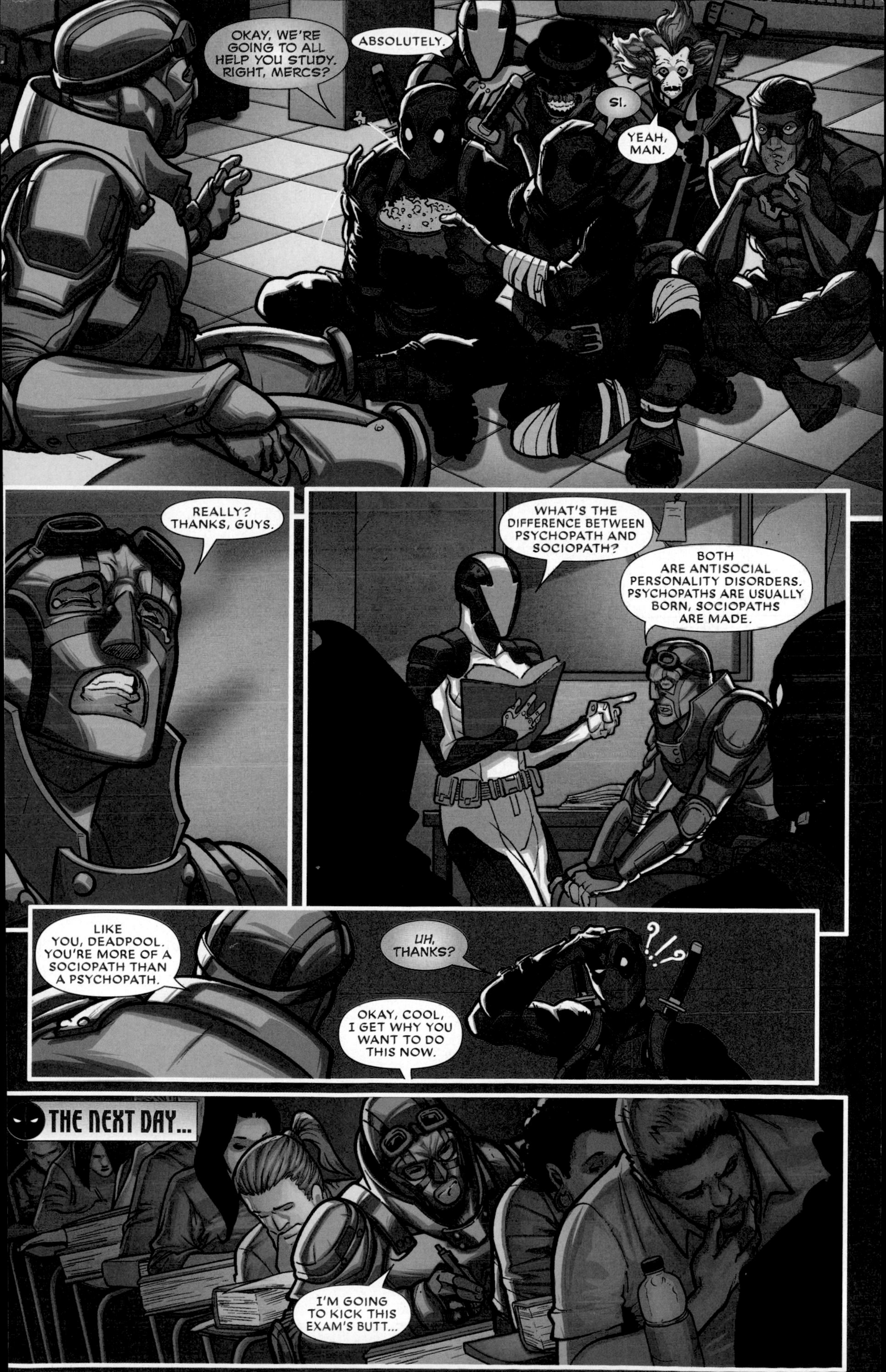

OKAY, WE'RE GOING TO ALL HELP YOU STUDY. RIGHT, MERCS?
ABSOLUTELY.
SI.
YEAH, MAN.
REALLY? THANKS, GUYS.
WHAT'S THE DIFFERENCE BETWEEN PSYCHOPATH AND SOCIOPATH?
BOTH ARE ANTISOCIAL PERSONALITY DISORDERS. PSYCHOPATHS ARE USUALLY BORN, SOCIOPATHS ARE MADE.
LIKE YOU, DEADPOOL. YOU'RE MORE OF A SOCIOPATH THAN A PSYCHOPATH.
UH, THANKS?
OKAY, COOL, I GET WHY YOU WANT TO DO THIS NOW.
THE NEXT DAY...
I'M GOING TO KICK THIS EXAM'S BUTT...

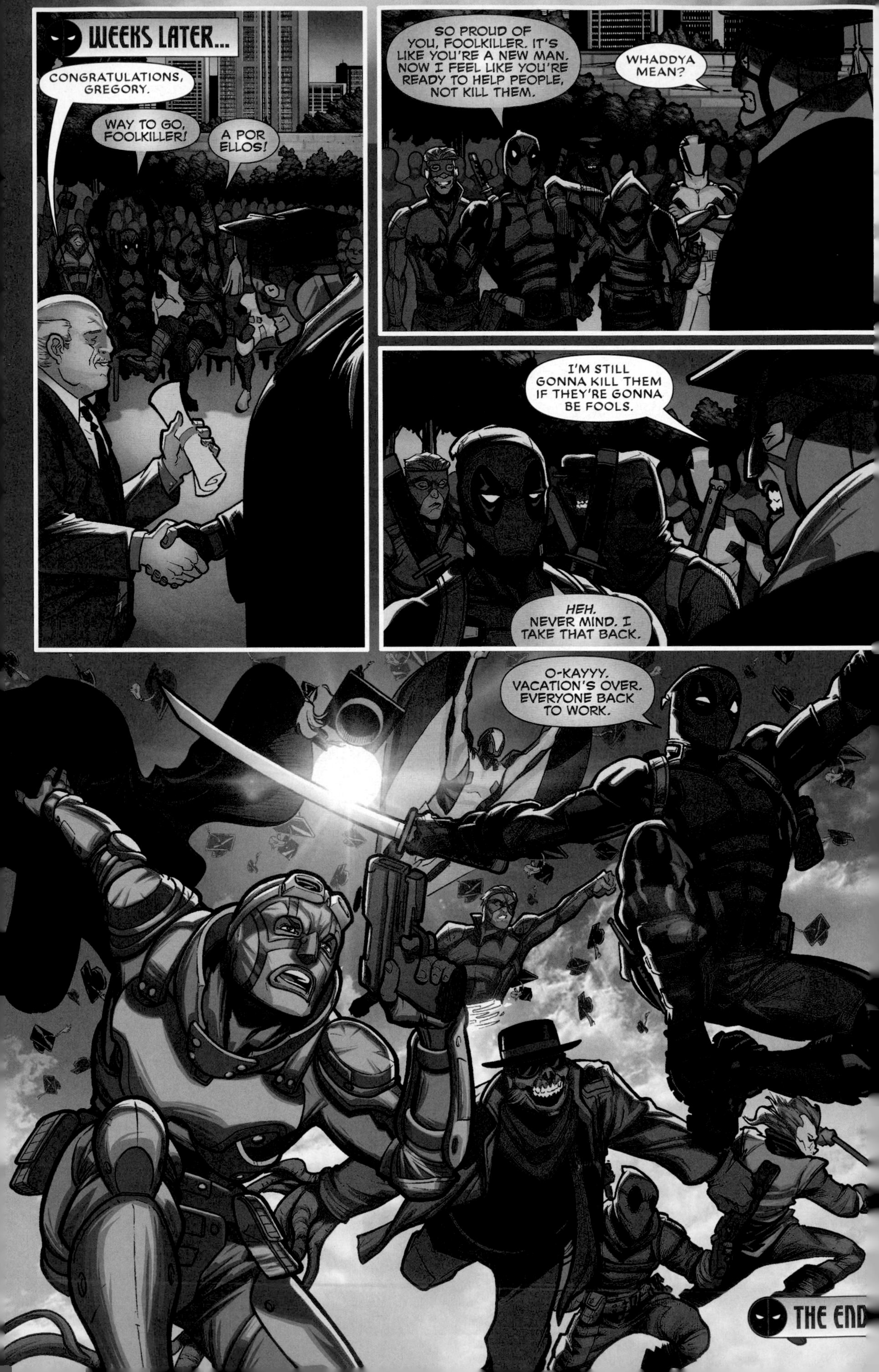
WEEKS LATER...
CONGRATULATIONS, GREGORY.
WAY TO GO, FOOLKILLER!
A POR ELLOS!
SO PROUD OF YOU, FOOLKILLER. IT'S LIKE YOU'RE A NEW MAN. NOW I FEEL LIKE YOU'RE READY TO HELP PEOPLE, NOT KILL THEM.
WHADDYA MEAN?
I'M STILL GONNA KILL THEM IF THEY'RE GONNA BE FOOLS.
HEH. NEVER MIND. I TAKE THAT BACK.
O-KAYYY. VACATION'S OVER. EVERYONE BACK TO WORK.
THE END

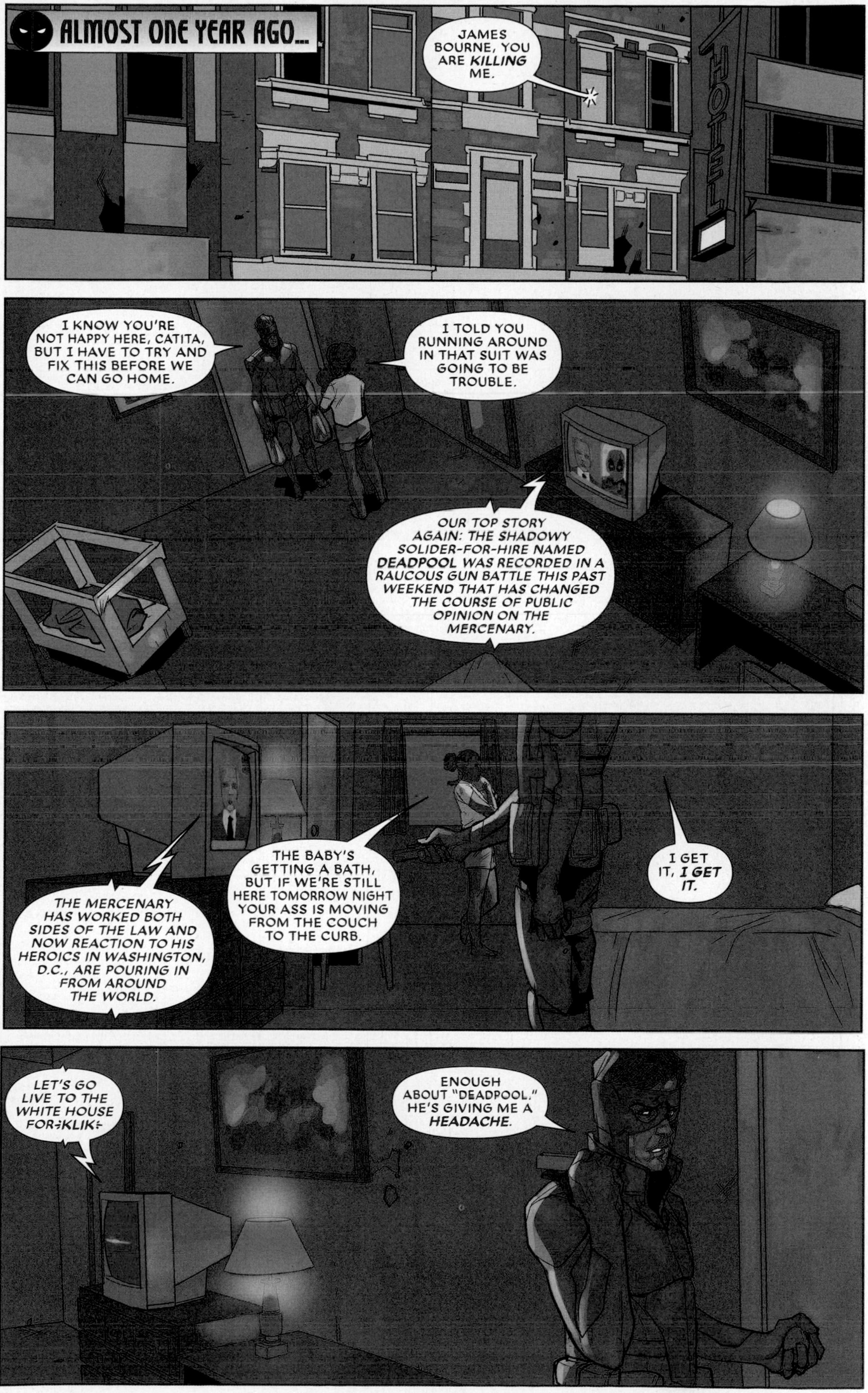

ALMOST ONE YEAR AGO...
JAMES BOURNE, YOU ARE KILLING ME.
HOTEL
I KNOW YOU'RE NOT HAPPY HERE, CATITA, BUT I HAVE TO TRY AND FIX THIS BEFORE WE CAN GO HOME.
I TOLD YOU RUNNING AROUND IN THAT SUIT WAS GOING TO BE TROUBLE.
OUR TOP STORY AGAIN: THE SHADOWY SOLIDER-FOR-HIRE NAMED DEADPOOL WAS RECORDED IN A RAUCOUS GUN BATTLE THIS PAST WEEKEND THAT HAS CHANGED THE COURSE OF PUBLIC OPINION ON THE MERCENARY.
THE MERCENARY HAS WORKED BOTH SIDES OF THE LAW AND NOW REACTION TO HIS HEROICS IN WASHINGTON, D.C., ARE POURING IN FROM AROUND THE WORLD.
THE BABY'S GETTING A BATH, BUT IF WE'RE STILL HERE TOMORROW NIGHT YOUR ASS IS MOVING FROM THE COUCH TO THE CURB.
I GET IT, I GET IT.
LET'S GO LIVE TO THE WHITE HOUSE FOR÷KLIK÷
ENOUGH ABOUT "DEADPOOL." HE'S GIVING ME A HEADACHE.

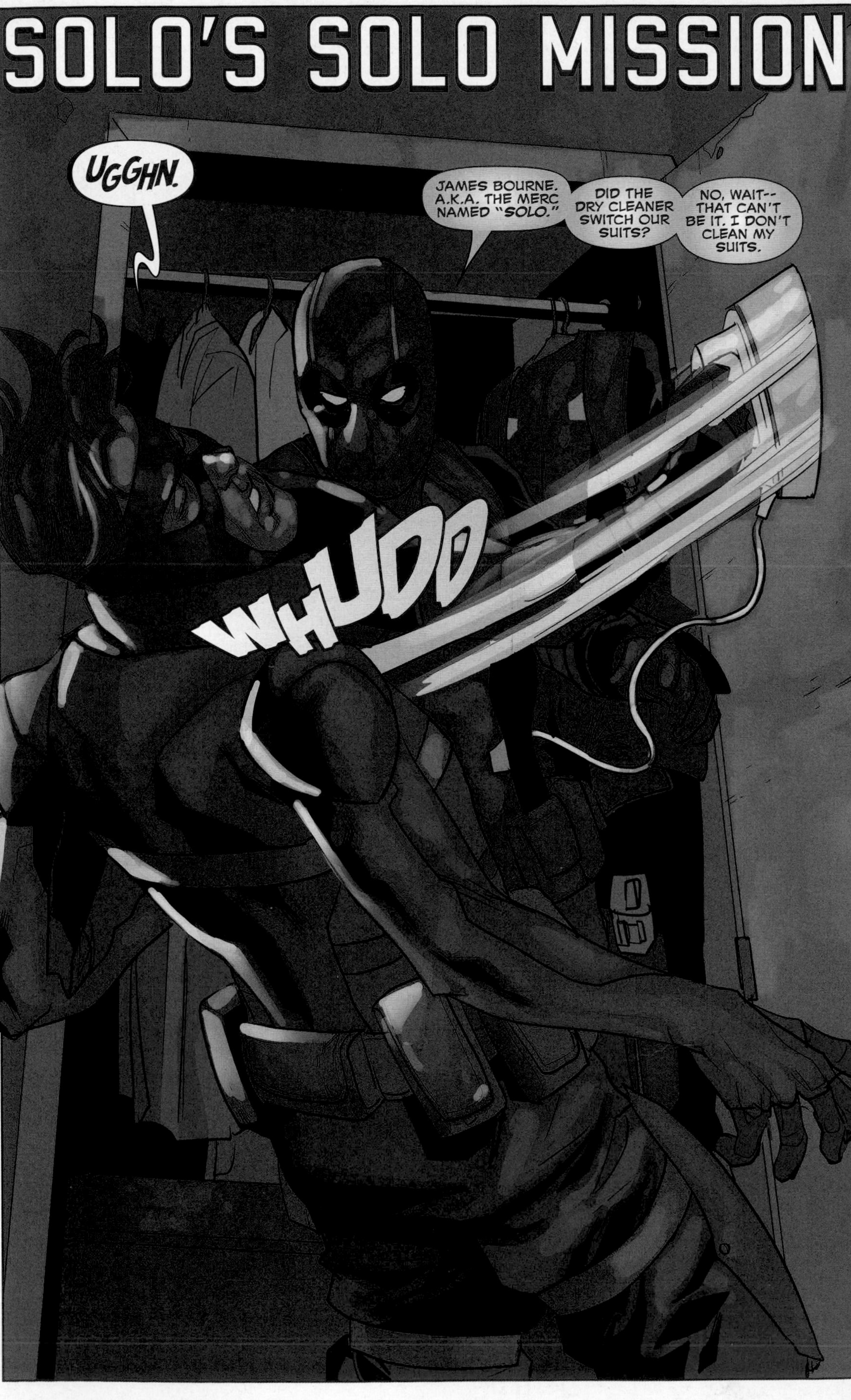
SOLO'S SOLO MISSION
UGGHN.
JAMES BOURNE. A.K.A. THE MERC NAMED "SOLO."
DID THE DRY CLEANER SWITCH OUR SUITS?
NO, WAIT-- THAT CAN'T BE IT. I DON'T CLEAN MY SUITS.
WHUDD

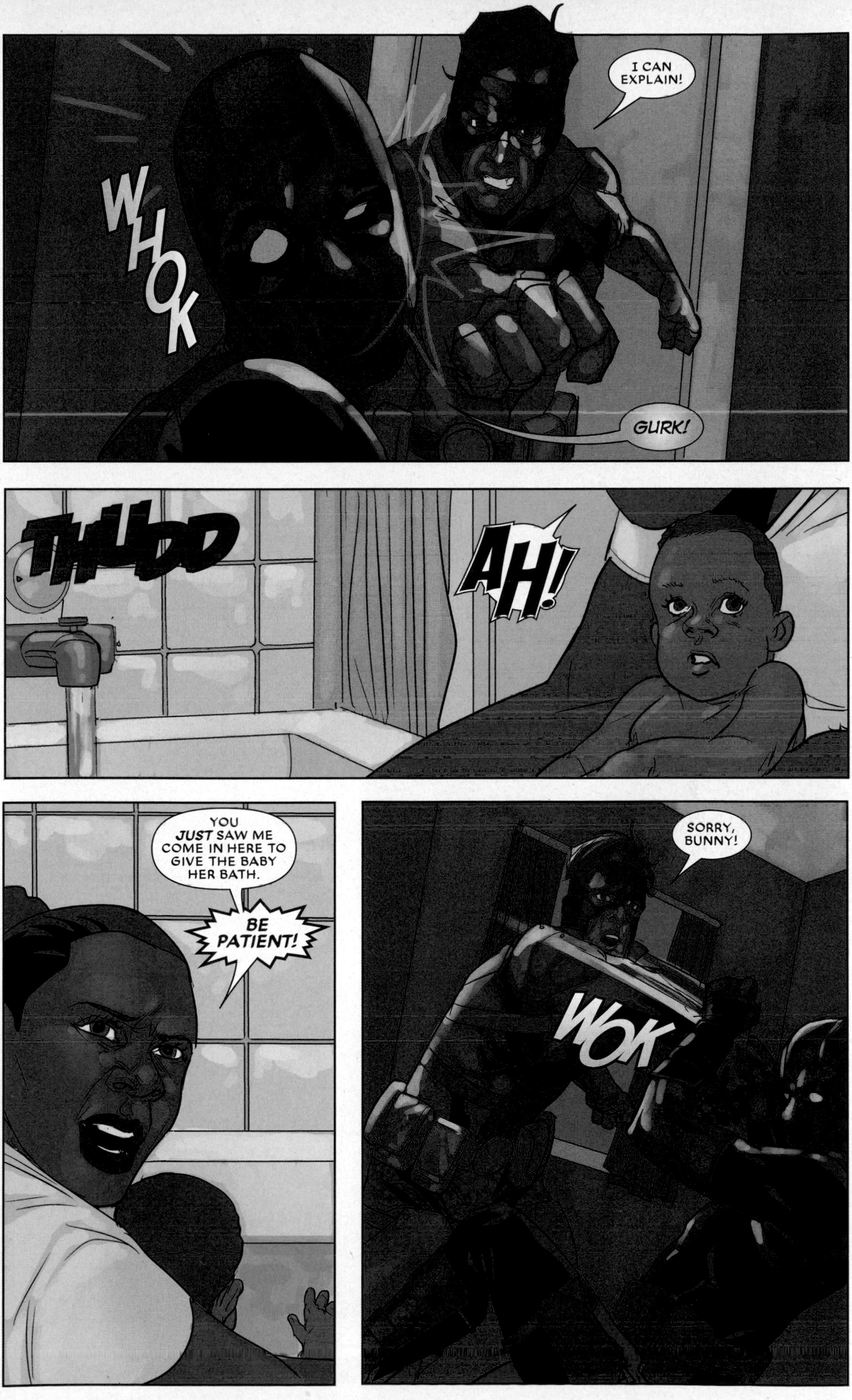
I CAN EXPLAIN!
WHOK
GURK!
THUDD
AH!
YOU JUST SAW ME COME IN HERE TO GIVE THE BABY HER BATH.
BE PATIENT!
SORRY, BUNNY!
WOK

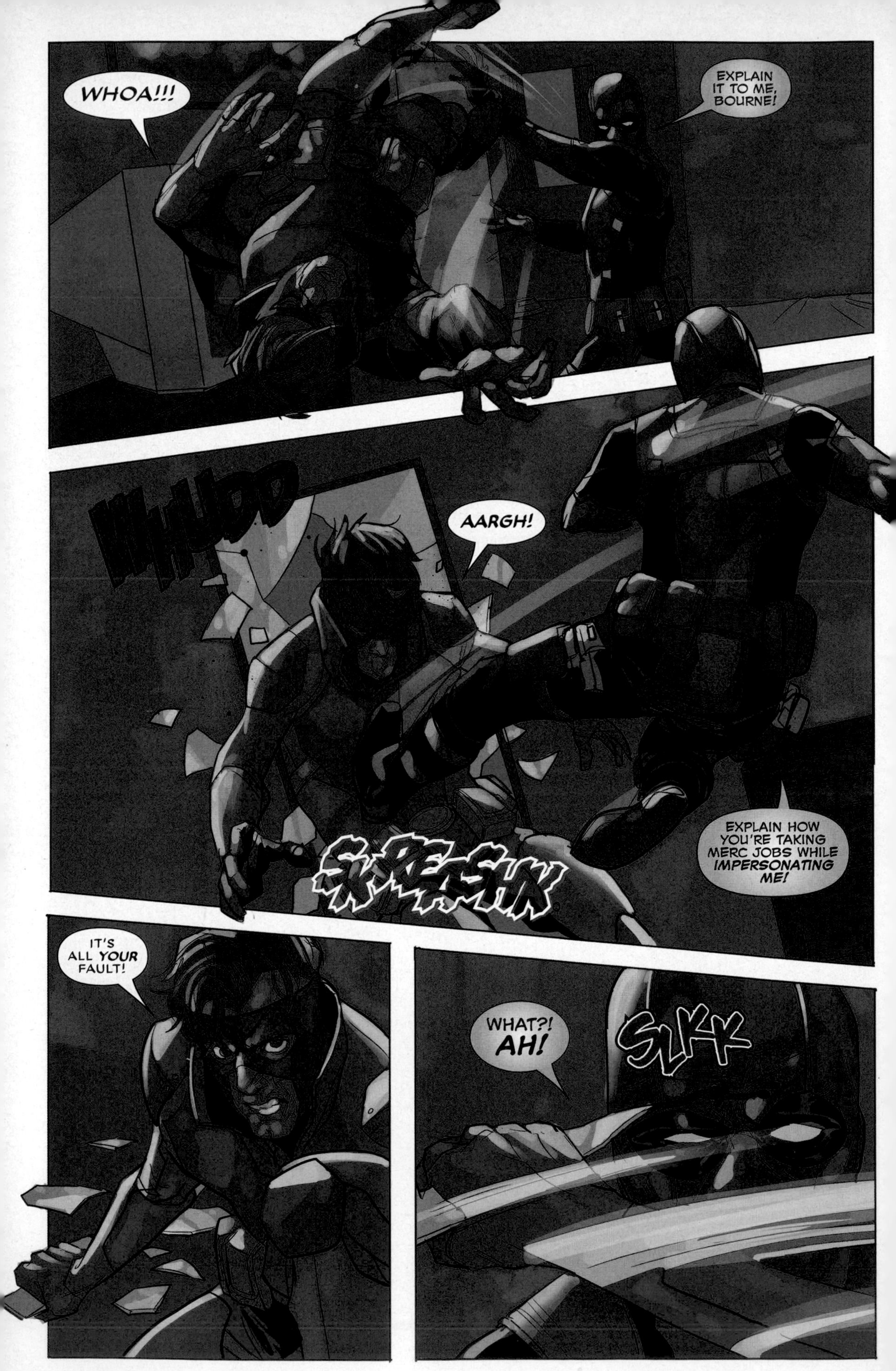
WHOA!!!
EXPLAIN IT TO ME, BOURNE!
AARGH!
EXPLAIN HOW YOU'RE TAKING MERC JOBS WHILE IMPERSONATING ME!
IT'S ALL YOUR FAULT!
WHAT?! AH!
SLKK

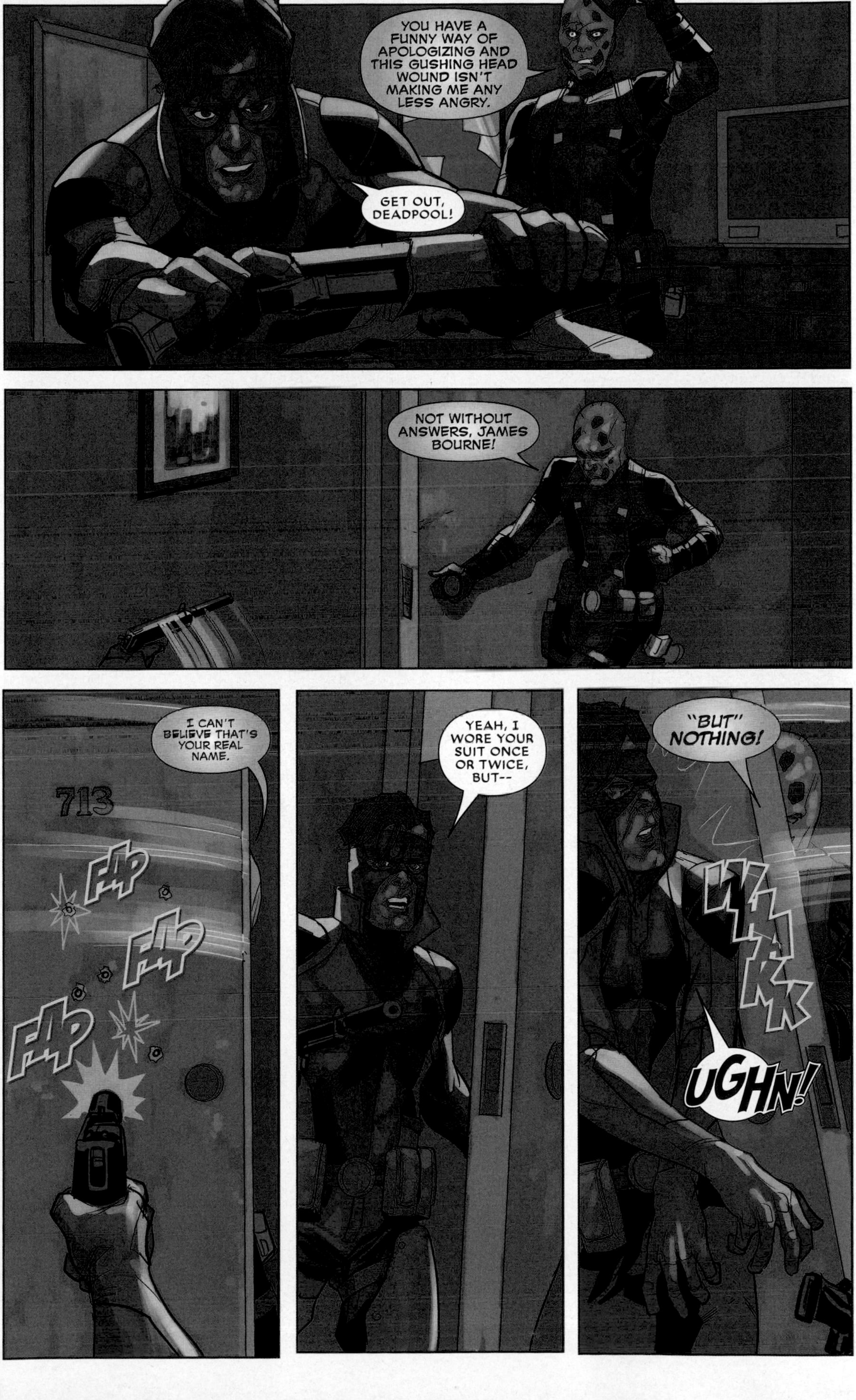
YOU HAVE A FUNNY WAY OF APOLOGIZING AND THIS GUSHING HEAD WOUND ISN'T MAKING ME ANY LESS ANGRY.
GET OUT, DEADPOOL!
NOT WITHOUT ANSWERS, JAMES BOURNE!
I CAN'T BELIEVE THAT'S YOUR REAL NAME.
713
FAP
FAP
FAP
YEAH, I WORE YOUR SUIT ONCE OR TWICE, BUT--
"BUT" NOTHING!
WHAKK
UGHN!

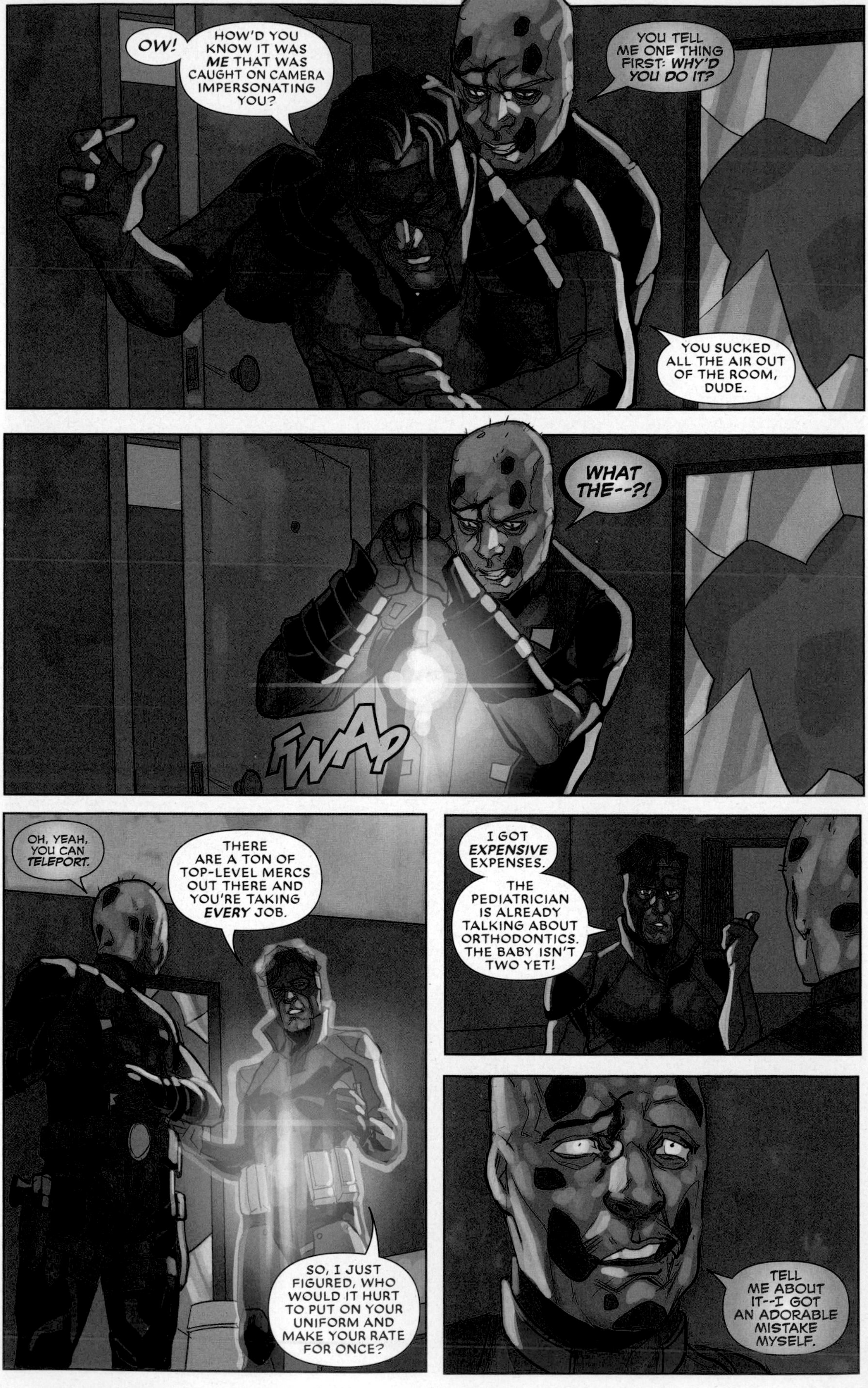
OW!
HOW'D YOU KNOW IT WAS ME THAT WAS CAUGHT ON CAMERA IMPERSONATING YOU?
YOU TELL ME ONE THING FIRST: WHY'D YOU DO IT?
YOU SUCKED ALL THE AIR OUT OF THE ROOM, DUDE.
WHAT THE--?!
FWAP
OH, YEAH, YOU CAN TELEPORT.
THERE ARE A TON OF TOP-LEVEL MERCS OUT THERE AND YOU'RE TAKING EVERY JOB.
SO, I JUST FIGURED, WHO WOULD IT HURT TO PUT ON YOUR UNIFORM AND MAKE YOUR RATE FOR ONCE?
I GOT EXPENSIVE EXPENSES.
THE PEDIATRICIAN IS ALREADY TALKING ABOUT ORTHODONTICS. THE BABY ISN'T TWO YET!
TELL ME ABOUT IT--I GOT AN ADORABLE MISTAKE MYSELF.

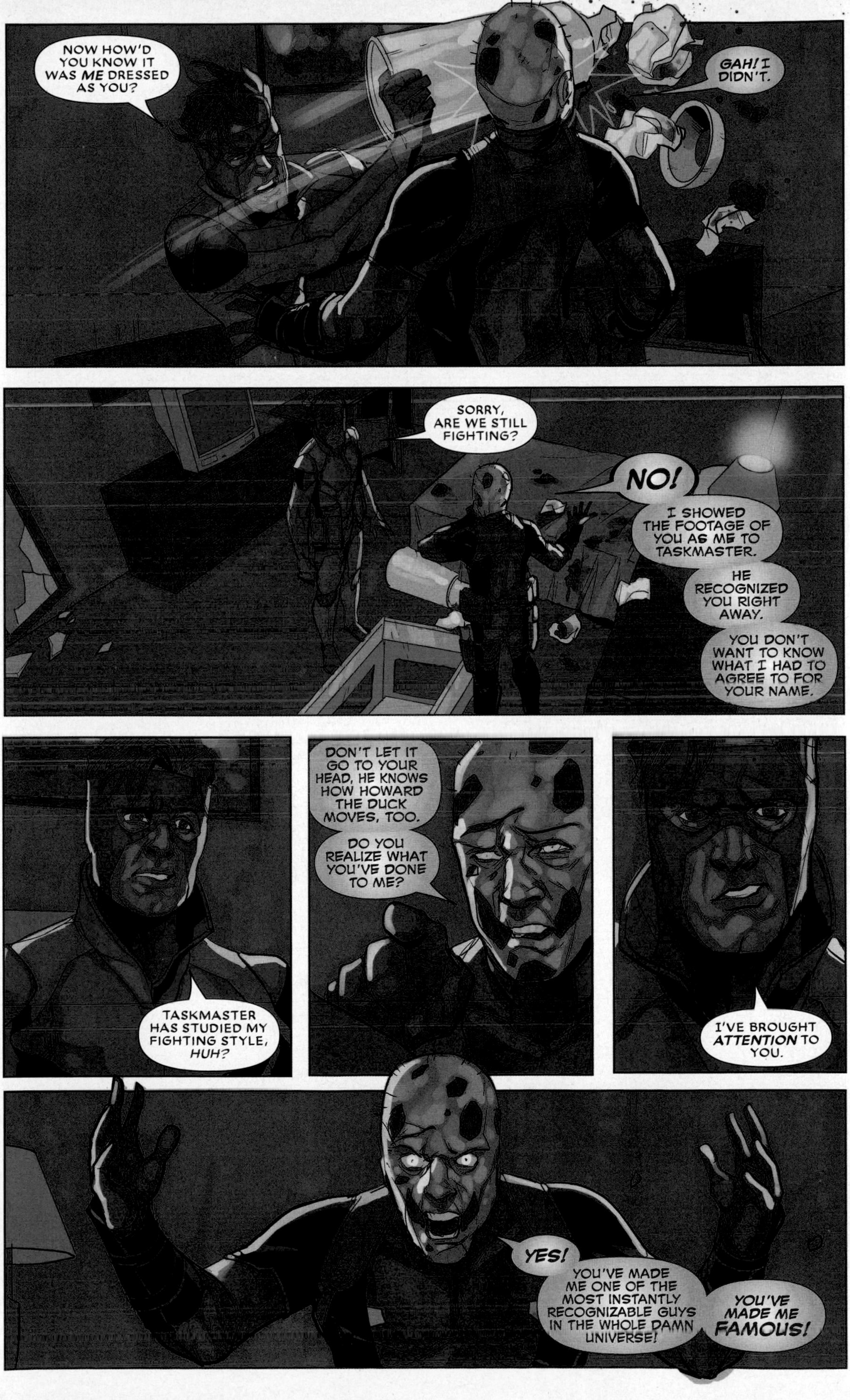
NOW HOW'D YOU KNOW IT WAS *ME* DRESSED AS YOU?
*GAH!* I DIDN'T.
SORRY, ARE WE STILL FIGHTING?
NO!
I SHOWED THE FOOTAGE OF YOU AS ME TO TASKMASTER.
HE RECOGNIZED YOU RIGHT AWAY.
YOU DON'T WANT TO KNOW WHAT I HAD TO AGREE TO FOR YOUR NAME.
TASKMASTER HAS STUDIED MY FIGHTING STYLE, *HUH?*
DON'T LET IT GO TO YOUR HEAD, HE KNOWS HOW HOWARD THE DUCK MOVES, TOO.
DO YOU REALIZE WHAT YOU'VE DONE TO ME?
I'VE BROUGHT *ATTENTION* TO YOU.
*YES!*
YOU'VE MADE ME ONE OF THE MOST INSTANTLY RECOGNIZABLE GUYS IN THE WHOLE DAMN UNIVERSE!
*YOU'VE MADE ME FAMOUS!*

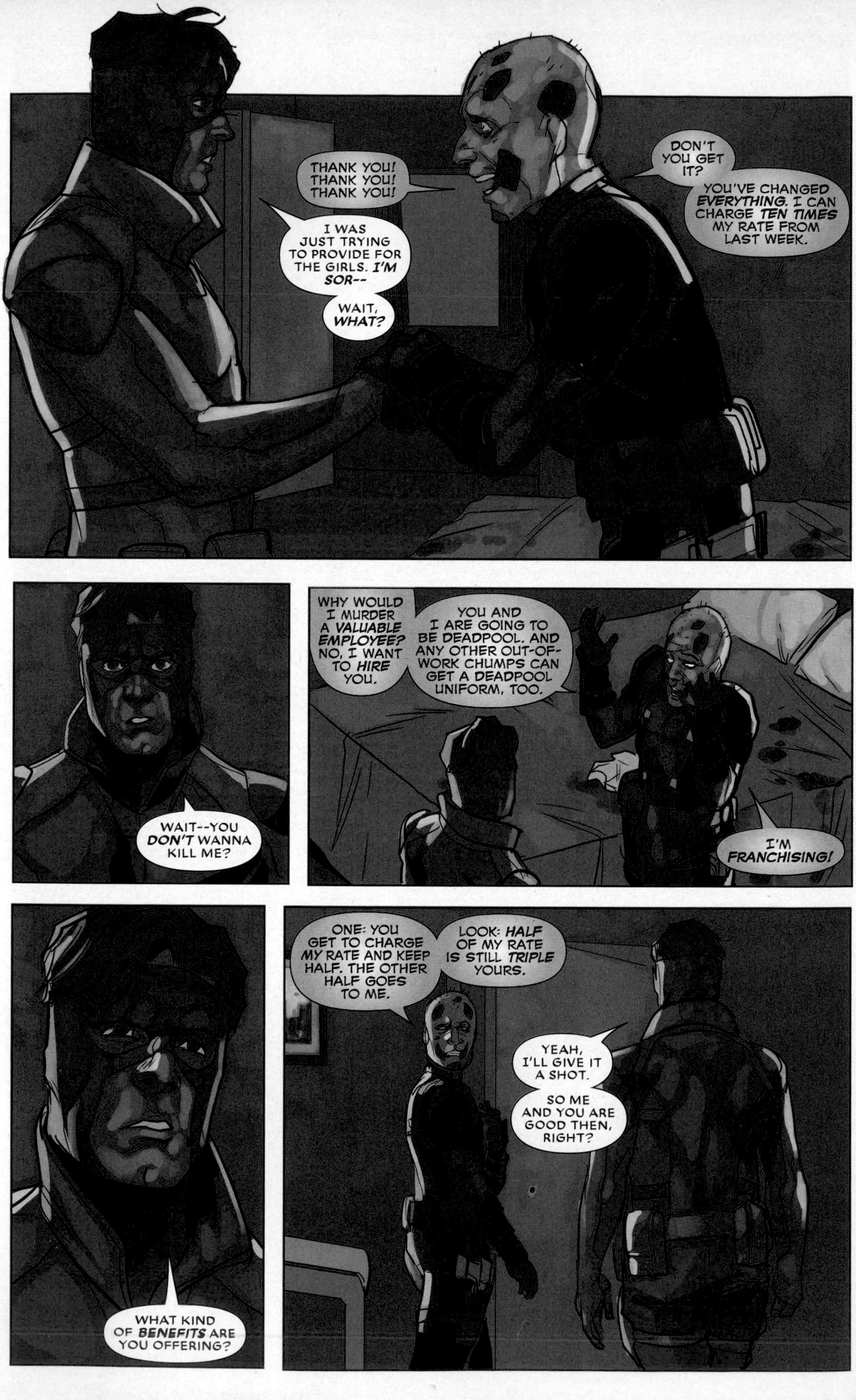
THANK YOU! THANK YOU! THANK YOU!
I WAS JUST TRYING TO PROVIDE FOR THE GIRLS. I'M SOR--
WAIT, WHAT?
DON'T YOU GET IT?
YOU'VE CHANGED EVERYTHING. I CAN CHARGE TEN TIMES MY RATE FROM LAST WEEK.
WAIT--YOU DON'T WANNA KILL ME?
WHY WOULD I MURDER A VALUABLE EMPLOYEE? NO, I WANT TO HIRE YOU.
YOU AND I ARE GOING TO BE DEADPOOL. AND ANY OTHER OUT-OF-WORK CHUMPS CAN GET A DEADPOOL UNIFORM, TOO.
I'M FRANCHISING!
WHAT KIND OF BENEFITS ARE YOU OFFERING?
ONE: YOU GET TO CHARGE MY RATE AND KEEP HALF. THE OTHER HALF GOES TO ME.
LOOK: HALF OF MY RATE IS STILL TRIPLE YOURS.
YEAH, I'LL GIVE IT A SHOT.
SO ME AND YOU ARE GOOD THEN, RIGHT?

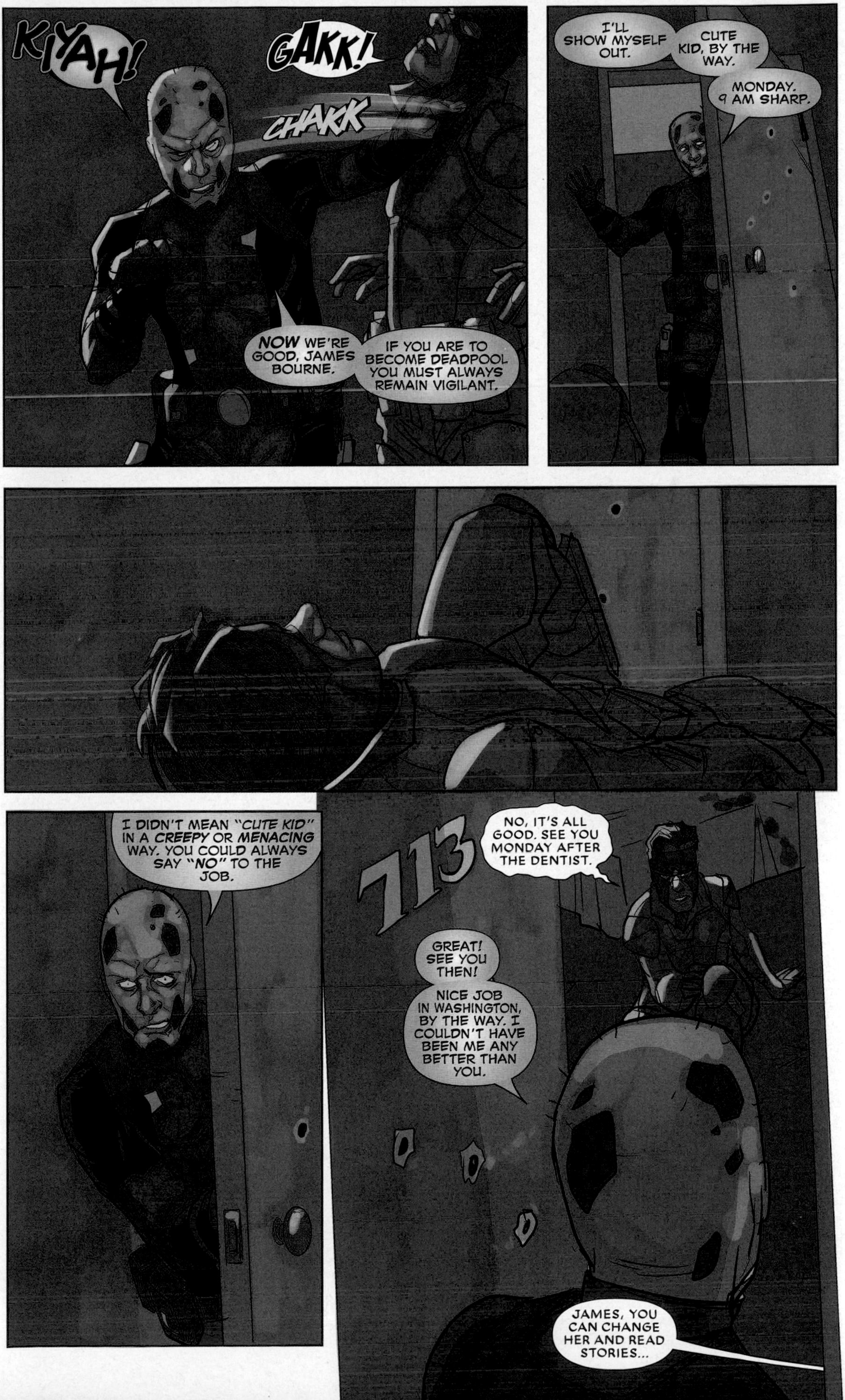
KIYAH!
GAKK!
CHAKK
NOW WE'RE GOOD, JAMES BOURNE.
IF YOU ARE TO BECOME DEADPOOL YOU MUST ALWAYS REMAIN VIGILANT.
I'LL SHOW MYSELF OUT.
CUTE KID, BY THE WAY.
MONDAY. 9 AM SHARP.
I DIDN'T MEAN "CUTE KID" IN A CREEPY OR MENACING WAY. YOU COULD ALWAYS SAY "NO" TO THE JOB.
713
NO, IT'S ALL GOOD. SEE YOU MONDAY AFTER THE DENTIST.
GREAT! SEE YOU THEN!
NICE JOB IN WASHINGTON, BY THE WAY. I COULDN'T HAVE BEEN ME ANY BETTER THAN YOU.
JAMES, YOU CAN CHANGE HER AND READ STORIES...

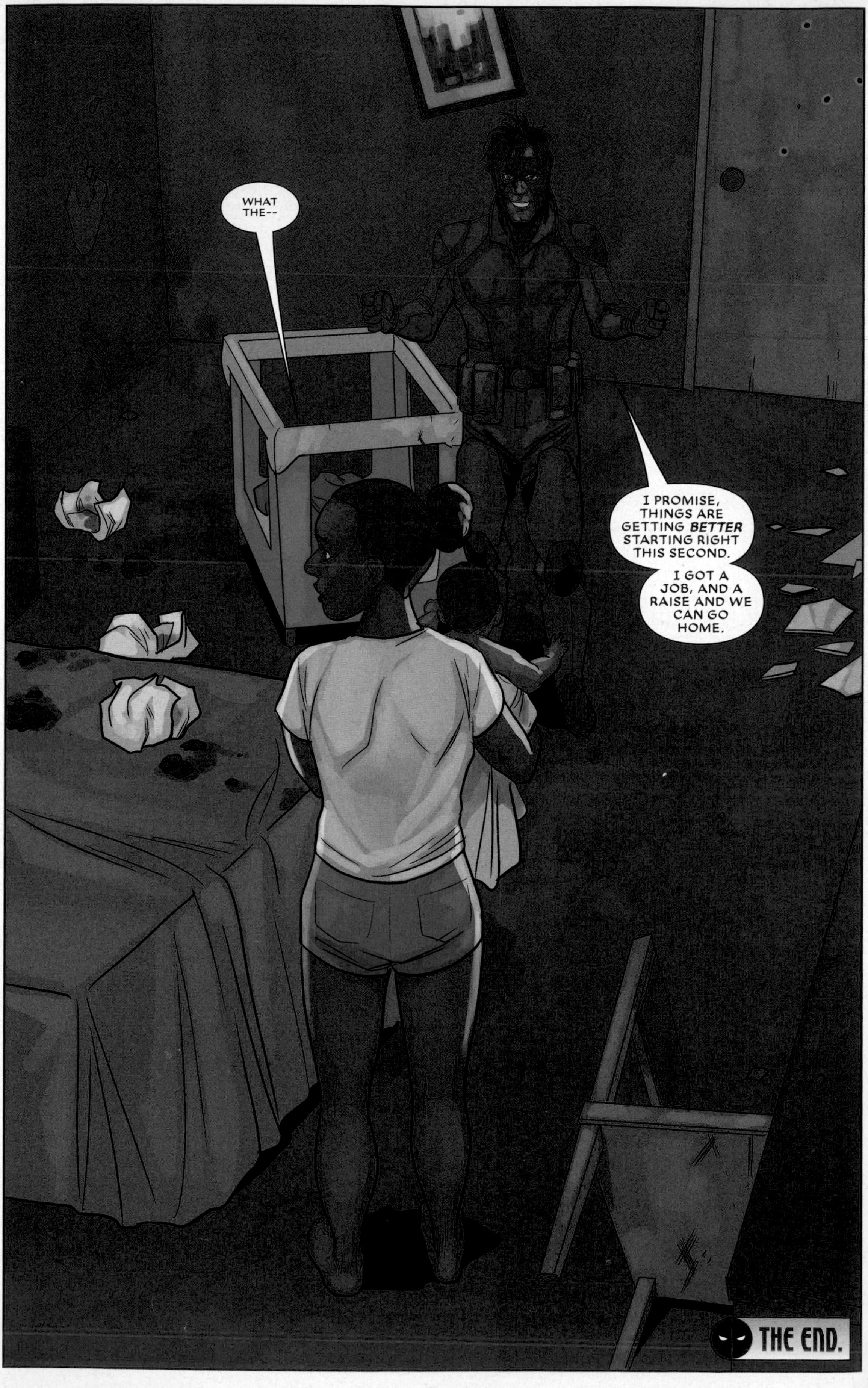

WHAT THE--
I PROMISE, THINGS ARE GETTING *BETTER* STARTING RIGHT THIS SECOND.
I GOT A JOB, AND A RAISE AND WE CAN GO HOME.
THE END.

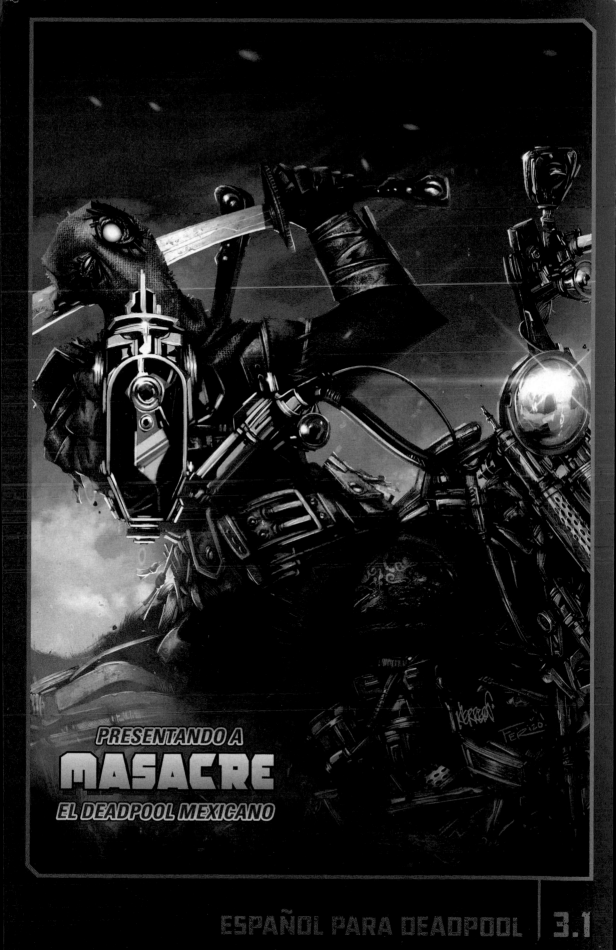

PRESENTANDO A

# MASACRE

EL DEADPOOL MEXICANO

Vengador...asesino... superestrella...apestoso... posiblemente el asesino más hábil y definitivamente el más fastidioso del mundo, Wade Wilson fue escogido para un programa ultra secreto en el gobierno, donde obtuvo el poder para recuperarse y sanar cualquier herida. De alguna forma, Wade se ha convertido en uno de los "héroes" mas queridos del mundo, aunque se gane la vida como matón. Llámenlo el Mercenario Bocón... llámenlo el Degenerado Regenerado... llámenlo...

# DEADPOOL

¡QUE ONDA! ¡AQUÍ DEADPOOL, Y LES TRAIGO ALGO ÚNICO!

¡ESTA EDICIÓN ESPECIAL ES PRESENTADA TOTALMENTE EN ESPAÑOL!

ES LA HISTORIA DE UN CHICO QUE CONOCÍ EN MÉXICO HACE YA ALGÚN TIEMPO... UN CHICO AL QUE QUIZÁ LE CAUSÉ UNA GRAN IMPRESIÓN.

SE HACE LLAMAR... ¡MASACRE!

¿ENTIENDEN LO QUE LES ESTOY DICIENDO? APUESTO A QUE MUCHOS DE USTEDES NO.

PUEDO DECIR LO QUE YO QUIERA, ¿NO ES CIERTO? FANTÁSTICO.

¡VEINTE MIL DELFINES GELATINOSOS DESTRUYERON CON FERVOR A NUMEROSOS PUERCOESPINES SIFILÍTICOS!

¡JE-JE, DIVERTIDO! Y USTEDES, LOS QUE HABLAN ESPAÑOL, NO CUENTEN LO QUE HE DICHO.

PEQUEÑO DEADPOOL POR
**IRENE Y. LEE**

# ESPAÑOL PARA DEADPOOL

**Brian Posehn y Gerry Duggan**
escritores

**Scott Koblish**
ilustrador

**Nick Filardi**
colorista

**VC's Joe Sabino**
rotulista

**Francisco Herrera y Fernando Rizo**
portada

**Arturo G. Aldama y Veronica Worrells**
traductores

**Heather Antos**
editora asistente

**Jordan D. White**
editor

**Axel Alonso**
director editorial

**Joe Quesada**
director creativo

**Dan Buckley**
publisher

**Alan Fine**
productor ejecutivo

Agradecimiento especial a Mike Hawthorne por el diseño de Masacre.

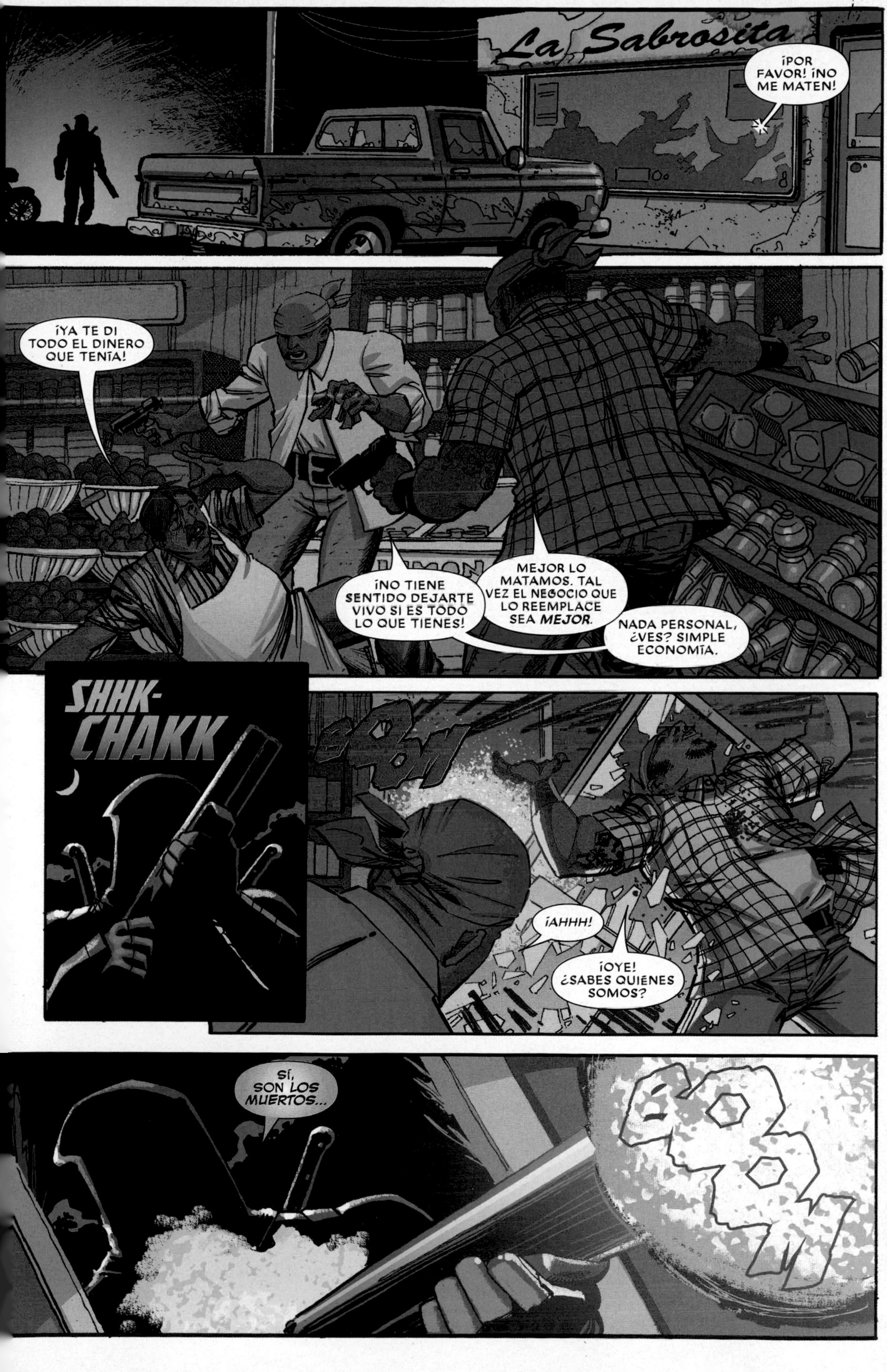
La Sabrosita
¡POR FAVOR! ¡NO ME MATEN!
¡YA TE DI TODO EL DINERO QUE TENÍA!
¡NO TIENE SENTIDO DEJARTE VIVO SI ES TODO LO QUE TIENES!
MEJOR LO MATAMOS. TAL VEZ EL NEGOCIO QUE LO REEMPLACE SEA *MEJOR*.
NADA PERSONAL, ¿VES? SIMPLE ECONOMÍA.
SHHK-CHAKK
¡AHHH!
¡OYE! ¿SABES QUIÉNES SOMOS?
SÍ, SON LOS MUERTOS...

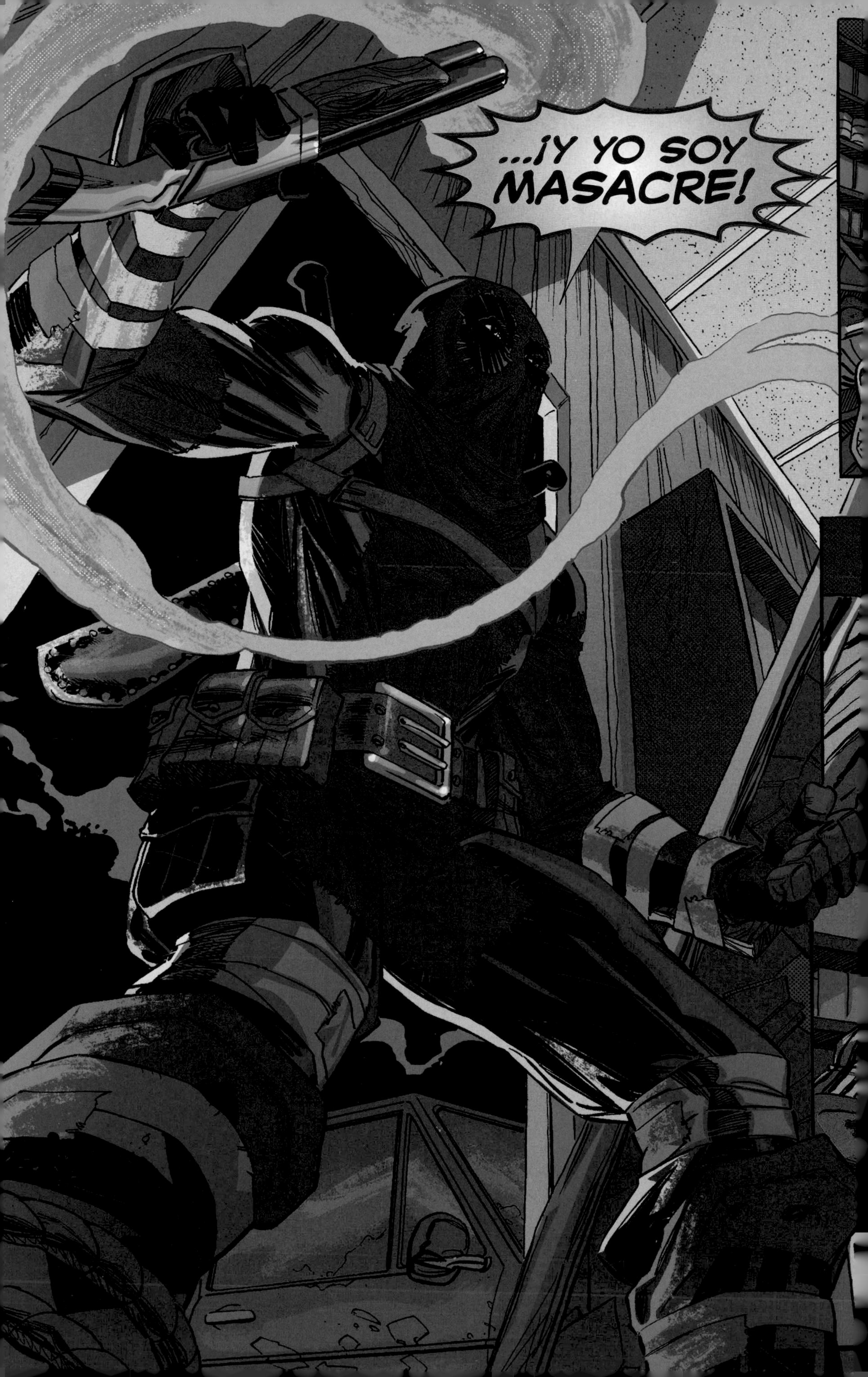
...¡Y YO SOY MASACRE!

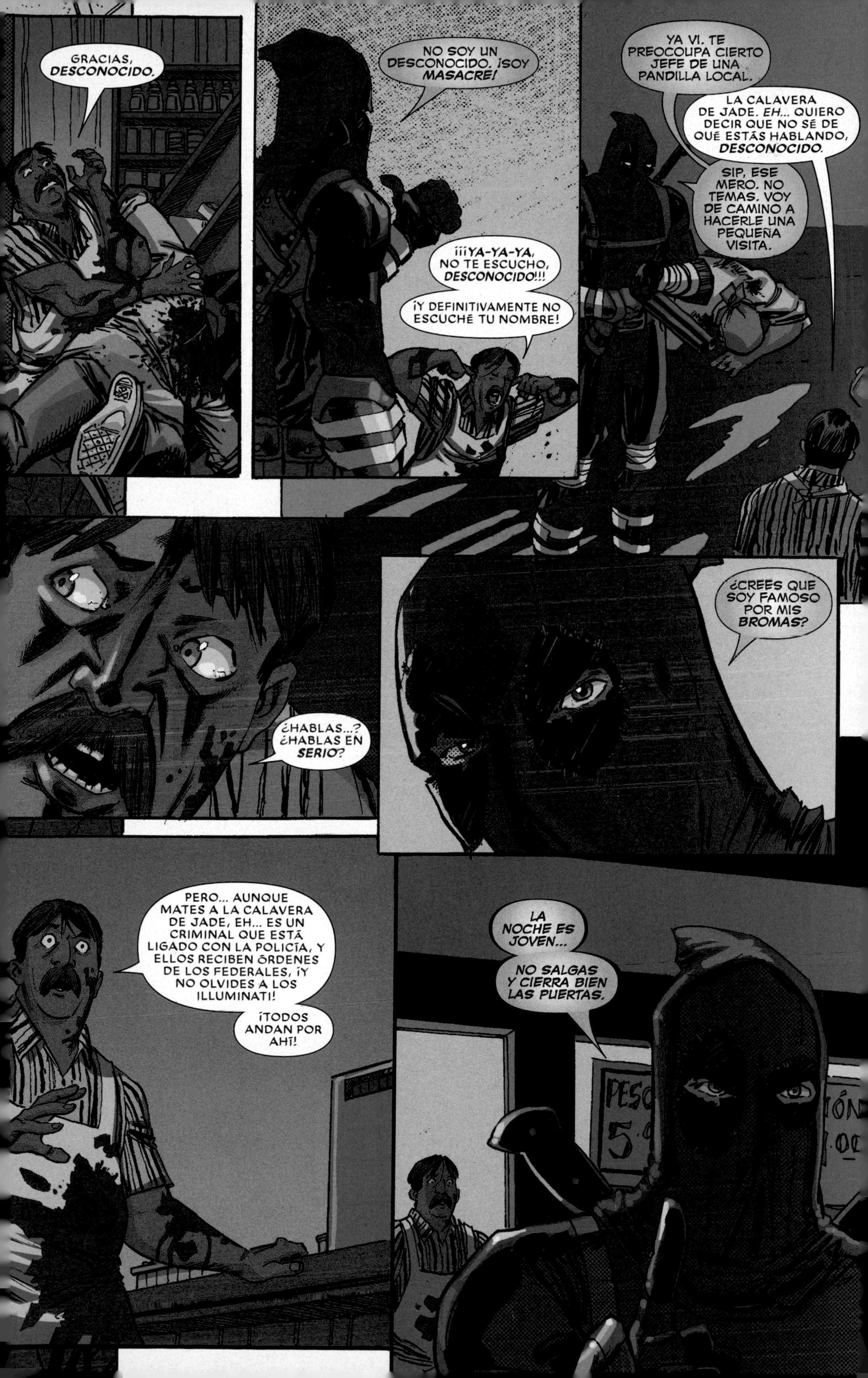
GRACIAS, *DESCONOCIDO.*
NO SOY UN DESCONOCIDO. ¡SOY *MASACRE!*
¡¡¡*YA-YA-YA*, NO TE ESCUCHO, *DESCONOCIDO*!!!
¡Y DEFINITIVAMENTE NO ESCUCHÉ TU NOMBRE!
YA VI. TE PREOCUPA CIERTO JEFE DE UNA PANDILLA LOCAL.
LA CALAVERA DE JADE. *EH*... QUIERO DECIR QUE NO SÉ DE QUÉ ESTÁS HABLANDO, *DESCONOCIDO.*
SIP, ESE MERO. NO TEMAS. VOY DE CAMINO A HACERLE UNA PEQUEÑA VISITA.
¿HABLAS...? ¿HABLAS EN *SERIO*?
¿CREES QUE SOY FAMOSO POR MIS *BROMAS*?
PERO... AUNQUE MATES A LA CALAVERA DE JADE, EH... ES UN CRIMINAL QUE ESTÁ LIGADO CON LA POLICÍA, Y ELLOS RECIBEN ÓRDENES DE LOS FEDERALES, ¡Y NO OLVIDES A LOS ILLUMINATI!
¡TODOS ANDAN POR AHÍ!
*LA NOCHE ES JOVEN...*
*NO SALGAS Y CIERRA BIEN LAS PUERTAS.*

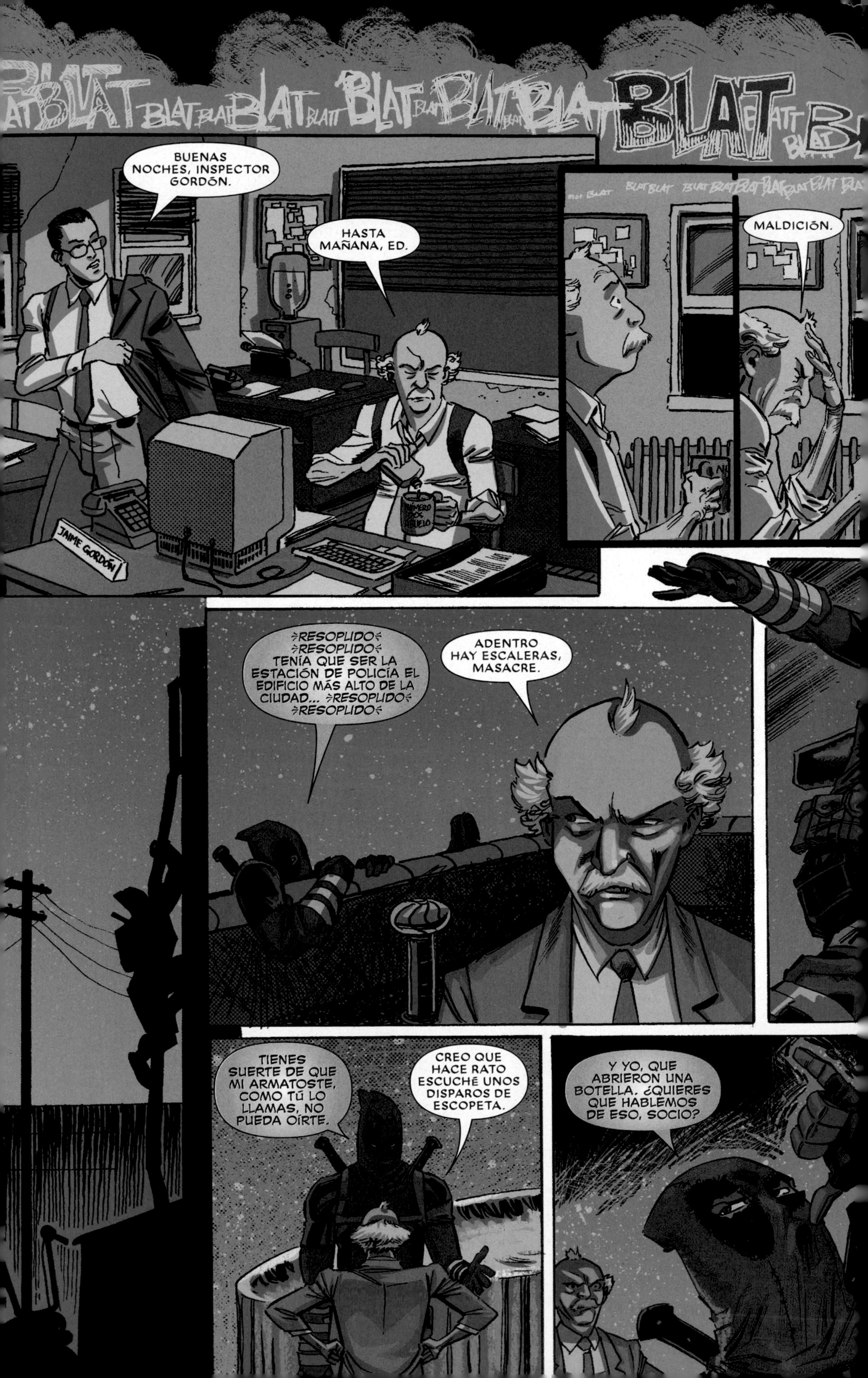
BLAT BLAT BLAT BLAT BLAT BLATT BLAT BLAT BLAT BLAT BLAT BLAT BLATT BLAT
BUENAS NOCHES, INSPECTOR GORDÓN.
HASTA MAÑANA, ED.
JAIME GORDÓN
BLAT BLAT BLAT BLAT BLAT BLAT BLAT BLAT BLAT BLAT
MALDICIÓN.
*RESOPLIDO* *RESOPLIDO* TENÍA QUE SER LA ESTACIÓN DE POLICÍA EL EDIFICIO MÁS ALTO DE LA CIUDAD... *RESOPLIDO* *RESOPLIDO*
ADENTRO HAY ESCALERAS, MASACRE.
TIENES SUERTE DE QUE MI ARMATOSTE, COMO TÚ LO LLAMAS, NO PUEDA OÍRTE.
CREO QUE HACE RATO ESCUCHÉ UNOS DISPAROS DE ESCOPETA.
Y YO, QUE ABRIERON UNA BOTELLA. ¿QUIERES QUE HABLEMOS DE ESO, SOCIO?

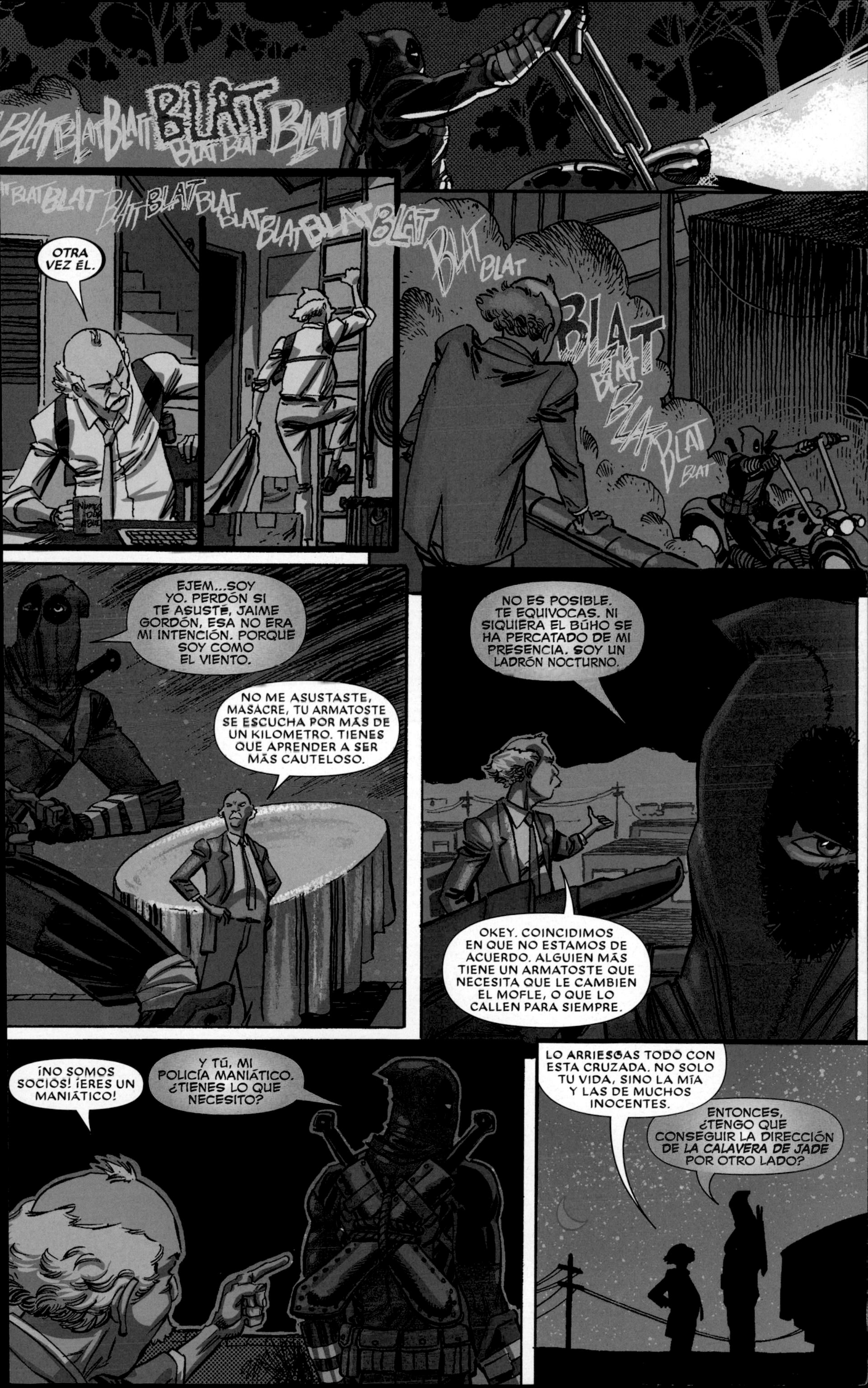
BLAT BLAT BLATT BLATT BLAT BLAT BLAT
BLAT BLAT BLATT BLAT BLAT BLAT BLAT BLAT BLAT BLAT BLAT
OTRA VEZ ÉL.
BLAT BLAT BLAT BLAT BLAT BLAT
EJEM...SOY YO. PERDÓN SI TE ASUSTÉ, JAIME GORDÓN, ESA NO ERA MI INTENCIÓN. PORQUE SOY COMO EL VIENTO.
NO ME ASUSTASTE, MASACRE, TU ARMATOSTE SE ESCUCHA POR MÁS DE UN KILOMETRO. TIENES QUE APRENDER A SER MÁS CAUTELOSO.
NO ES POSIBLE. TE EQUIVOCAS. NI SIQUIERA EL BÚHO SE HA PERCATADO DE MI PRESENCIA. SOY UN LADRÓN NOCTURNO.
OKEY. COINCIDIMOS EN QUE NO ESTAMOS DE ACUERDO. ALGUIEN MÁS TIENE UN ARMATOSTE QUE NECESITA QUE LE CAMBIEN EL MOFLE, O QUE LO CALLEN PARA SIEMPRE.
¡NO SOMOS SOCIOS! ¡ERES UN MANIÁTICO!
Y TÚ, MI POLICÍA MANIÁTICO. ¿TIENES LO QUE NECESITO?
LO ARRIESGAS TODO CON ESTA CRUZADA. NO SOLO TU VIDA, SINO LA MÍA Y LAS DE MUCHOS INOCENTES.
ENTONCES, ¿TENGO QUE CONSEGUIR LA DIRECCIÓN DE *LA CALAVERA DE JADE* POR OTRO LADO?

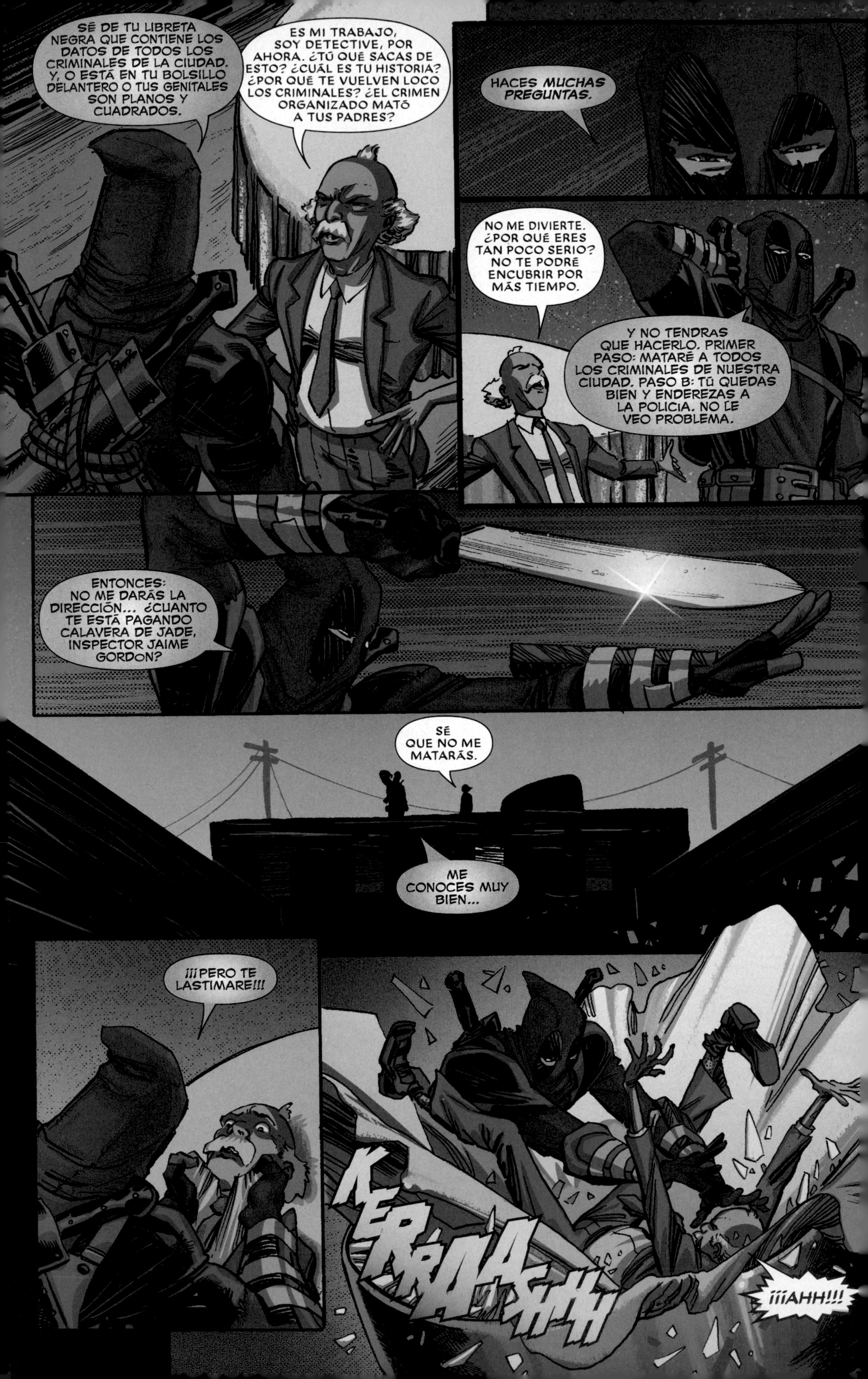
SÉ DE TU LIBRETA NEGRA QUE CONTIENE LOS DATOS DE TODOS LOS CRIMINALES DE LA CIUDAD. Y, O ESTÁ EN TU BOLSILLO DELANTERO O TUS GENITALES SON PLANOS Y CUADRADOS.
ES MI TRABAJO, SOY DETECTIVE, POR AHORA. ¿TÚ QUÉ SACAS DE ESTO? ¿CUÁL ES TU HISTORIA? ¿POR QUÉ TE VUELVEN LOCO LOS CRIMINALES? ¿EL CRIMEN ORGANIZADO MATÓ A TUS PADRES?
HACES *MUCHAS PREGUNTAS.*
NO ME DIVIERTE. ¿POR QUÉ ERES TAN POCO SERIO? NO TE PODRÉ ENCUBRIR POR MÁS TIEMPO.
Y NO TENDRAS QUE HACERLO. PRIMER PASO: MATARÉ A TODOS LOS CRIMINALES DE NUESTRA CIUDAD. PASO B: TÚ QUEDAS BIEN Y ENDEREZAS A LA POLICIA. NO LE VEO PROBLEMA.
ENTONCES: NO ME DARÁS LA DIRECCIÓN... ¿CUANTO TE ESTÁ PAGANDO CALAVERA DE JADE, INSPECTOR JAIME GORDON?
SÉ QUE NO ME MATARÁS.
ME CONOCES MUY BIEN...
¡¡¡PERO TE LASTIMARE!!!
KERRAASHHH
¡¡¡AHH!!!

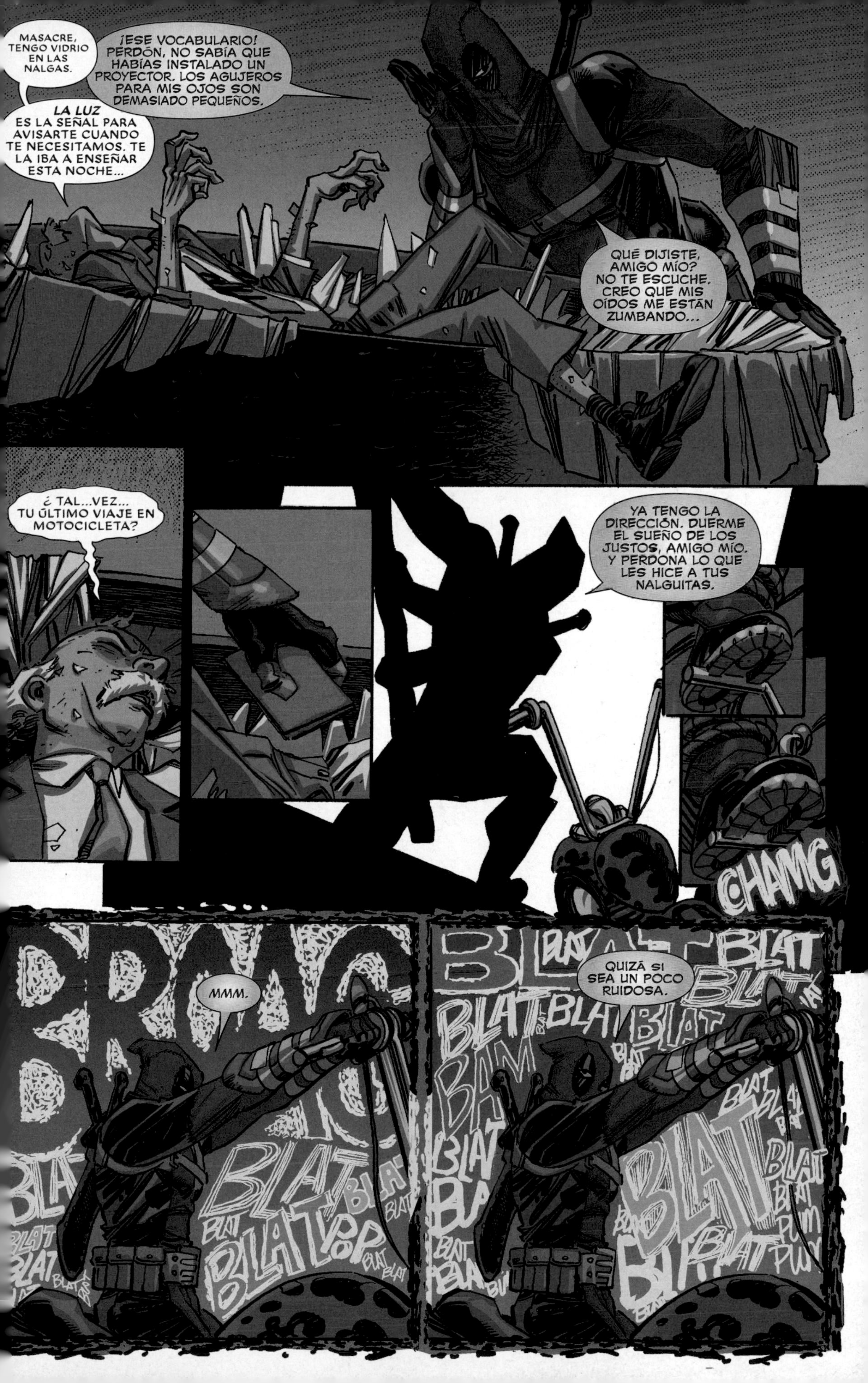
MASACRE, TENGO VIDRIO EN LAS NALGAS.
¡ESE VOCABULARIO! PERDÓN, NO SABÍA QUE HABÍAS INSTALADO UN PROYECTOR. LOS AGUJEROS PARA MIS OJOS SON DEMASIADO PEQUEÑOS.
*LA LUZ* ES LA SEÑAL PARA AVISARTE CUANDO TE NECESITAMOS. TE LA IBA A ENSEÑAR ESTA NOCHE...
QUÉ DIJISTE, AMIGO MÍO? NO TE ESCUCHE. CREO QUE MIS OÍDOS ME ESTÁN ZUMBANDO...
¿ TAL...VEZ... TU ÚLTIMO VIAJE EN MOTOCICLETA?
YA TENGO LA DIRECCIÓN. DUERME EL SUEÑO DE LOS JUSTOS, AMIGO MÍO. Y PERDONA LO QUE LES HICE A TUS NALGUITAS.
CHAMG
MMM.
BLAT BLAT BLAT POP
QUIZÁ SI SEA UN POCO RUIDOSA.
BLAT BLAT BAM BLAT BLAT

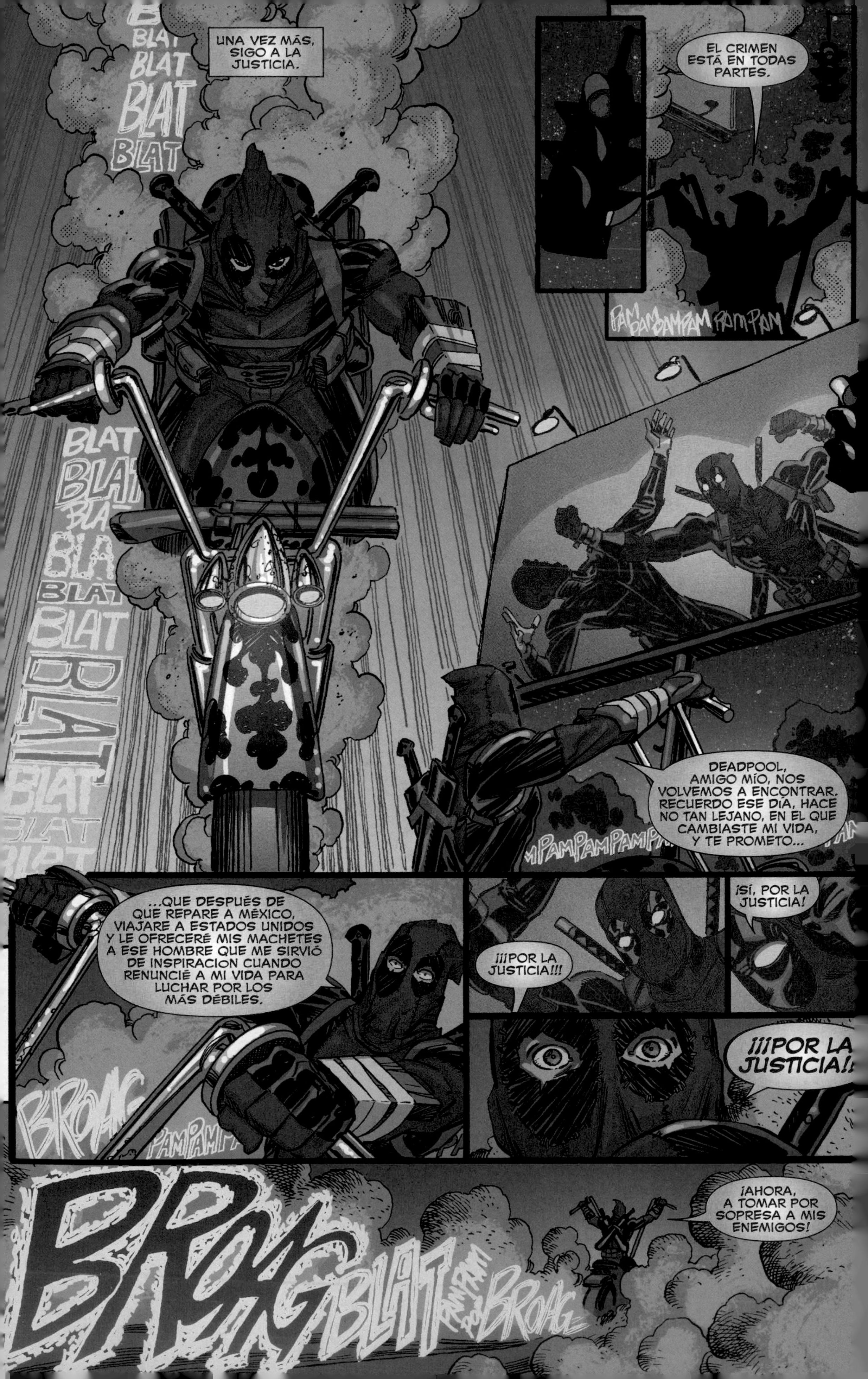
BLAT BLAT BLAT BLAT BLAT
UNA VEZ MÁS, SIGO A LA JUSTICIA.
EL CRIMEN ESTÁ EN TODAS PARTES.
PAMPAMBAMPAM PAMPAM
BLAT BLAT BLAT BLAT BLAT BLAT BLAT BLAT BLAT
DEADPOOL, AMIGO MÍO, NOS VOLVEMOS A ENCONTRAR. RECUERDO ESE DÍA, HACE NO TAN LEJANO, EN EL QUE CAMBIASTE MI VIDA, Y TE PROMETO...
...QUE DESPUÉS DE QUE REPARE A MÉXICO, VIAJARE A ESTADOS UNIDOS Y LE OFRECERÉ MIS MACHETES A ESE HOMBRE QUE ME SIRVIÓ DE INSPIRACION CUANDO RENUNCIÉ A MI VIDA PARA LUCHAR POR LOS MÁS DÉBILES.
BROAG
¡¡¡POR LA JUSTICIA!!!
¡SÍ, POR LA JUSTICIA!
¡¡¡POR LA JUSTICIA!!
¡AHORA, A TOMAR POR SOPRESA A MIS ENEMIGOS!
BROAG BLAT BROAG

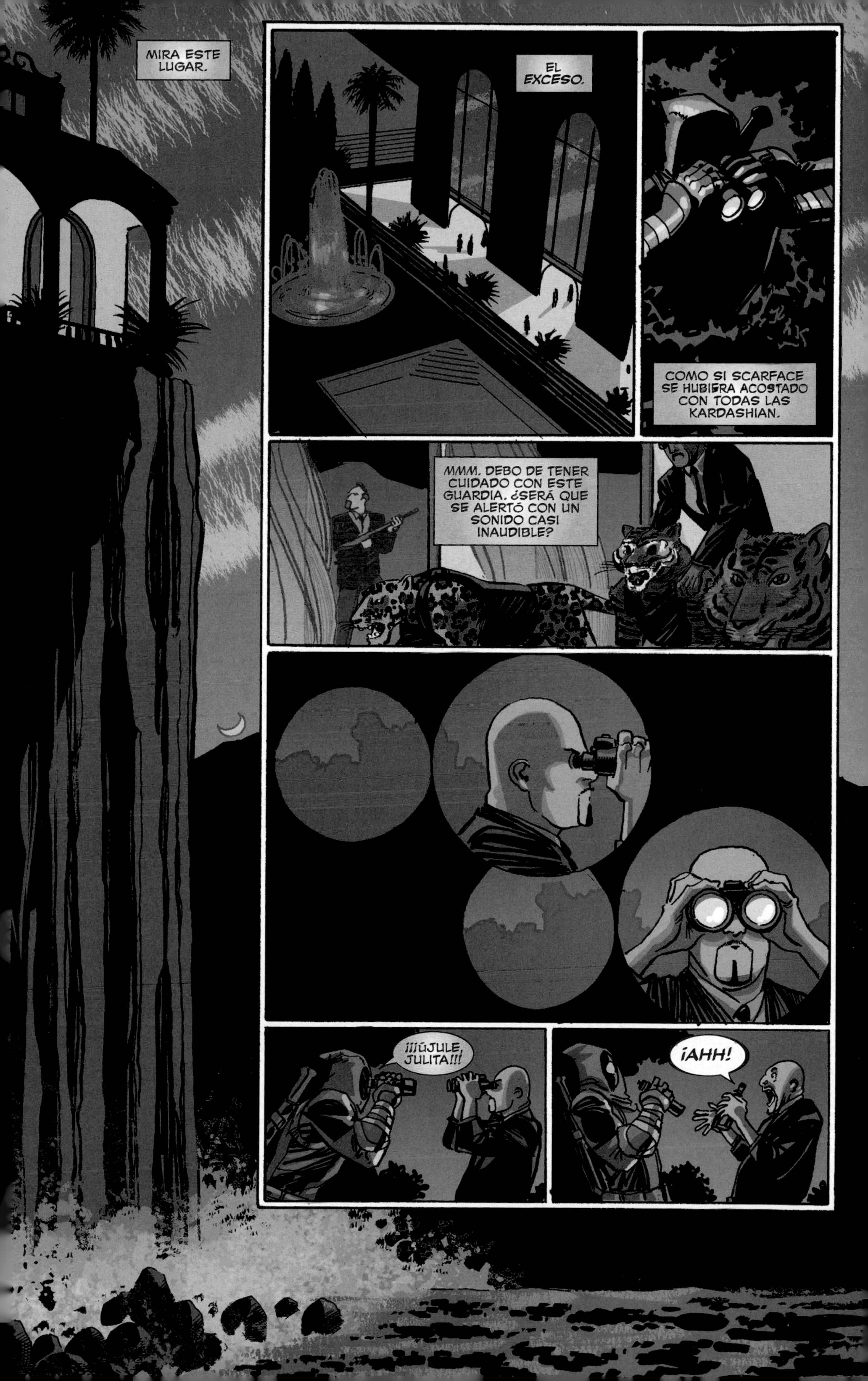
MIRA ESTE LUGAR.
EL EXCESO.
COMO SI SCARFACE SE HUBIERA ACOSTADO CON TODAS LAS KARDASHIAN.
MMM. DEBO DE TENER CUIDADO CON ESTE GUARDIA. ¿SERÁ QUE SE ALERTÓ CON UN SONIDO CASI INAUDIBLE?
¡¡¡ÚJULE, JULITA!!!
¡AHH!

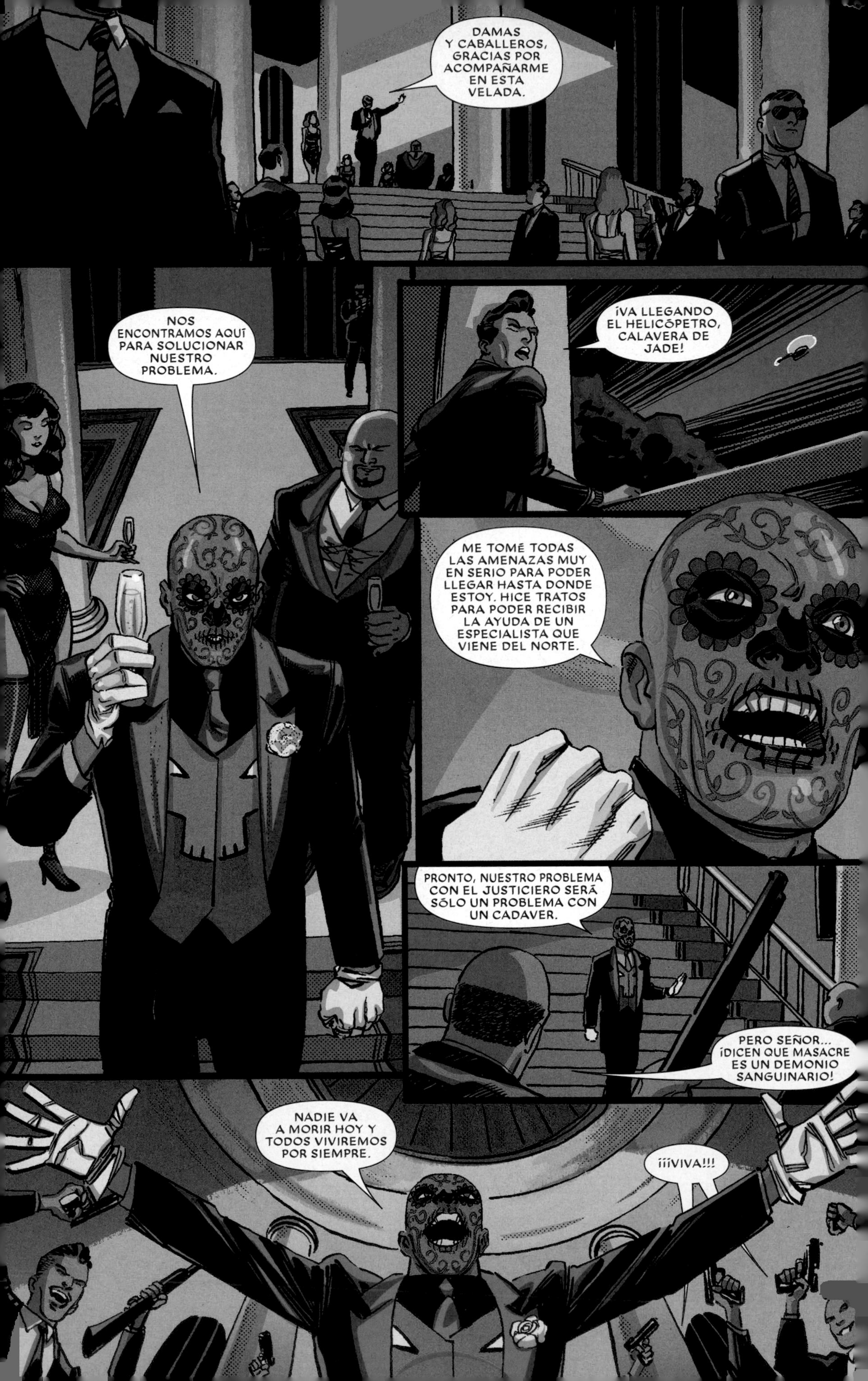
DAMAS Y CABALLEROS, GRACIAS POR ACOMPAÑARME EN ESTA VELADA.
NOS ENCONTRAMOS AQUÍ PARA SOLUCIONAR NUESTRO PROBLEMA.
¡VA LLEGANDO EL HELICÓPETRO, CALAVERA DE JADE!
ME TOMÉ TODAS LAS AMENAZAS MUY EN SERIO PARA PODER LLEGAR HASTA DONDE ESTOY. HICE TRATOS PARA PODER RECIBIR LA AYUDA DE UN ESPECIALISTA QUE VIENE DEL NORTE.
PRONTO, NUESTRO PROBLEMA CON EL JUSTICIERO SERÁ SÓLO UN PROBLEMA CON UN CADÁVER.
PERO SEÑOR... ¡DICEN QUE MASACRE ES UN DEMONIO SANGUINARIO!
NADIE VA A MORIR HOY Y TODOS VIVIREMOS POR SIEMPRE.
¡¡¡VIVA!!!

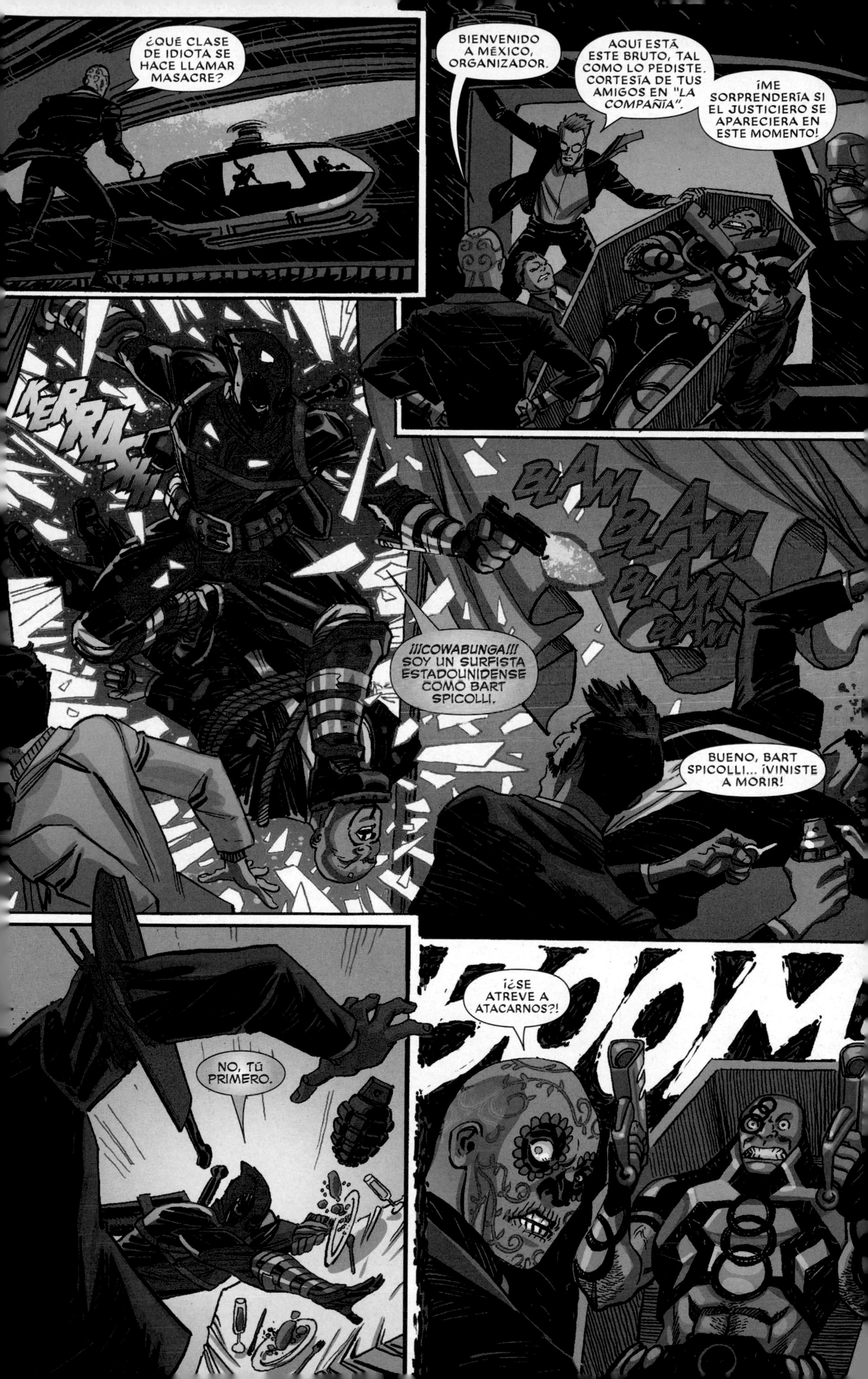
¿QUÉ CLASE DE IDIOTA SE HACE LLAMAR MASACRE?
BIENVENIDO A MÉXICO, ORGANIZADOR.
AQUÍ ESTÁ ESTE BRUTO, TAL COMO LO PEDISTE. CORTESÍA DE TUS AMIGOS EN "LA COMPAÑÍA".
¡ME SORPRENDERÍA SI EL JUSTICIERO SE APARECIERA EN ESTE MOMENTO!
KERRASHH
BLAM BLAM BLAM BLAM BLAM
¡¡¡COWABUNGA!!! SOY UN SURFISTA ESTADOUNIDENSE COMO BART SPICOLLI.
BUENO, BART SPICOLLI... ¡VINISTE A MORIR!
¡¿SE ATREVE A ATACARNOS?!
NO, TÚ PRIMERO.

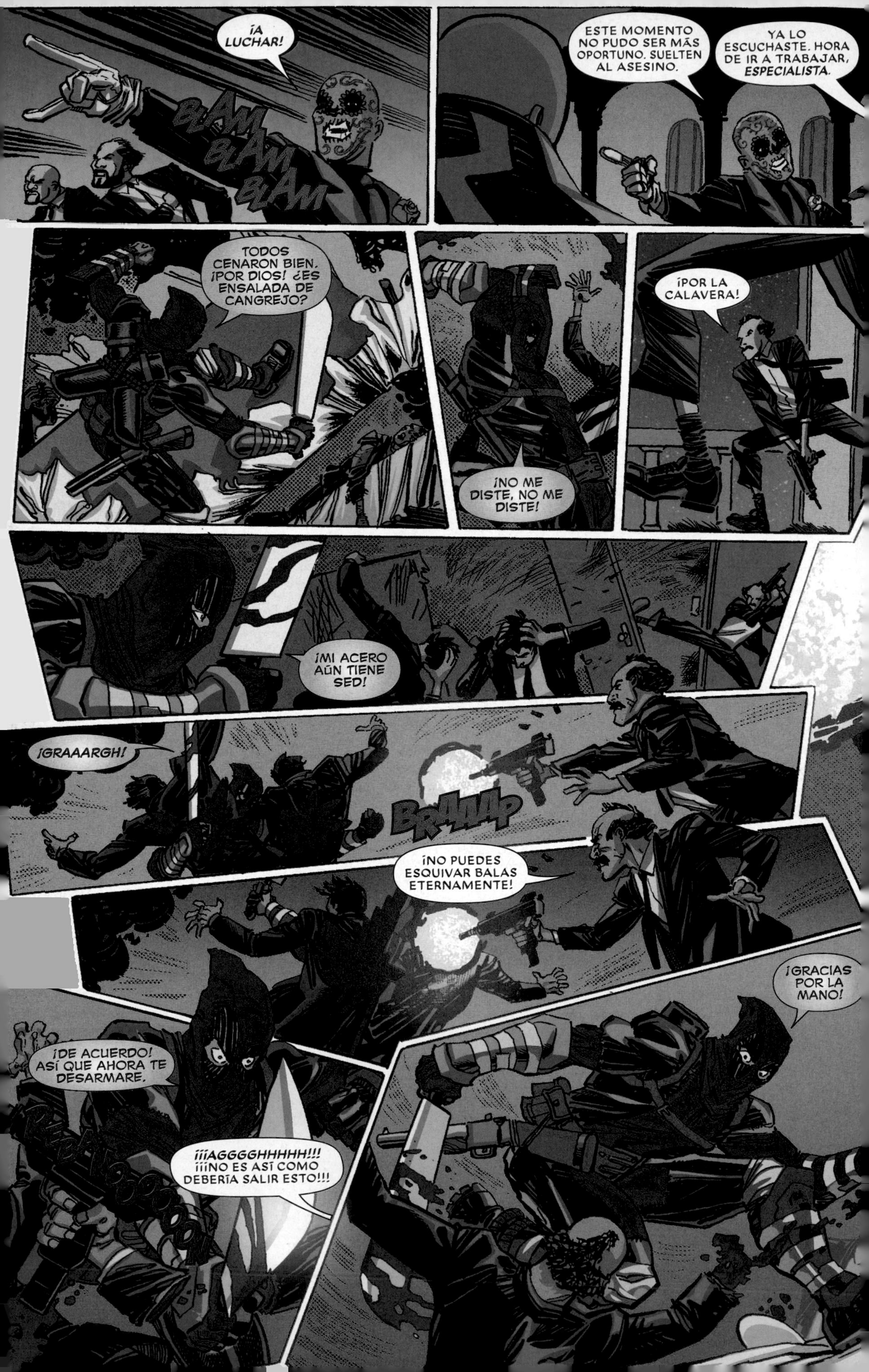

¡A LUCHAR!
BLAM BLAM BLAM
ESTE MOMENTO NO PUDO SER MÁS OPORTUNO. SUELTEN AL ASESINO.
YA LO ESCUCHASTE. HORA DE IR A TRABAJAR, ESPECIALISTA.
TODOS CENARON BIEN. ¡POR DIOS! ¿ES ENSALADA DE CANGREJO?
¡NO ME DISTE, NO ME DISTE!
¡POR LA CALAVERA!
¡MI ACERO AÚN TIENE SED!
¡GRAAARGH!
BRAAAP
¡NO PUEDES ESQUIVAR BALAS ETERNAMENTE!
¡GRACIAS POR LA MANO!
¡DE ACUERDO! ASÍ QUE AHORA TE DESARMARE.
¡¡¡AGGGGHHHHH!!! ¡¡¡NO ES ASÍ COMO DEBERÍA SALIR ESTO!!!

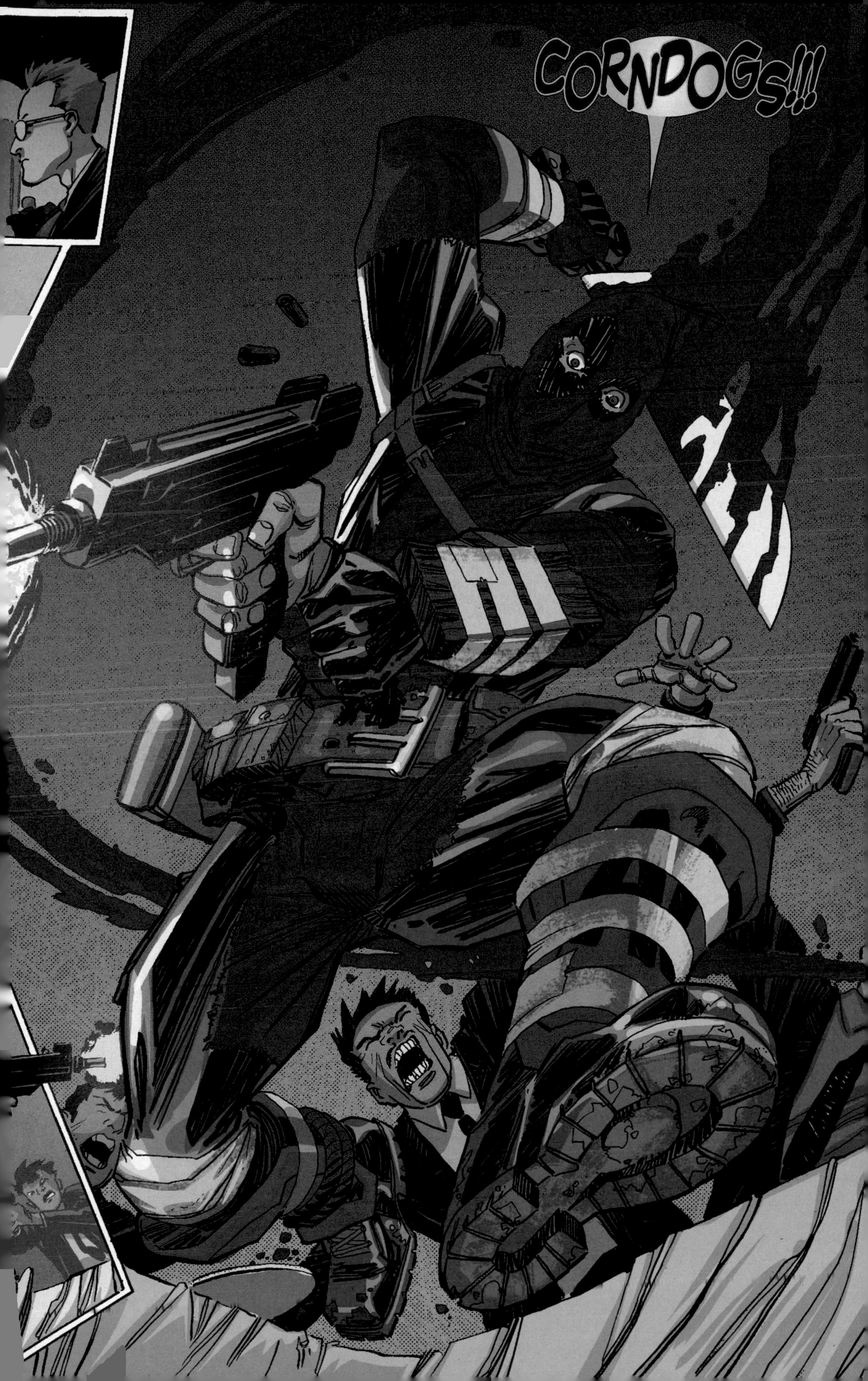
CORNDOGS!!!

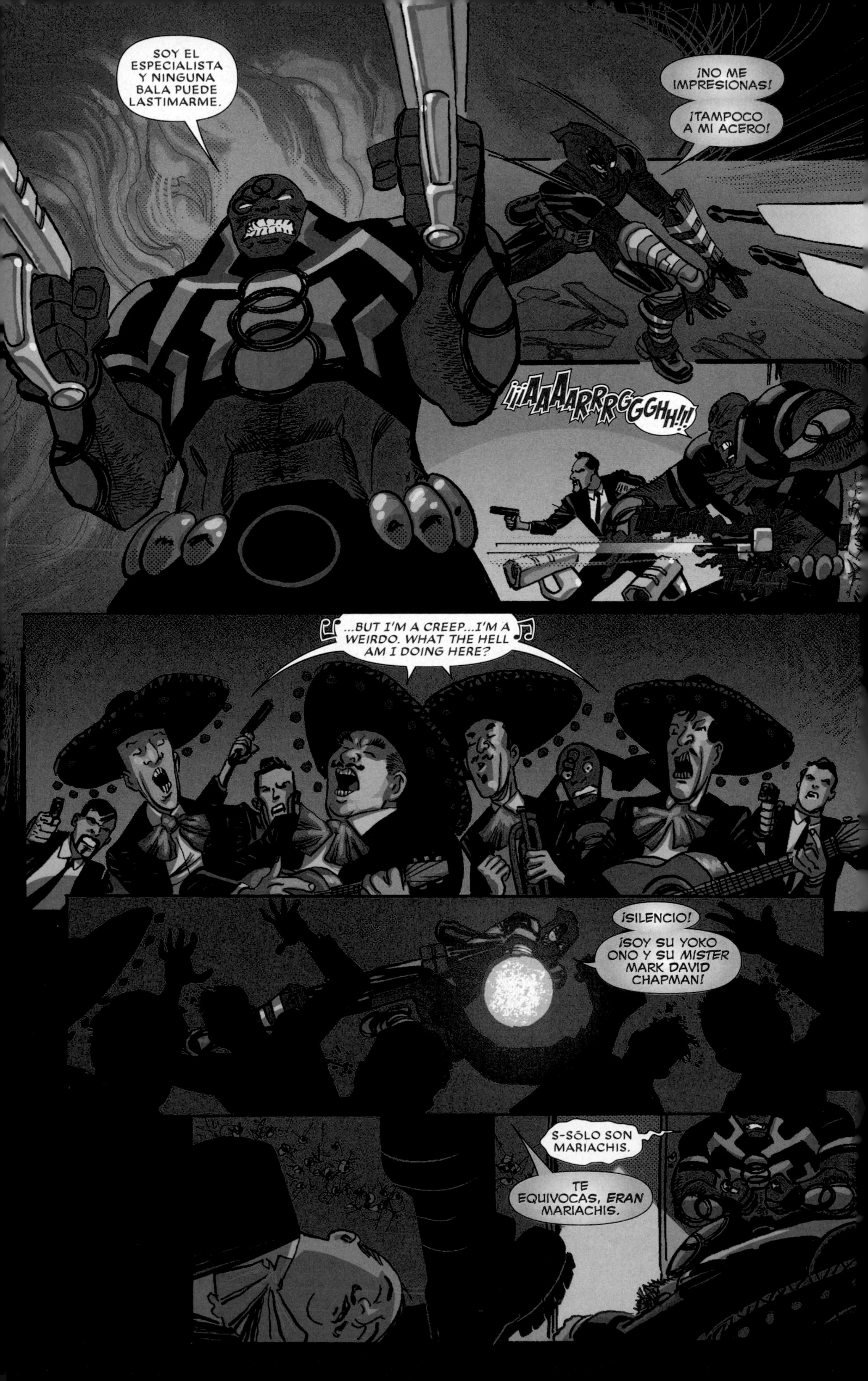
SOY EL ESPECIALISTA Y NINGUNA BALA PUEDE LASTIMARME.
¡NO ME IMPRESIONAS!
¡TAMPOCO A MI ACERO!
¡¡¡AAAARRRGGGHH!!!
...BUT I'M A CREEP...I'M A WEIRDO. WHAT THE HELL AM I DOING HERE?
¡SILENCIO!
¡SOY SU YOKO ONO Y SU MISTER MARK DAVID CHAPMAN!
S-SÓLO SON MARIACHIS.
TE EQUIVOCAS, ERAN MARIACHIS.

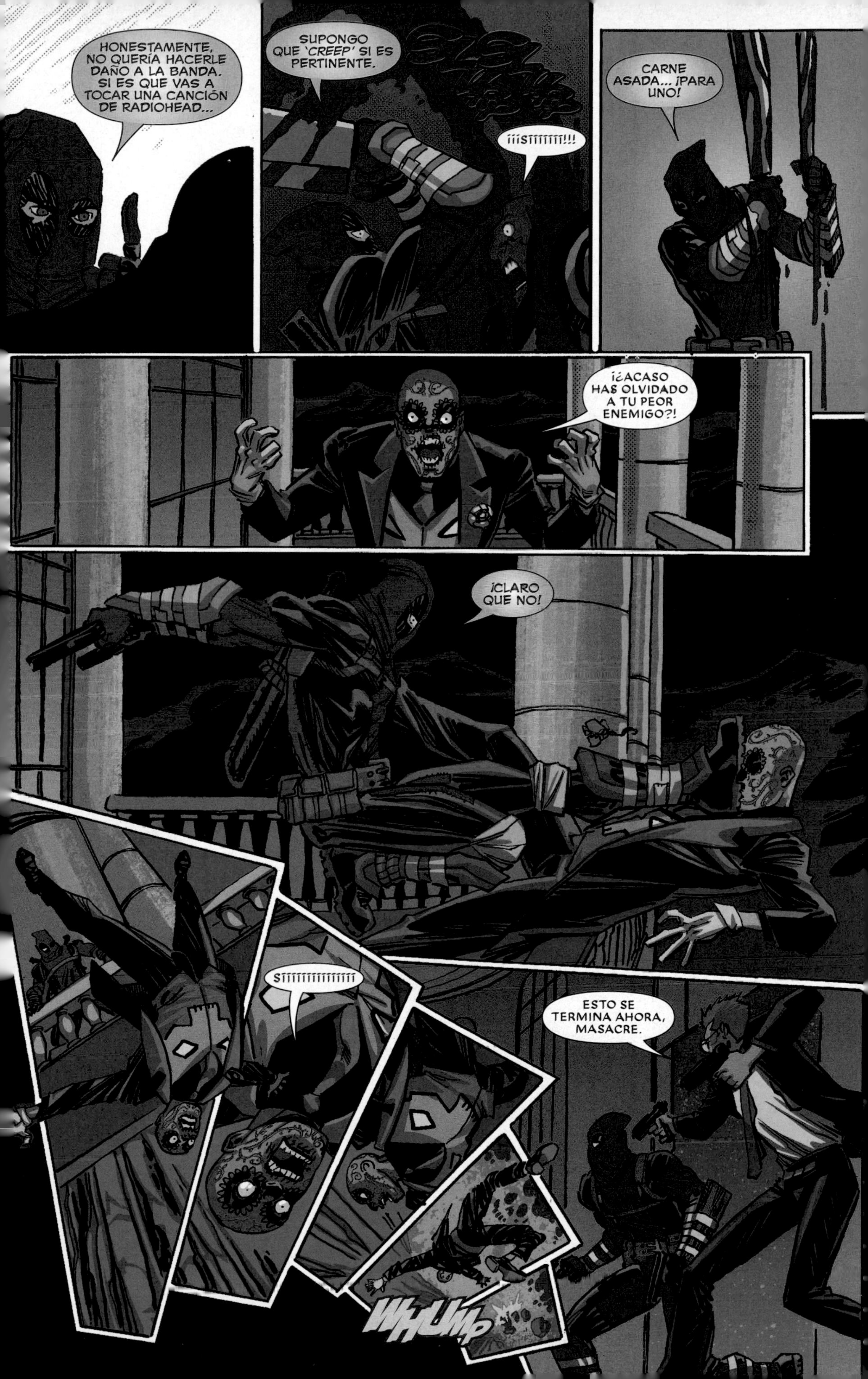
HONESTAMENTE, NO QUERÍA HACERLE DAÑO A LA BANDA. SI ES QUE VAS A TOCAR UNA CANCIÓN DE RADIOHEAD...
SUPONGO QUE 'CREEP' SI ES PERTINENTE.
¡¡¡SÍÍÍÍÍÍÍ!!!
CARNE ASADA... ¡PARA UNO!
¡¿ACASO HAS OLVIDADO A TU PEOR ENEMIGO?!
¡CLARO QUE NO!
SÍÍÍÍÍÍÍÍÍÍÍÍÍÍ
ESTO SE TERMINA AHORA, MASACRE.
WHUMP

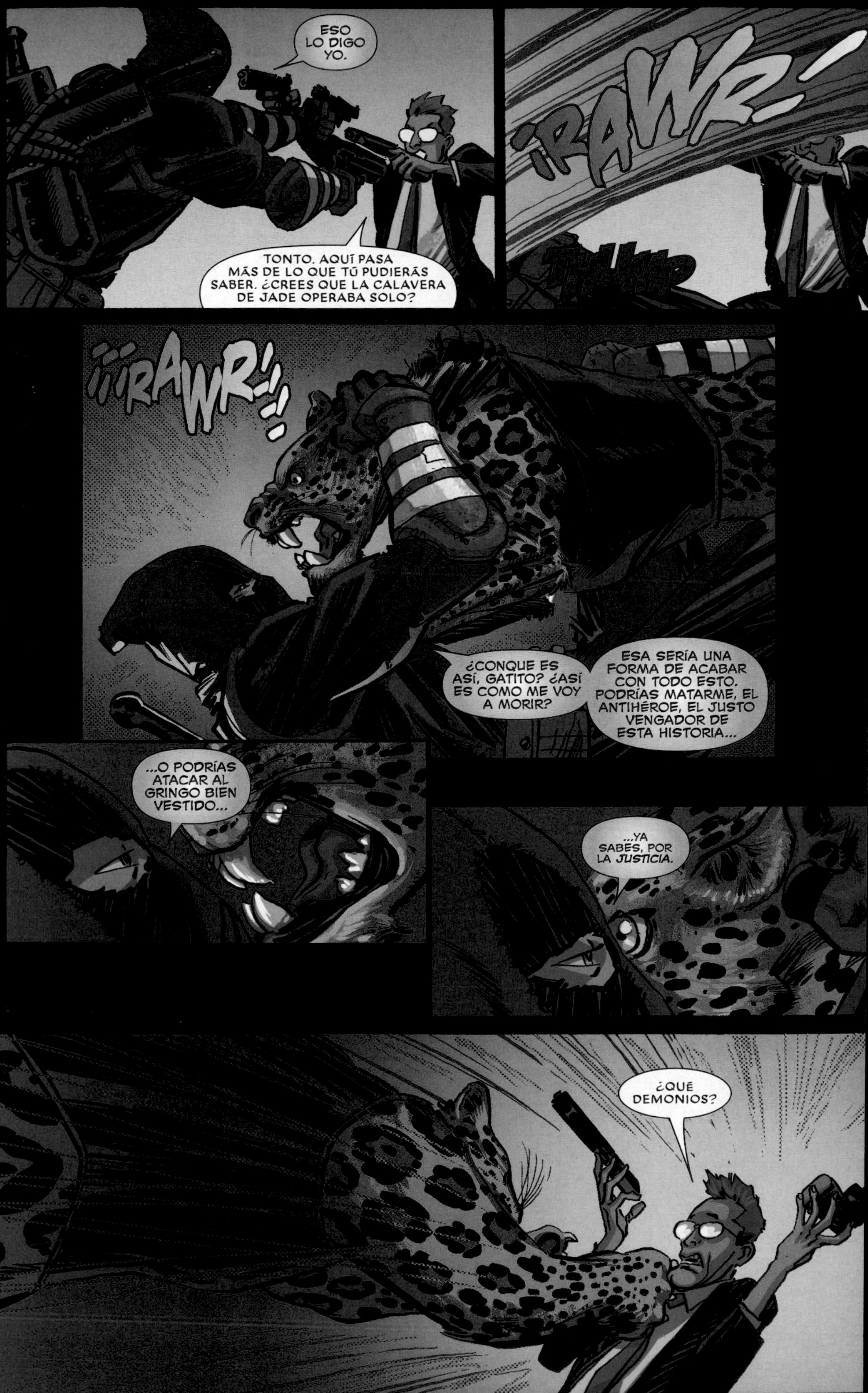
ESO LO DIGO YO.
TONTO. AQUÍ PASA MÁS DE LO QUE TÚ PUDIERÁS SABER. ¿CREES QUE LA CALAVERA DE JADE OPERABA SOLO?
¡RAWR!
¡¡¡RAWR!!!
¿CONQUE ES ASÍ, GATITO? ¿ASÍ ES COMO ME VOY A MORIR?
ESA SERÍA UNA FORMA DE ACABAR CON TODO ESTO. PODRÍAS MATARME, EL ANTIHÉROE, EL JUSTO VENGADOR DE ESTA HISTORIA...
...O PODRÍAS ATACAR AL GRINGO BIEN VESTIDO...
...YA SABES, POR LA *JUSTICIA*.
¿QUÉ DEMONIOS?

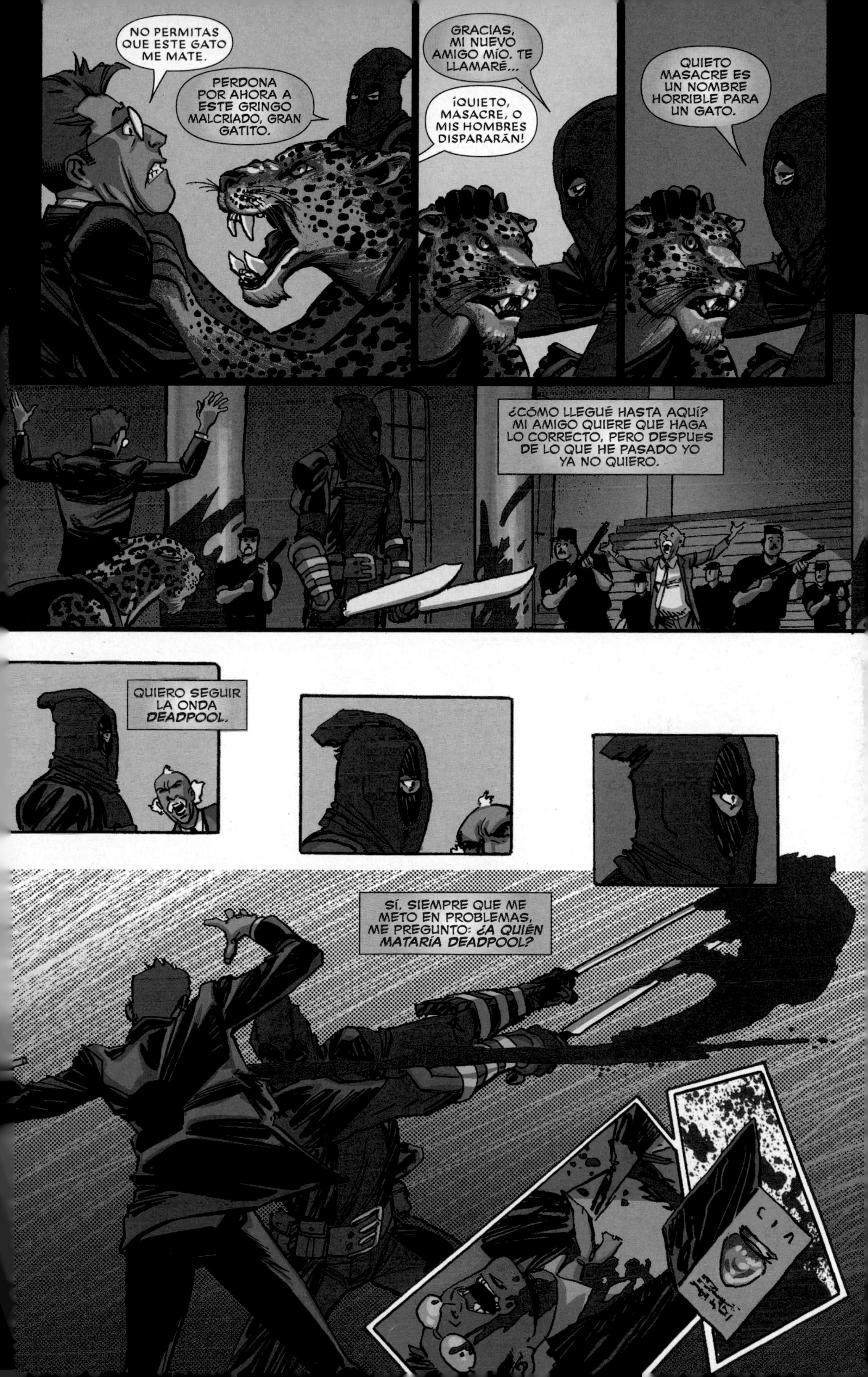
NO PERMITAS QUE ESTE GATO ME MATE.
PERDONA POR AHORA A ESTE GRINGO MALCRIADO, GRAN GATITO.
GRACIAS, MI NUEVO AMIGO MÍO. TE LLAMARÉ...
¡QUIETO, MASACRE, O MIS HOMBRES DISPARARÁN!
QUIETO MASACRE ES UN NOMBRE HORRIBLE PARA UN GATO.
¿CÓMO LLEGUÉ HASTA AQUÍ? MI AMIGO QUIERE QUE HAGA LO CORRECTO, PERO DESPUÉS DE LO QUE HE PASADO YO YA NO QUIERO.
QUIERO SEGUIR LA ONDA *DEADPOOL.*
SÍ, SIEMPRE QUE ME METO EN PROBLEMAS, ME PREGUNTO: *¿A QUIÉN MATARÍA DEADPOOL?*

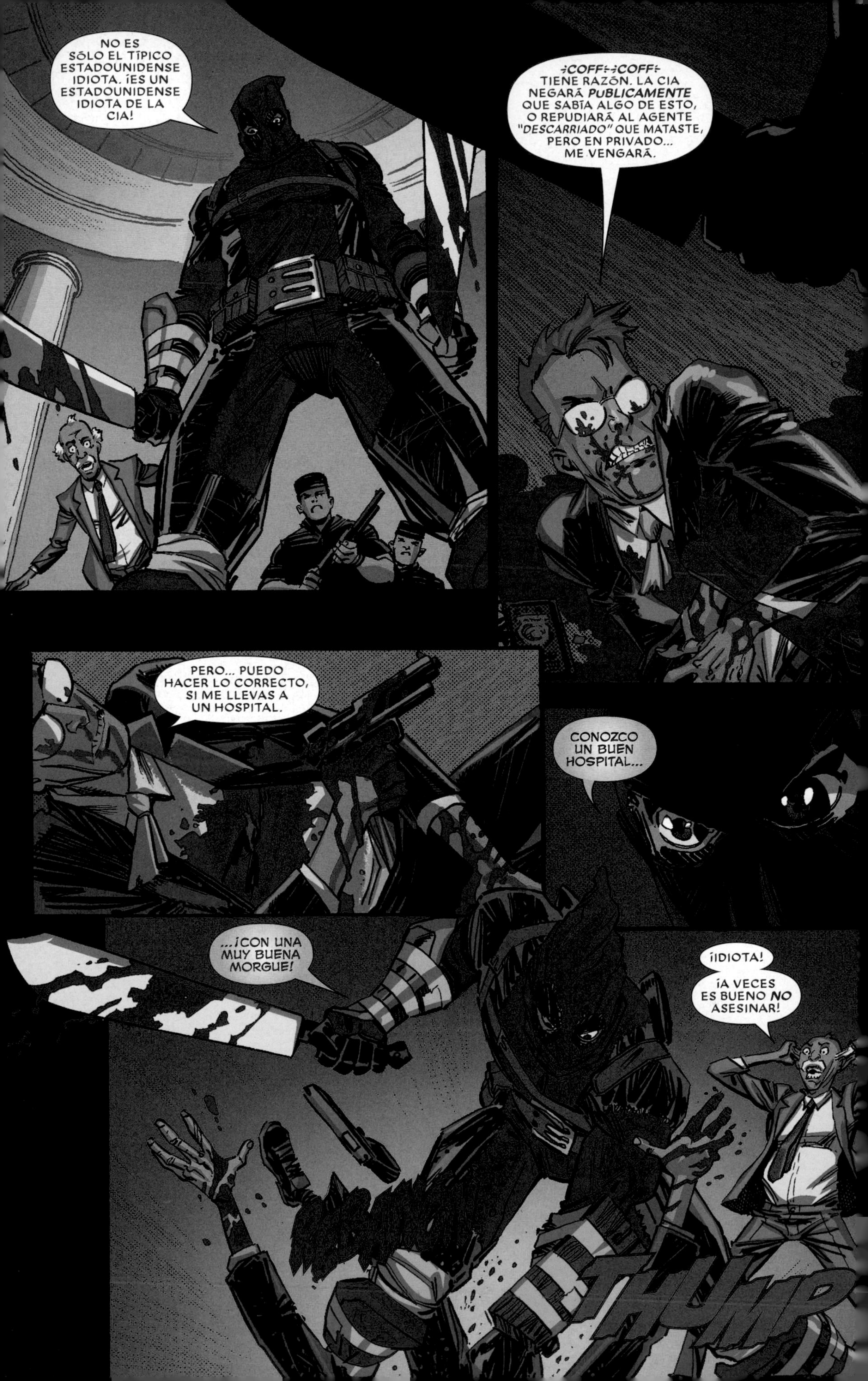
NO ES SÓLO EL TÍPICO ESTADOUNIDENSE IDIOTA. ¡ES UN ESTADOUNIDENSE IDIOTA DE LA CIA!
¡COFF! ¡COFF! TIENE RAZÓN. LA CIA NEGARÁ PUBLICAMENTE QUE SABÍA ALGO DE ESTO, O REPUDIARÁ AL AGENTE "DESCARRIADO" QUE MATASTE, PERO EN PRIVADO... ME VENGARÁ.
PERO... PUEDO HACER LO CORRECTO, SI ME LLEVAS A UN HOSPITAL.
CONOZCO UN BUEN HOSPITAL...
...¡CON UNA MUY BUENA MORGUE!
¡IDIOTA!
¡A VECES ES BUENO NO ASESINAR!
THUMP

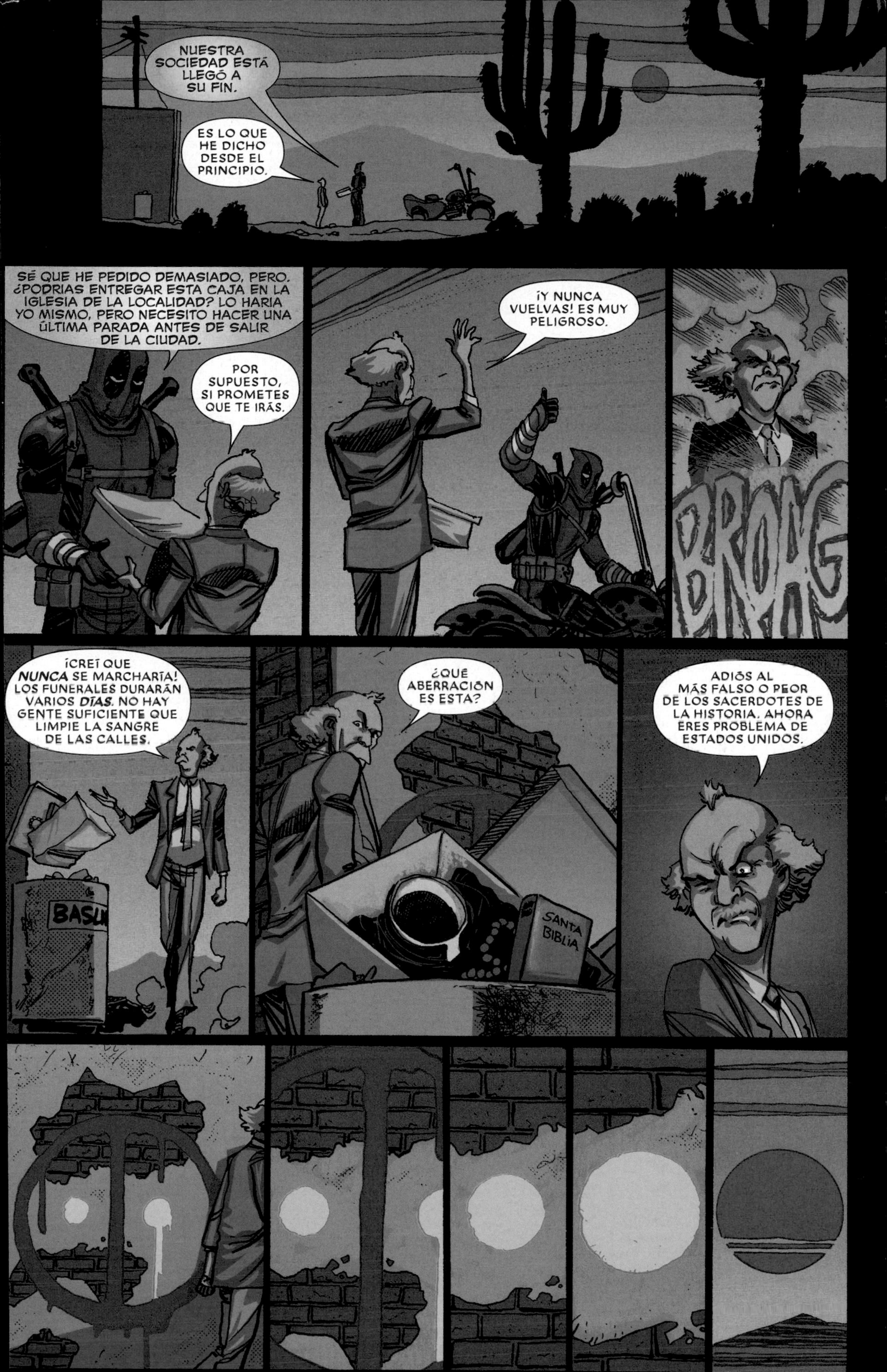
NUESTRA SOCIEDAD ESTÁ LLEGÓ A SU FIN.
ES LO QUE HE DICHO DESDE EL PRINCIPIO.
SÉ QUE HE PEDIDO DEMASIADO, PERO. ¿PODRIAS ENTREGAR ESTA CAJA EN LA IGLESIA DE LA LOCALIDAD? LO HARIA YO MISMO, PERO NECESITO HACER UNA ÚLTIMA PARADA ANTES DE SALIR DE LA CIUDAD.
POR SUPUESTO, SI PROMETES QUE TE IRÁS.
¡Y NUNCA VUELVAS! ES MUY PELIGROSO.
BRONG
¡CREÍ QUE *NUNCA* SE MARCHARÍA! LOS FUNERALES DURARÁN VARIOS *DÍAS*. NO HAY GENTE SUFICIENTE QUE LIMPIE LA SANGRE DE LAS CALLES.
BASU
¿QUÉ ABERRACIÓN ES ESTA?
SANTA BIBLIA
ADIÓS AL MÁS FALSO O PEOR DE LOS SACERDOTES DE LA HISTORIA. AHORA ERES PROBLEMA DE ESTADOS UNIDOS.

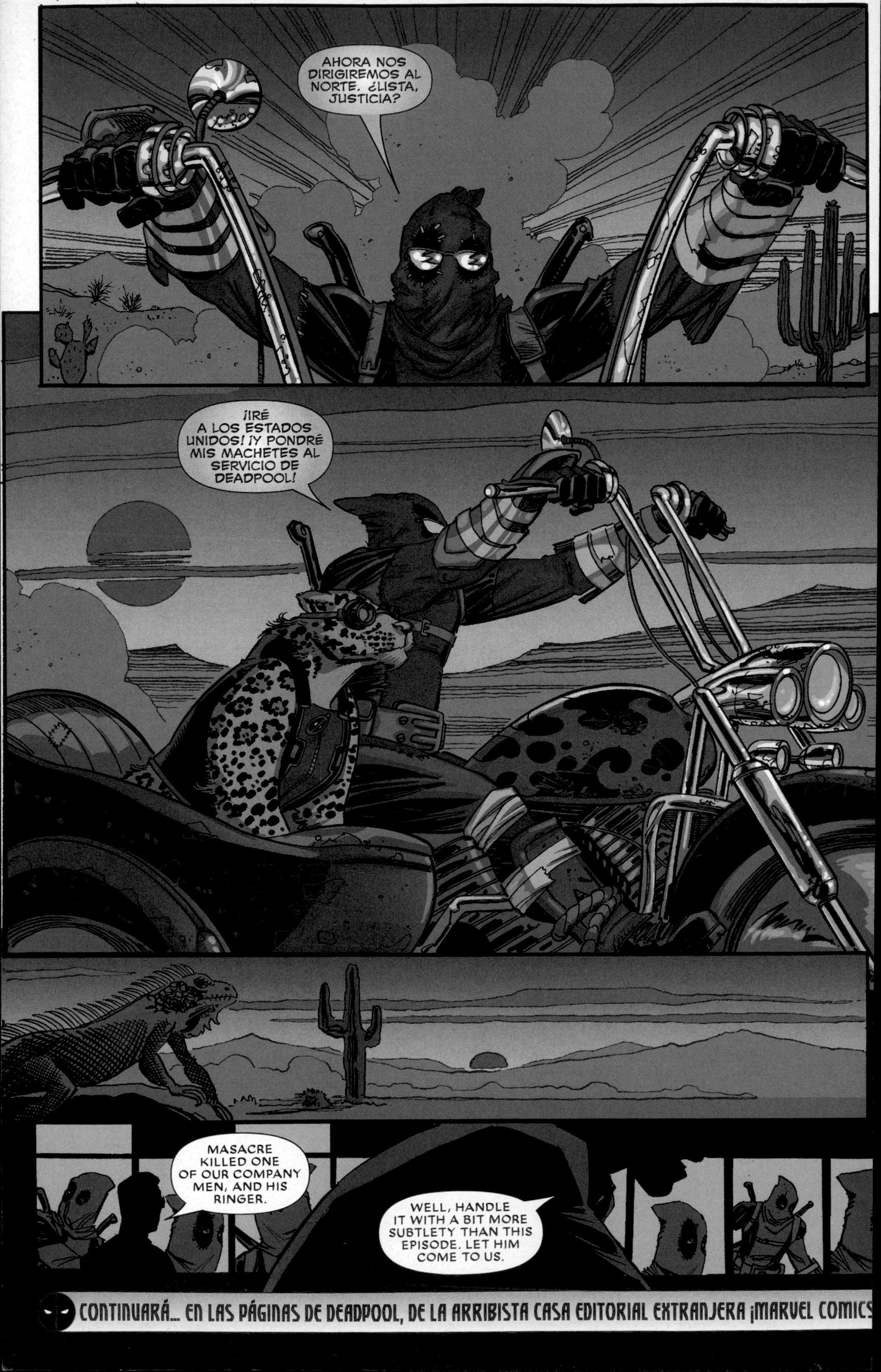
AHORA NOS DIRIGIREMOS AL NORTE. ¿LISTA, JUSTICIA?
¡IRÉ A LOS ESTADOS UNIDOS! ¡Y PONDRÉ MIS MACHETES AL SERVICIO DE DEADPOOL!
MASACRE KILLED ONE OF OUR COMPANY MEN, AND HIS RINGER.
WELL, HANDLE IT WITH A BIT MORE SUBTLETY THAN THIS EPISODE. LET HIM COME TO US.
CONTINUARÁ... EN LAS PÁGINAS DE DEADPOOL, DE LA ARRIBISTA CASA EDITORIAL EXTRANJERA ¡MARVEL COMICS

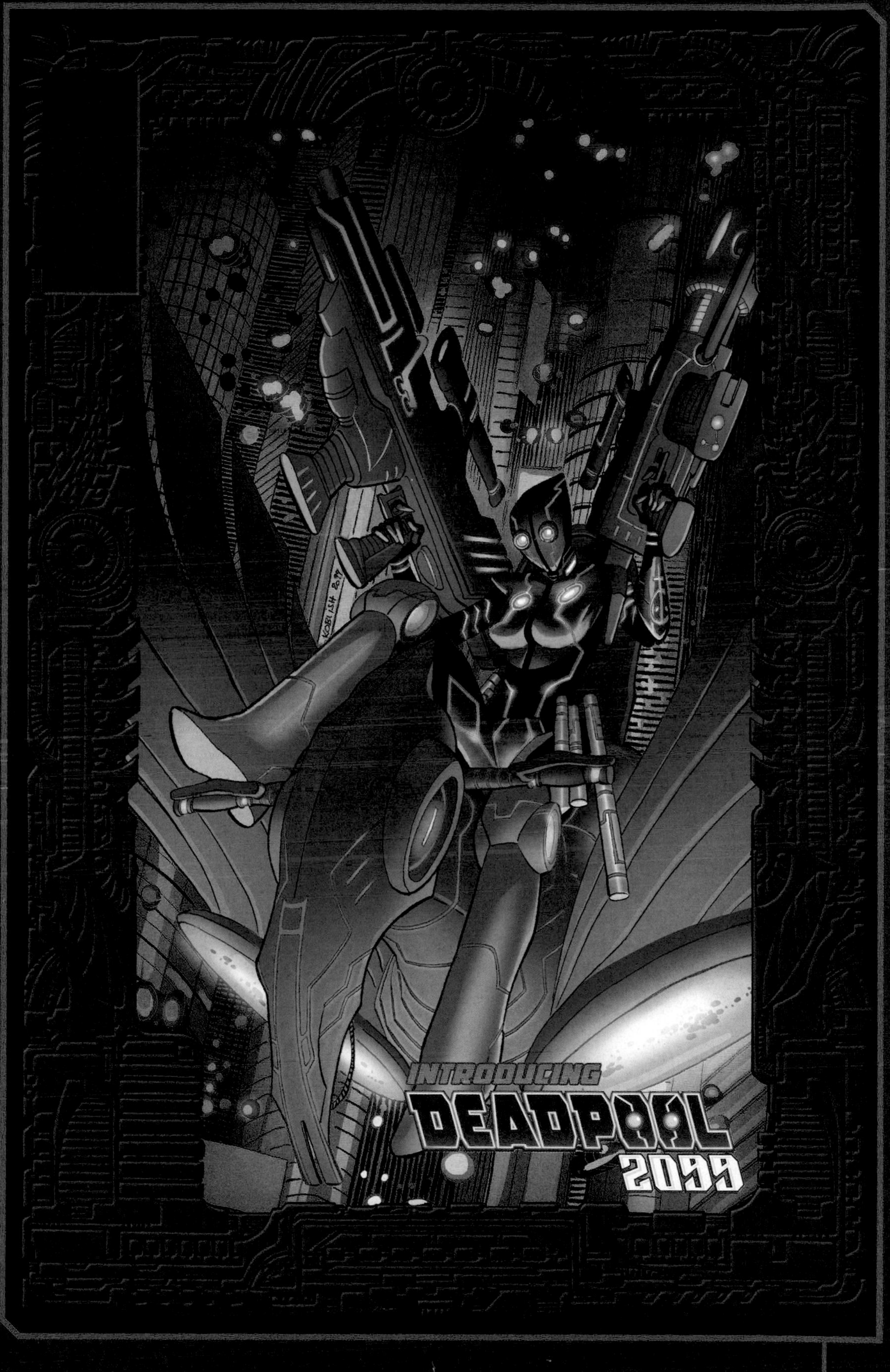
INTRODUCING
DEADPOOL
2099

AVENGER...ASSASSIN...SUPERSTAR...SMELLY PERSON...POSSIBLY THE WORLD'S MOST SKILLED MERCENARY. DEFINITELY THE WORLD'S MOST ANNOYING, WADE WILSON WAS CHOSEN FOR A TOP-SECRET GOVERNMENT PROGRAM THAT GAVE HIM A HEALING FACTOR ALLOWING HIM TO HEAL FROM ANY WOUND. SOMEHOW, DESPITE MAKING HIS MONEY AS A GUN FOR HIRE, WADE HAS BECOME ONE OF THE MOST BELOVED "HEROES" IN THE WORLD. CALL HIM THE MERC WITH THE MOUTH...CALL HIM THE REGENERATIN' DEGENERATE...CALL HIM...

# DEADPOOL

WHAT'S UP, POOL-PORTERS! I'M *DEADPOOL.*

NO, NOT THE DEADPOOL BEING DESCRIBED UP ABOVE. THAT'S SOME...LAME, *OLD-TIMEY* DEADPOOL.

I'M THE DEADPOOL OF NOW--THE YEAR 2099.

WANNA KNOW MORE? READ ON, MOTHERSHOCKERS!

LI'L DEADPOOL 2099 ART BY
IRENE Y. LEE 2099

GERRY DUGGAN 2099
WRITER

SCOTT KOBLISH 2099
ARTIST

NICK FILARDI 2099
COLORIST

VC'S JOE SABINO 209
LETTERER

SKOTT KOBLISH 2099 & GURU-EFX 2099
COVER

GERRY DUGGAN 2099, SCOTT KOBLISH 2099, GURU-EFX 2099 & VC'S JOE SABINO 209
#SECRETCOMIC VARIANT

HEATHER ANTOS 2099
ASSISTANT EDITOR

JORDAN D. WHITE 2099
EDITOR

AXEL ALONSO 2099
EDITOR IN CHIEF

JOE QUESADA 2099
CHIEF CREATIVE OFFICER

DAN BUCKLEY 2099
PUBLISHER

ALAN FINE 2099
EXECUTIVE PRODUC

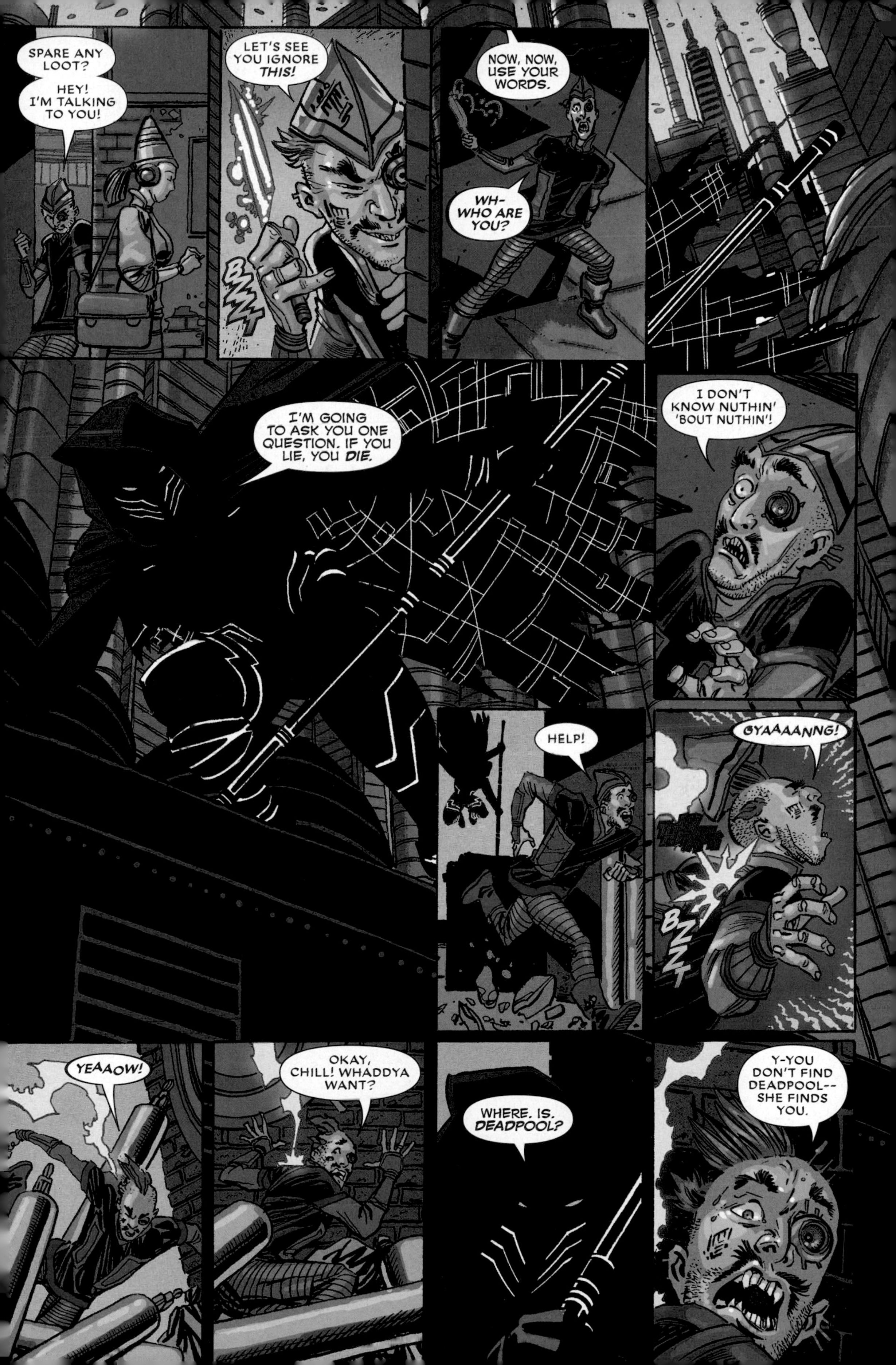
SPARE ANY LOOT?
HEY! I'M TALKING TO YOU!
LET'S SEE YOU IGNORE *THIS!*
BZZK
NOW, NOW, USE YOUR WORDS.
WH-WHO ARE YOU?
I'M GOING TO ASK YOU ONE QUESTION. IF YOU LIE, YOU *DIE.*
I DON'T KNOW NUTHIN' 'BOUT NUTHIN'!
HELP!
GYAAAANNG!
BZZT
YEAAOW!
OKAY, CHILL! WHADDYA WANT?
WHERE. IS. *DEADPOOL?*
Y-YOU DON'T FIND DEADPOOL-- SHE FINDS YOU.

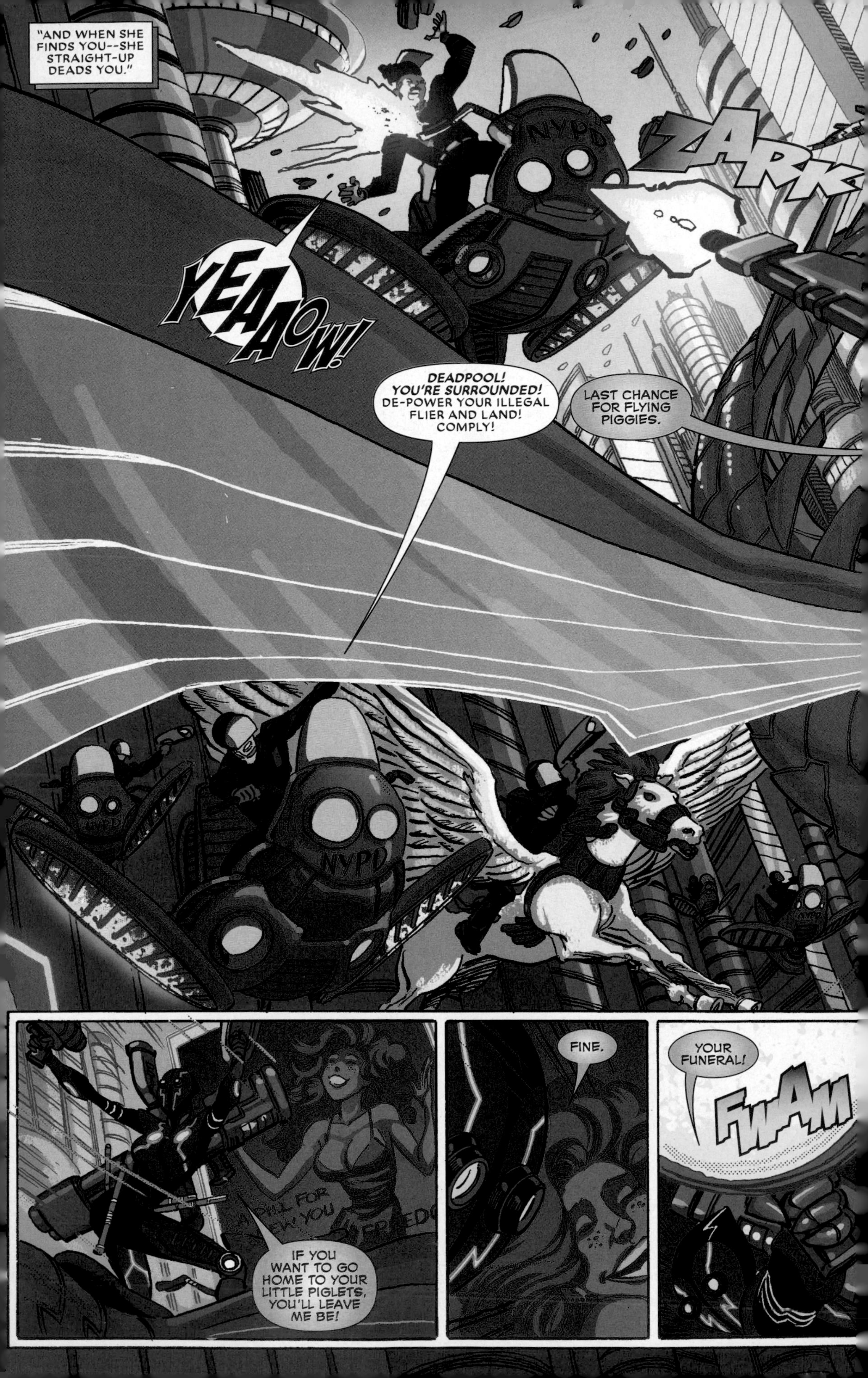
"AND WHEN SHE FINDS YOU--SHE STRAIGHT-UP DEADS YOU."
ZARK
YEAAOW!
DEADPOOL! YOU'RE SURROUNDED! DE-POWER YOUR ILLEGAL FLIER AND LAND! COMPLY!
LAST CHANCE FOR FLYING PIGGIES.
NYPD
IF YOU WANT TO GO HOME TO YOUR LITTLE PIGLETS, YOU'LL LEAVE ME BE!
FINE.
YOUR FUNERAL!
FWAM

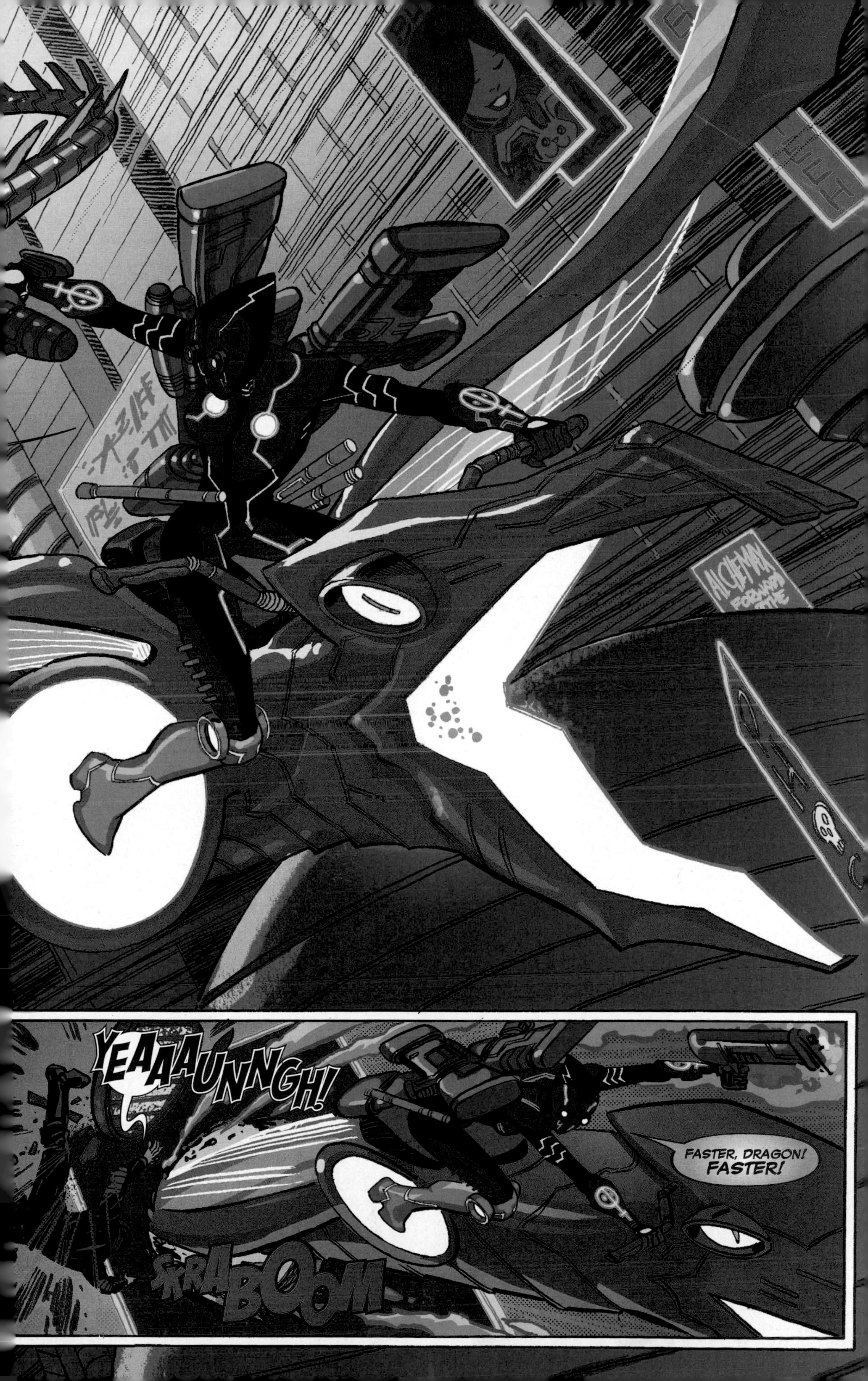
ALCHEMAX
YEAAAUNNGH!
FASTER, DRAGON! FASTER!
SKRABOOM

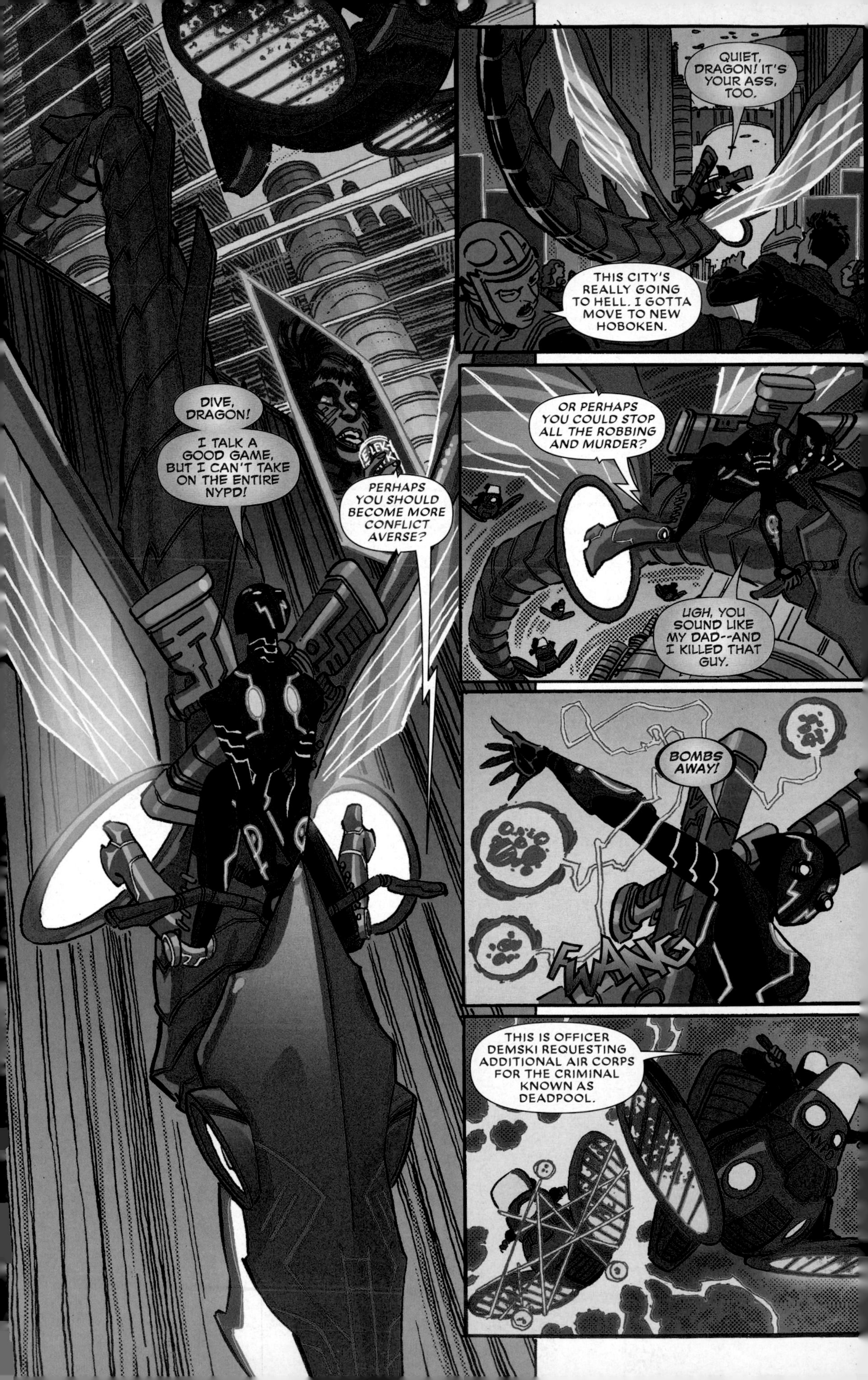
QUIET, DRAGON! IT'S YOUR ASS, TOO.
THIS CITY'S REALLY GOING TO HELL. I GOTTA MOVE TO NEW HOBOKEN.
DIVE, DRAGON!
I TALK A GOOD GAME, BUT I CAN'T TAKE ON THE ENTIRE NYPD!
PERHAPS YOU SHOULD BECOME MORE CONFLICT AVERSE?
OR PERHAPS YOU COULD STOP ALL THE ROBBING AND MURDER?
UGH, YOU SOUND LIKE MY DAD--AND I KILLED THAT GUY.
BOMBS AWAY!
FWANG
THIS IS OFFICER DEMSKI REQUESTING ADDITIONAL AIR CORPS FOR THE CRIMINAL KNOWN AS DEADPOOL.

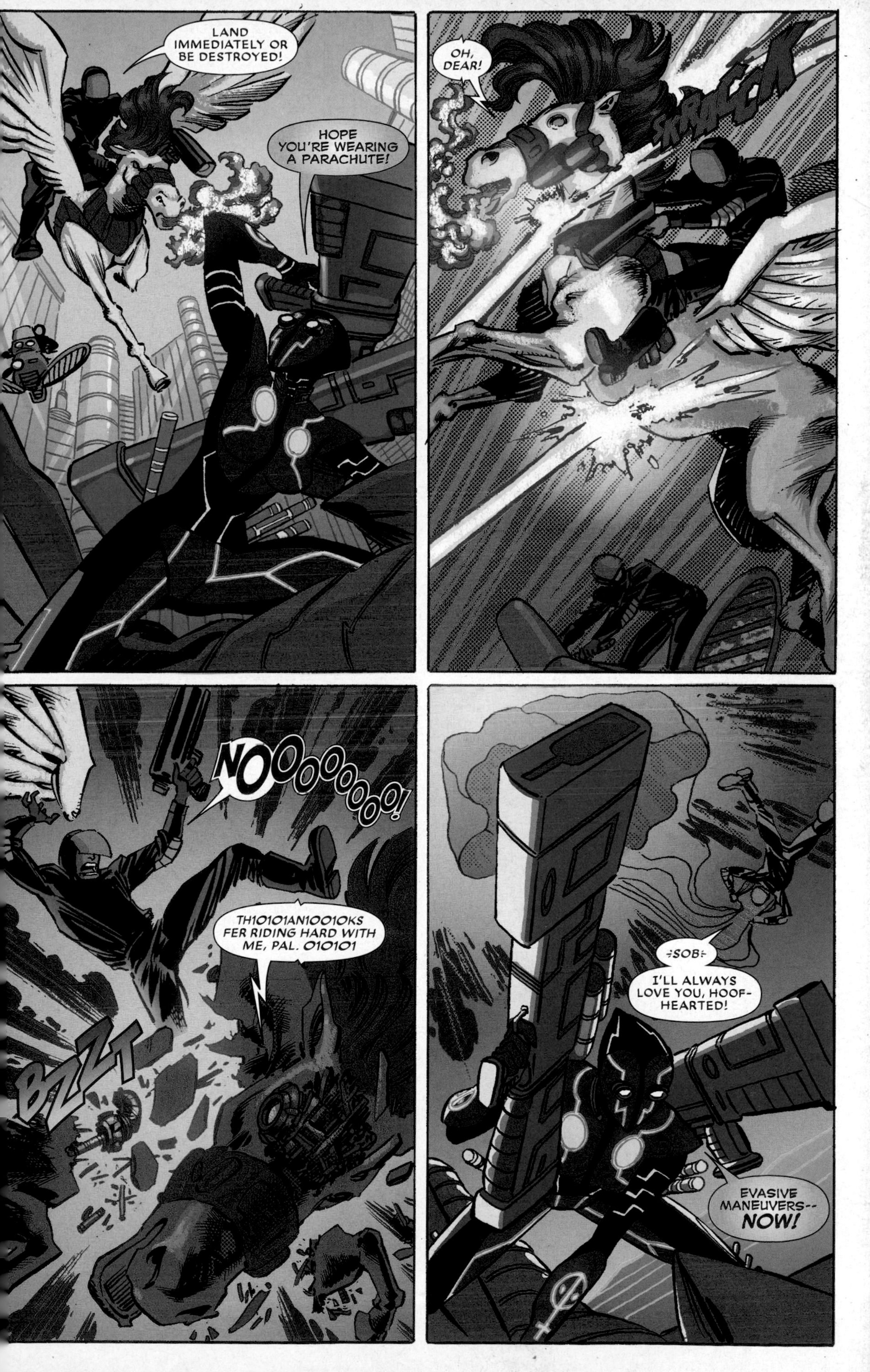
LAND IMMEDIATELY OR BE DESTROYED!
HOPE YOU'RE WEARING A PARACHUTE!
OH, DEAR!
SKRACCK
NOOOOOOOO!
THI0101AN10010KS FER RIDING HARD WITH ME, PAL. 010101
BZZT
SOB
I'LL ALWAYS LOVE YOU, HOOF-HEARTED!
EVASIVE MANEUVERS-- NOW!

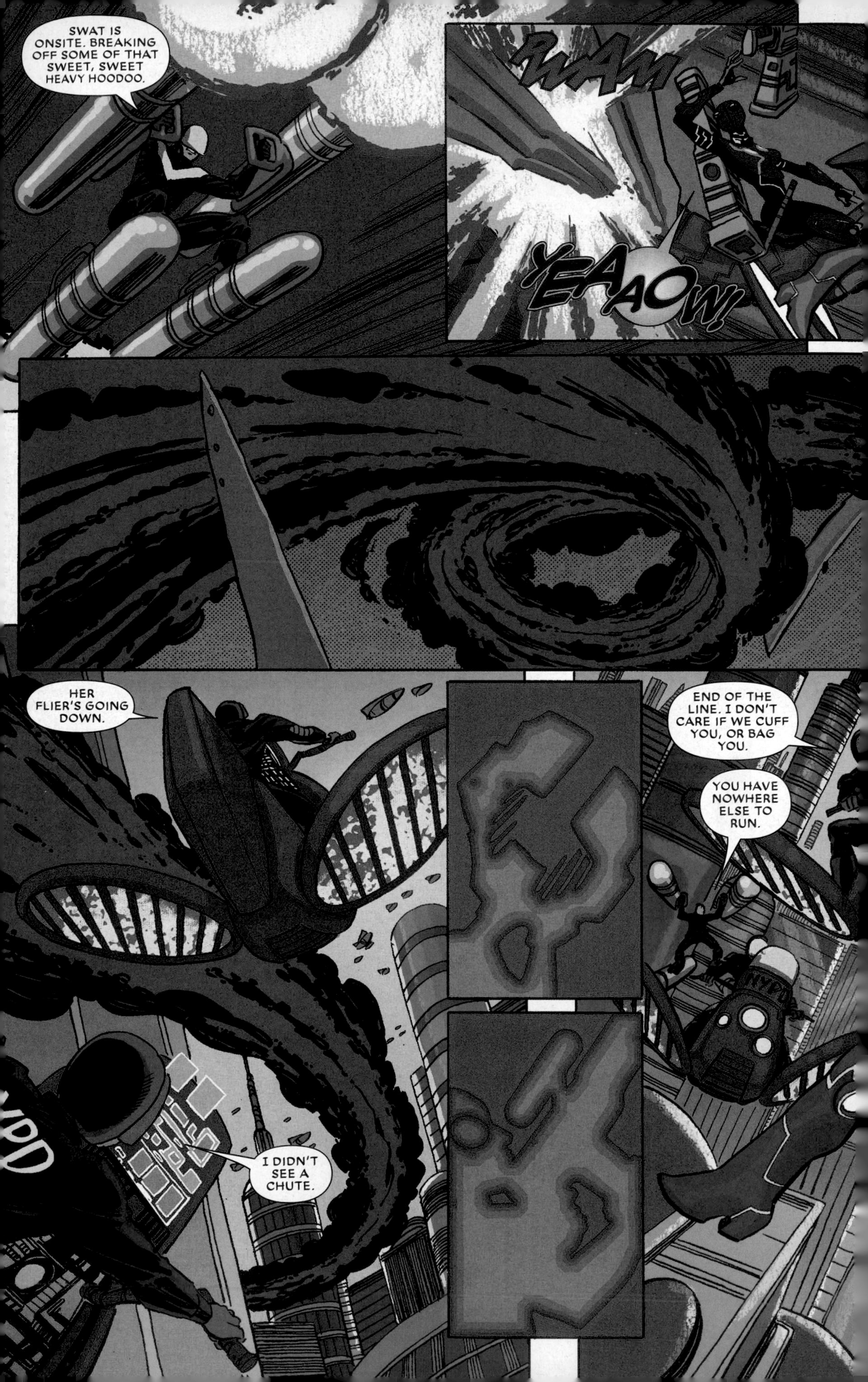
SWAT IS ONSITE. BREAKING OFF SOME OF THAT SWEET, SWEET HEAVY HOODOO.
RWAM
YEAAAOW!
HER FLIER'S GOING DOWN.
I DIDN'T SEE A CHUTE.
END OF THE LINE. I DON'T CARE IF WE CUFF YOU, OR BAG YOU.
YOU HAVE NOWHERE ELSE TO RUN.

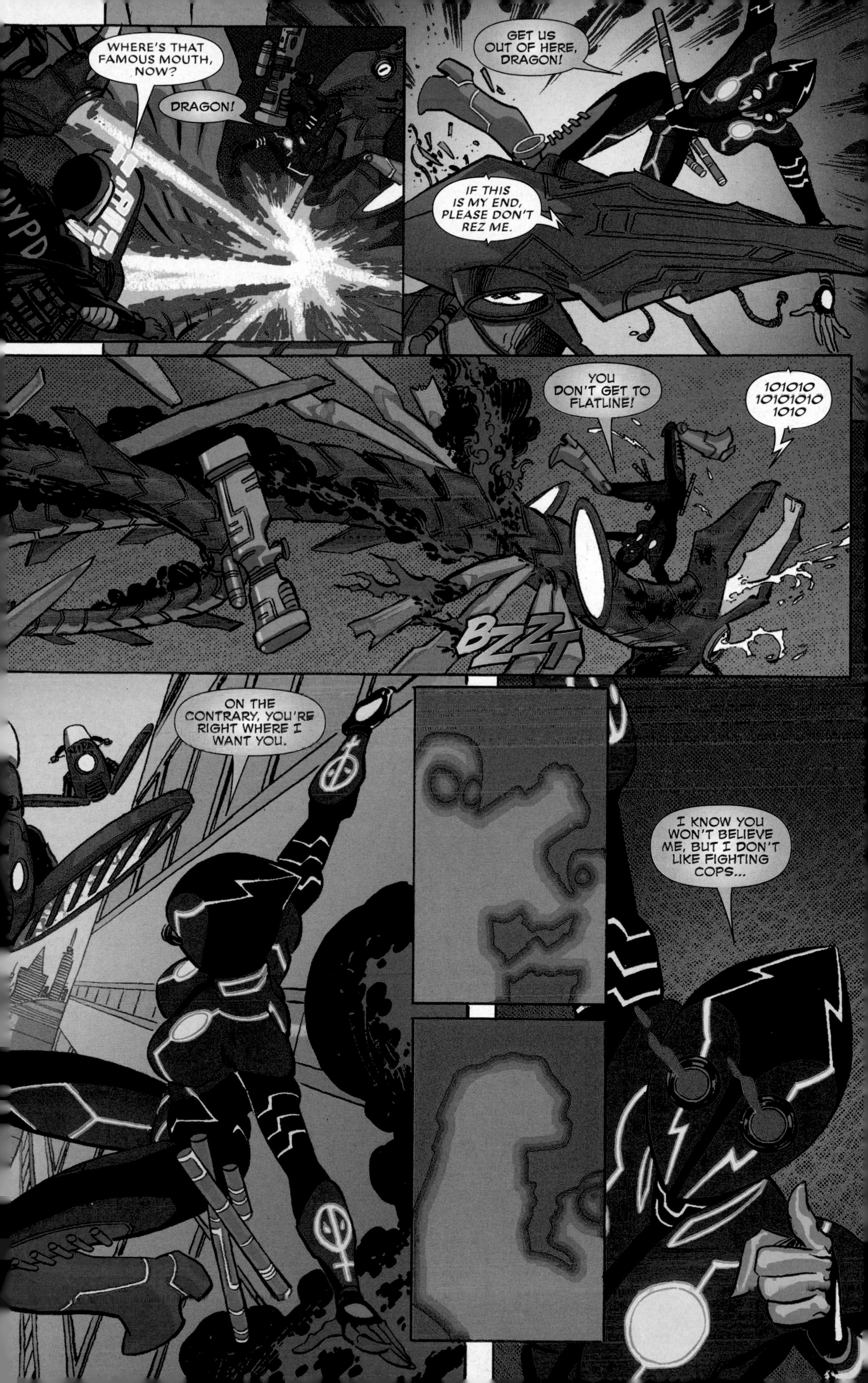
WHERE'S THAT FAMOUS MOUTH, NOW?
DRAGON!
GET US OUT OF HERE, DRAGON!
IF THIS IS MY END, PLEASE DON'T REZ ME.
YOU DON'T GET TO FLATLINE!
101010 10101010 1010
BZZZT
ON THE CONTRARY, YOU'RE RIGHT WHERE I WANT YOU.
I KNOW YOU WON'T BELIEVE ME, BUT I DON'T LIKE FIGHTING COPS...

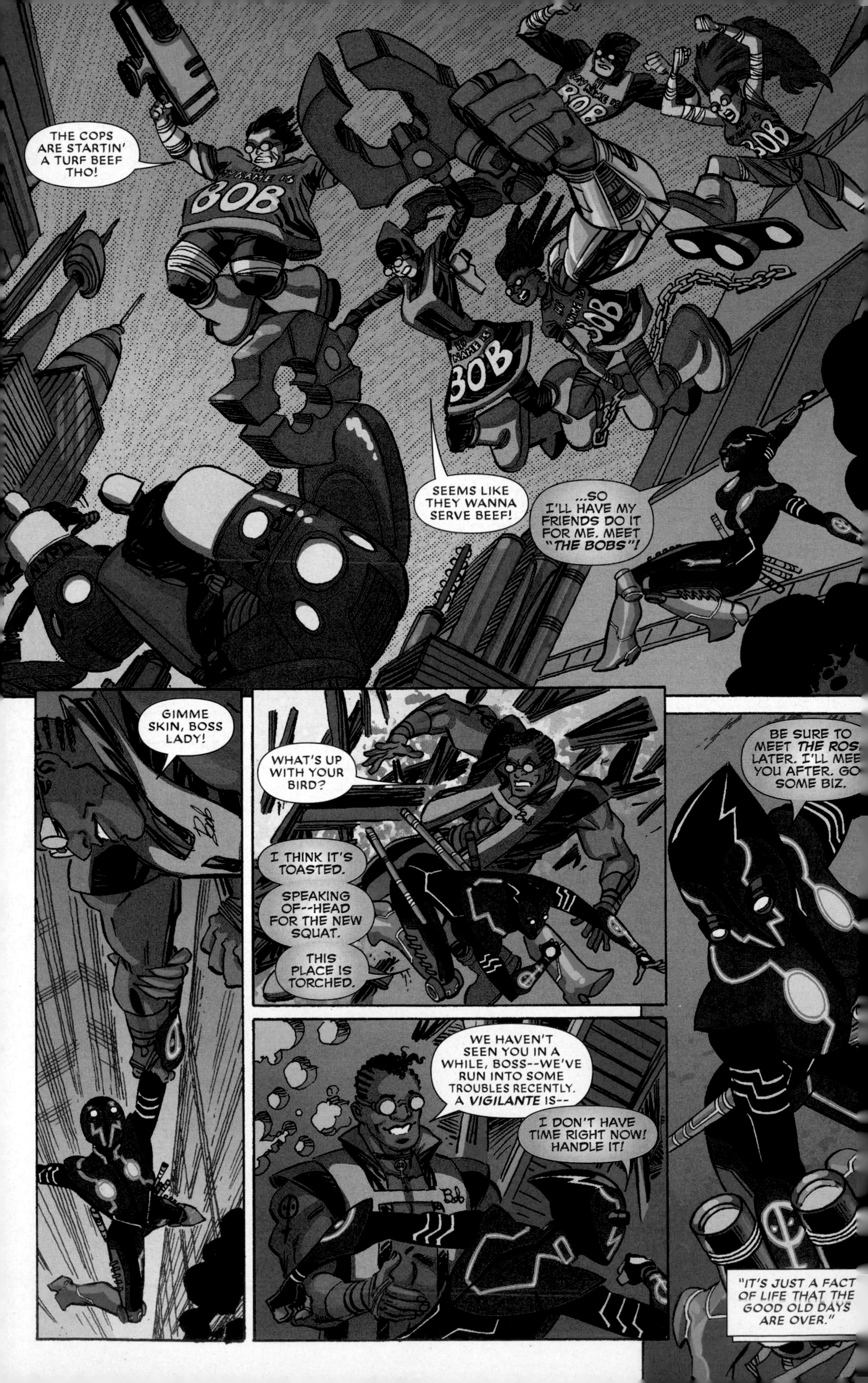
THE COPS ARE STARTIN' A TURF BEEF THO!
SEEMS LIKE THEY WANNA SERVE BEEF!
...SO I'LL HAVE MY FRIENDS DO IT FOR ME. MEET "THE BOBS"!
GIMME SKIN, BOSS LADY!
WHAT'S UP WITH YOUR BIRD?
I THINK IT'S TOASTED.
SPEAKING OF--HEAD FOR THE NEW SQUAT.
THIS PLACE IS TORCHED.
WE HAVEN'T SEEN YOU IN A WHILE, BOSS--WE'VE RUN INTO SOME TROUBLES RECENTLY. A VIGILANTE IS--
I DON'T HAVE TIME RIGHT NOW! HANDLE IT!
BE SURE TO MEET THE ROS LATER. I'LL MEE YOU AFTER. GO SOME BIZ.
"IT'S JUST A FACT OF LIFE THAT THE GOOD OLD DAYS ARE OVER."

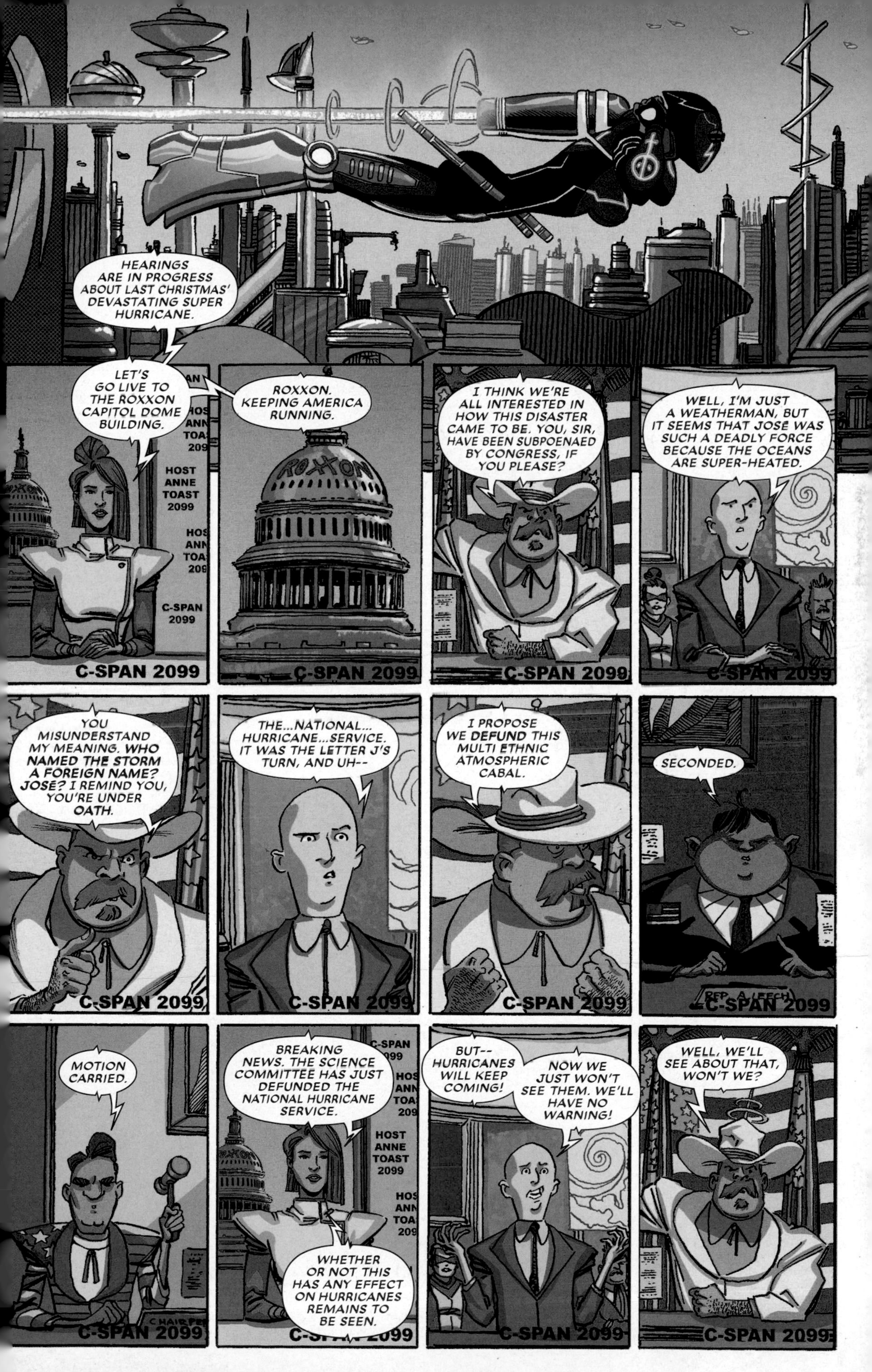
HEARINGS ARE IN PROGRESS ABOUT LAST CHRISTMAS' DEVASTATING SUPER HURRICANE.
LET'S GO LIVE TO THE ROXXON CAPITOL DOME BUILDING.
HOST ANNE TOAST 2099
C-SPAN 2099
ROXXON. KEEPING AMERICA RUNNING.
ROXXON
C-SPAN 2099
I THINK WE'RE ALL INTERESTED IN HOW THIS DISASTER CAME TO BE. YOU, SIR, HAVE BEEN SUBPOENAED BY CONGRESS, IF YOU PLEASE?
C-SPAN 2099
WELL, I'M JUST A WEATHERMAN, BUT IT SEEMS THAT JOSÉ WAS SUCH A DEADLY FORCE BECAUSE THE OCEANS ARE SUPER-HEATED.
C-SPAN 2099
YOU MISUNDERSTAND MY MEANING. WHO NAMED THE STORM A FOREIGN NAME? JOSÉ? I REMIND YOU, YOU'RE UNDER OATH.
C-SPAN 2099
THE...NATIONAL... HURRICANE...SERVICE. IT WAS THE LETTER J'S TURN, AND UH--
C-SPAN 2099
I PROPOSE WE DEFUND THIS MULTI ETHNIC ATMOSPHERIC CABAL.
C-SPAN 2099
SECONDED.
REP. A. LEECH
C-SPAN 2099
MOTION CARRIED.
C-SPAN 2099
BREAKING NEWS. THE SCIENCE COMMITTEE HAS JUST DEFUNDED THE NATIONAL HURRICANE SERVICE.
HOST ANNE TOAST 2099
WHETHER OR NOT THIS HAS ANY EFFECT ON HURRICANES REMAINS TO BE SEEN.
C-SPAN 2099
BUT-- HURRICANES WILL KEEP COMING!
NOW WE JUST WON'T SEE THEM. WE'LL HAVE NO WARNING!
C-SPAN 2099
WELL, WE'LL SEE ABOUT THAT, WON'T WE?
C-SPAN 2099

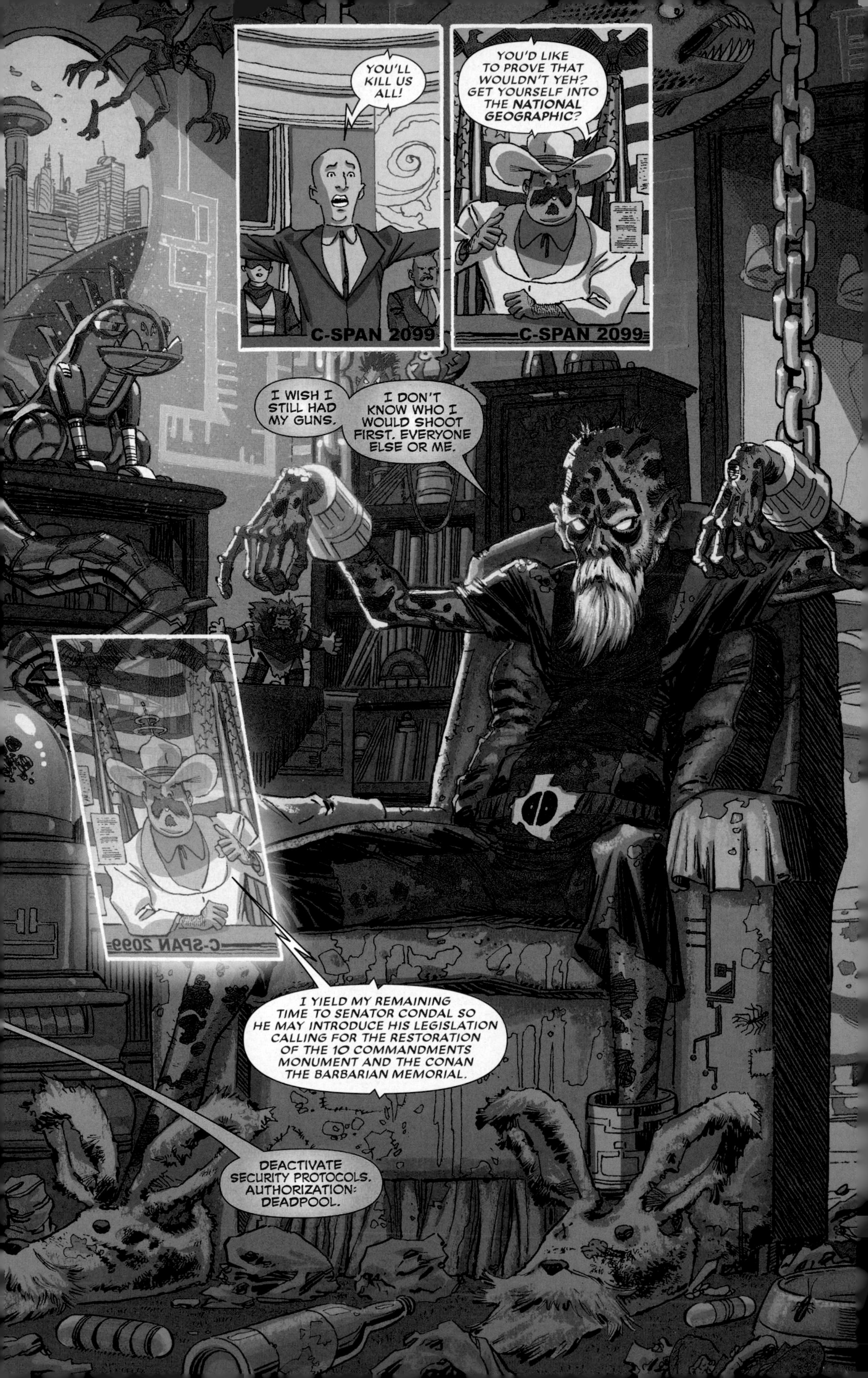
YOU'LL KILL US ALL!
C-SPAN 2099
YOU'D LIKE TO PROVE THAT WOULDN'T YEH? GET YOURSELF INTO THE NATIONAL GEOGRAPHIC?
C-SPAN 2099
I WISH I STILL HAD MY GUNS.
I DON'T KNOW WHO I WOULD SHOOT FIRST. EVERYONE ELSE OR ME.
C-SPAN 2099
I YIELD MY REMAINING TIME TO SENATOR CONDAL SO HE MAY INTRODUCE HIS LEGISLATION CALLING FOR THE RESTORATION OF THE 10 COMMANDMENTS MONUMENT AND THE CONAN THE BARBARIAN MEMORIAL.
DEACTIVATE SECURITY PROTOCOLS. AUTHORIZATION: DEADPOOL.

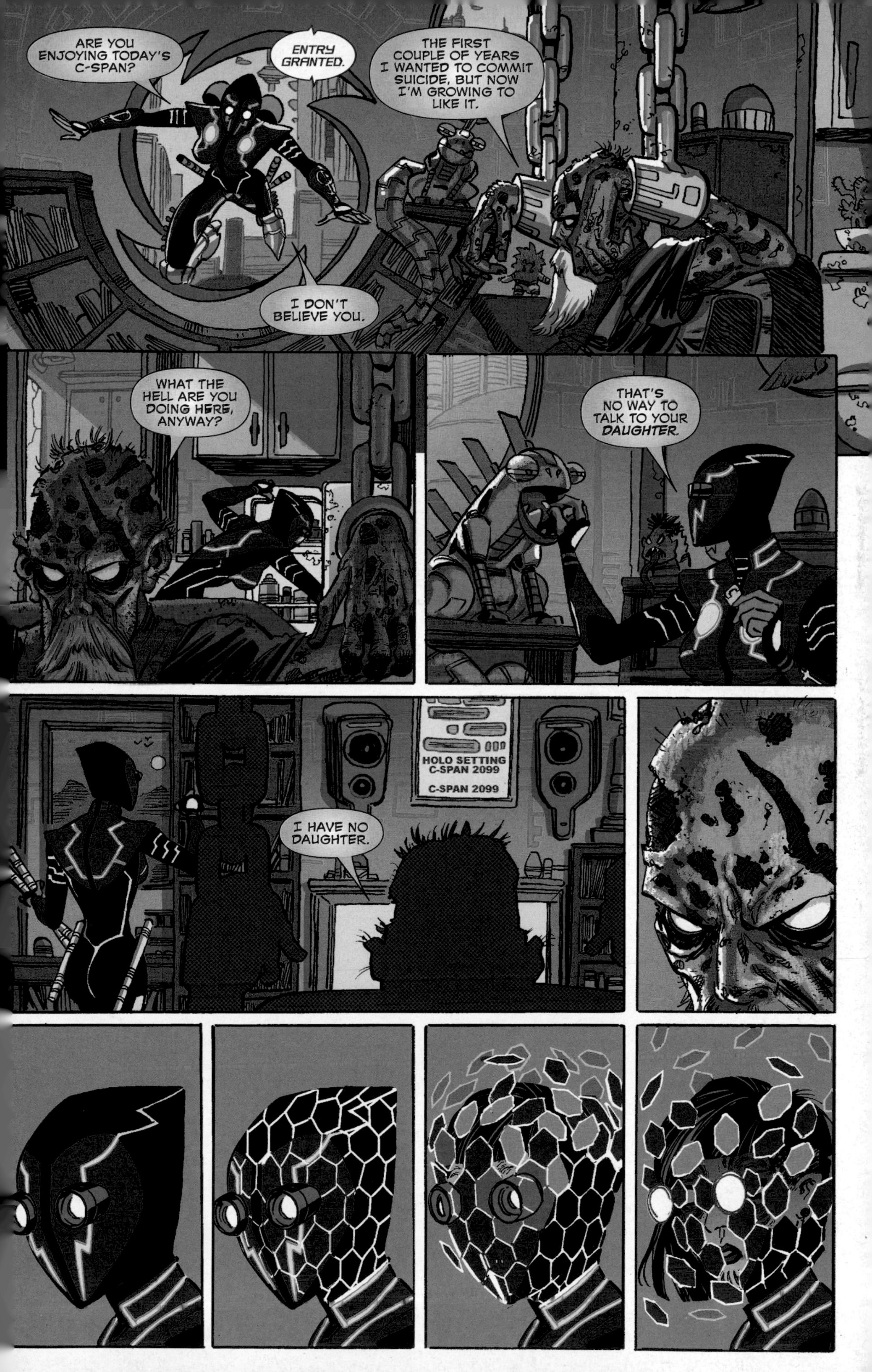
ARE YOU ENJOYING TODAY'S C-SPAN?
ENTRY GRANTED.
THE FIRST COUPLE OF YEARS I WANTED TO COMMIT SUICIDE, BUT NOW I'M GROWING TO LIKE IT.
I DON'T BELIEVE YOU.
WHAT THE HELL ARE YOU DOING HERE, ANYWAY?
THAT'S NO WAY TO TALK TO YOUR DAUGHTER.
HOLO SETTING C-SPAN 2099
C-SPAN 2099
I HAVE NO DAUGHTER.

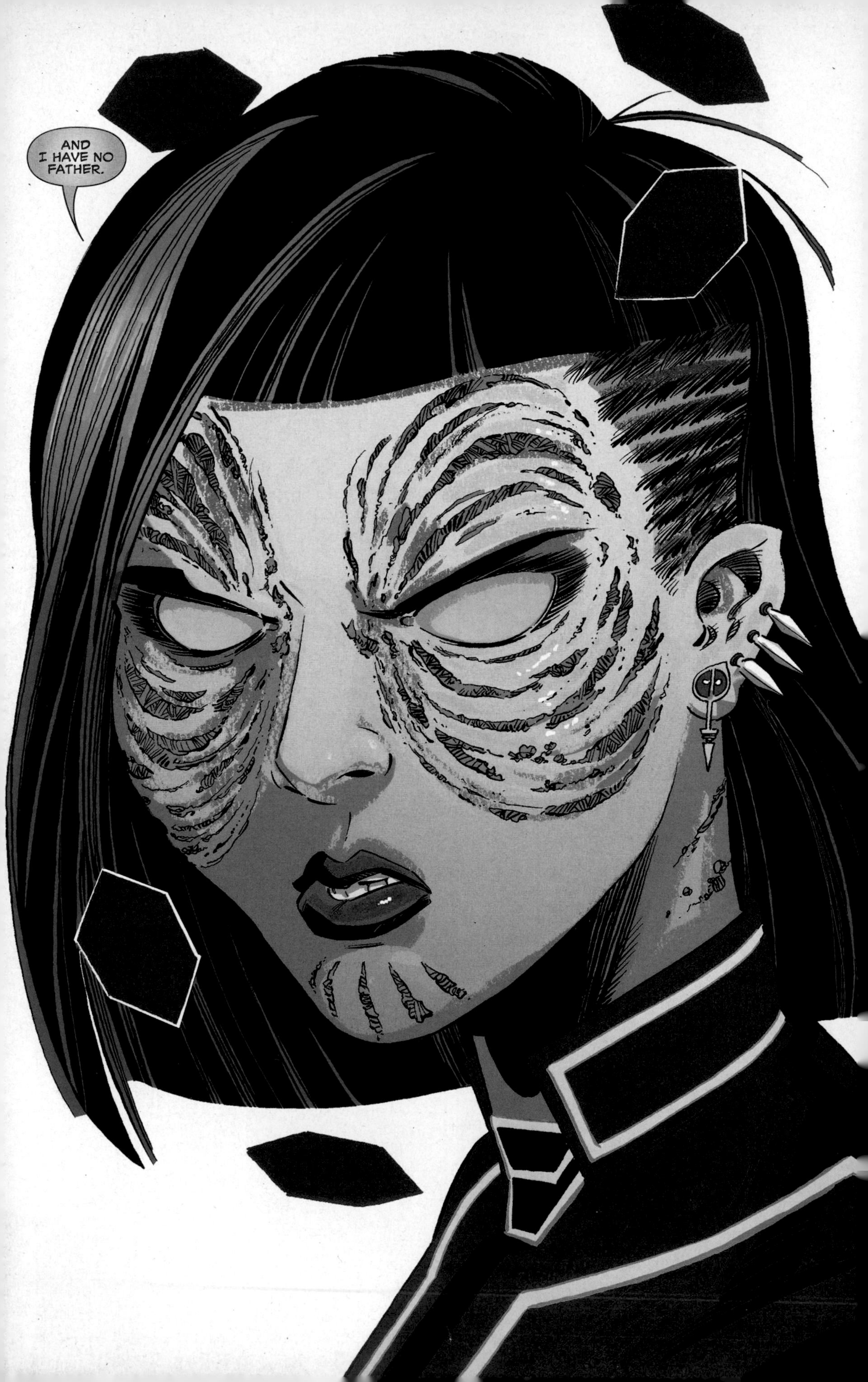
AND I HAVE NO FATHER.

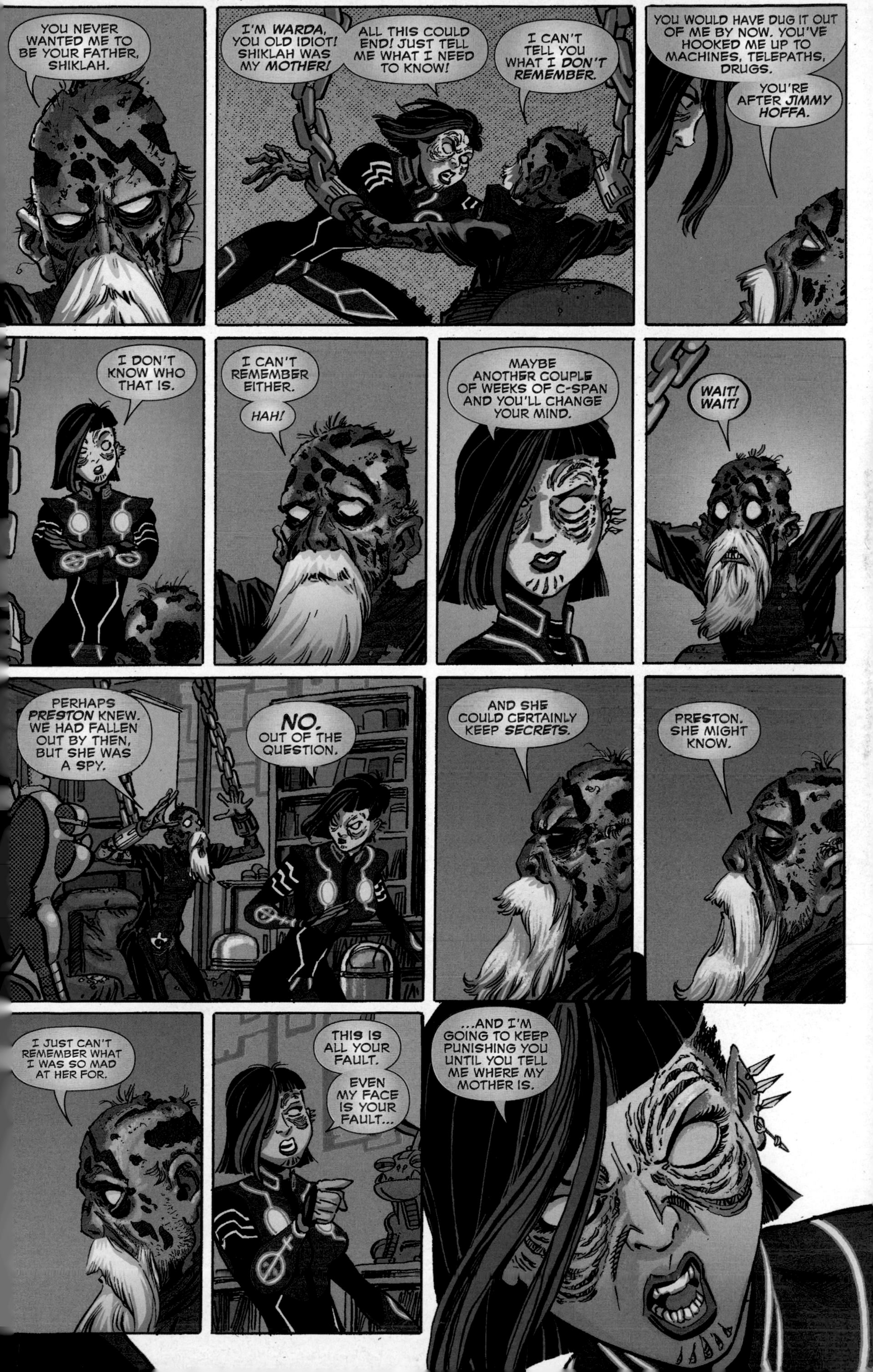
YOU NEVER WANTED ME TO BE YOUR FATHER, SHIKLAH.
I'M WARDA, YOU OLD IDIOT! SHIKLAH WAS MY MOTHER!
ALL THIS COULD END! JUST TELL ME WHAT I NEED TO KNOW!
I CAN'T TELL YOU WHAT I DON'T REMEMBER.
YOU WOULD HAVE DUG IT OUT OF ME BY NOW. YOU'VE HOOKED ME UP TO MACHINES, TELEPATHS, DRUGS.
YOU'RE AFTER JIMMY HOFFA.
I DON'T KNOW WHO THAT IS.
I CAN'T REMEMBER EITHER.
HAH!
MAYBE ANOTHER COUPLE OF WEEKS OF C-SPAN AND YOU'LL CHANGE YOUR MIND.
WAIT! WAIT!
PERHAPS PRESTON KNEW. WE HAD FALLEN OUT BY THEN, BUT SHE WAS A SPY.
NO. OUT OF THE QUESTION.
AND SHE COULD CERTAINLY KEEP SECRETS.
PRESTON. SHE MIGHT KNOW.
I JUST CAN'T REMEMBER WHAT I WAS SO MAD AT HER FOR.
THIS IS ALL YOUR FAULT.
EVEN MY FACE IS YOUR FAULT...
...AND I'M GOING TO KEEP PUNISHING YOU UNTIL YOU TELL ME WHERE MY MOTHER IS.

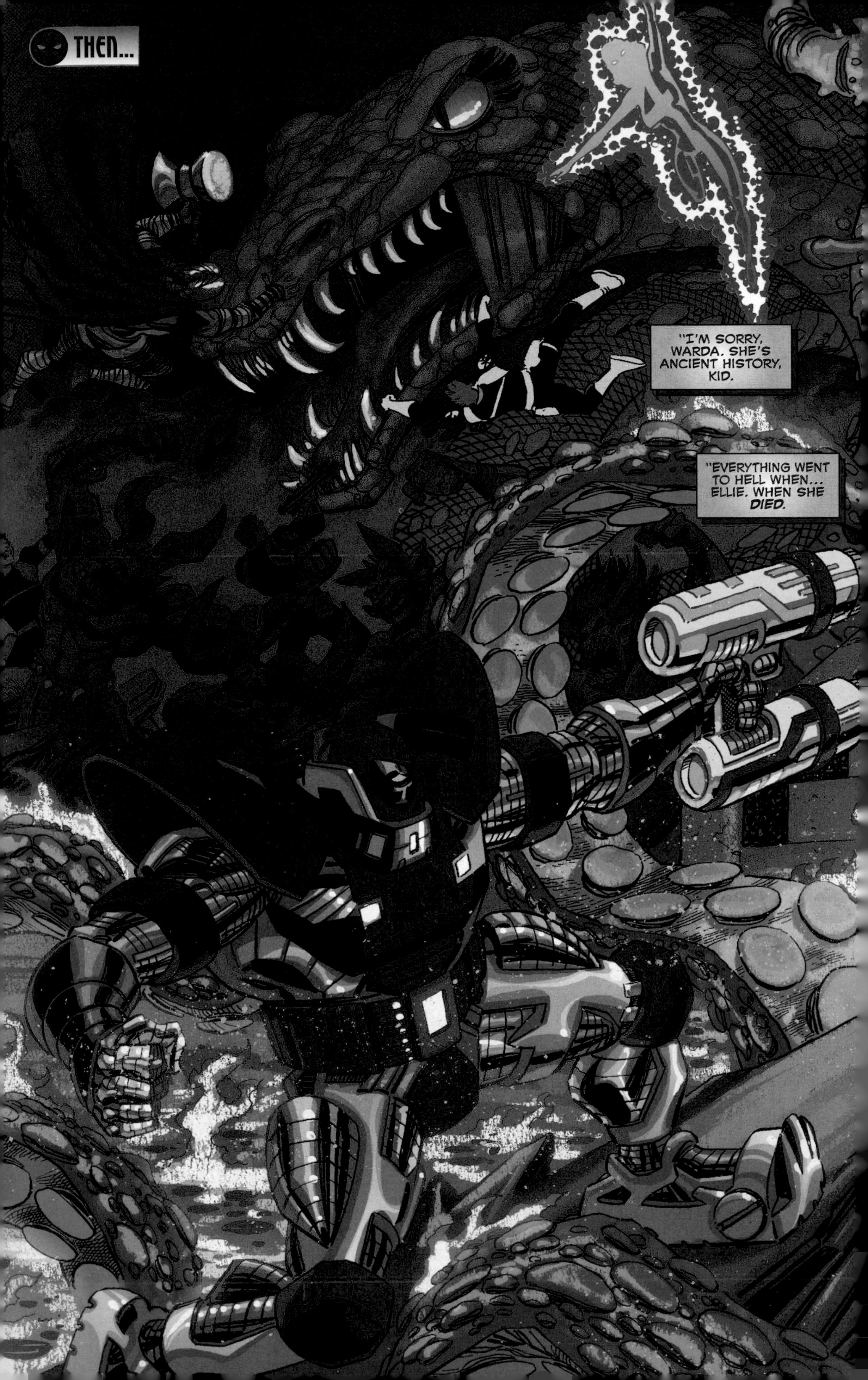
THEN...
"I'M SORRY, WARDA. SHE'S ANCIENT HISTORY, KID.
"EVERYTHING WENT TO HELL WHEN... ELLIE. WHEN SHE *DIED*.

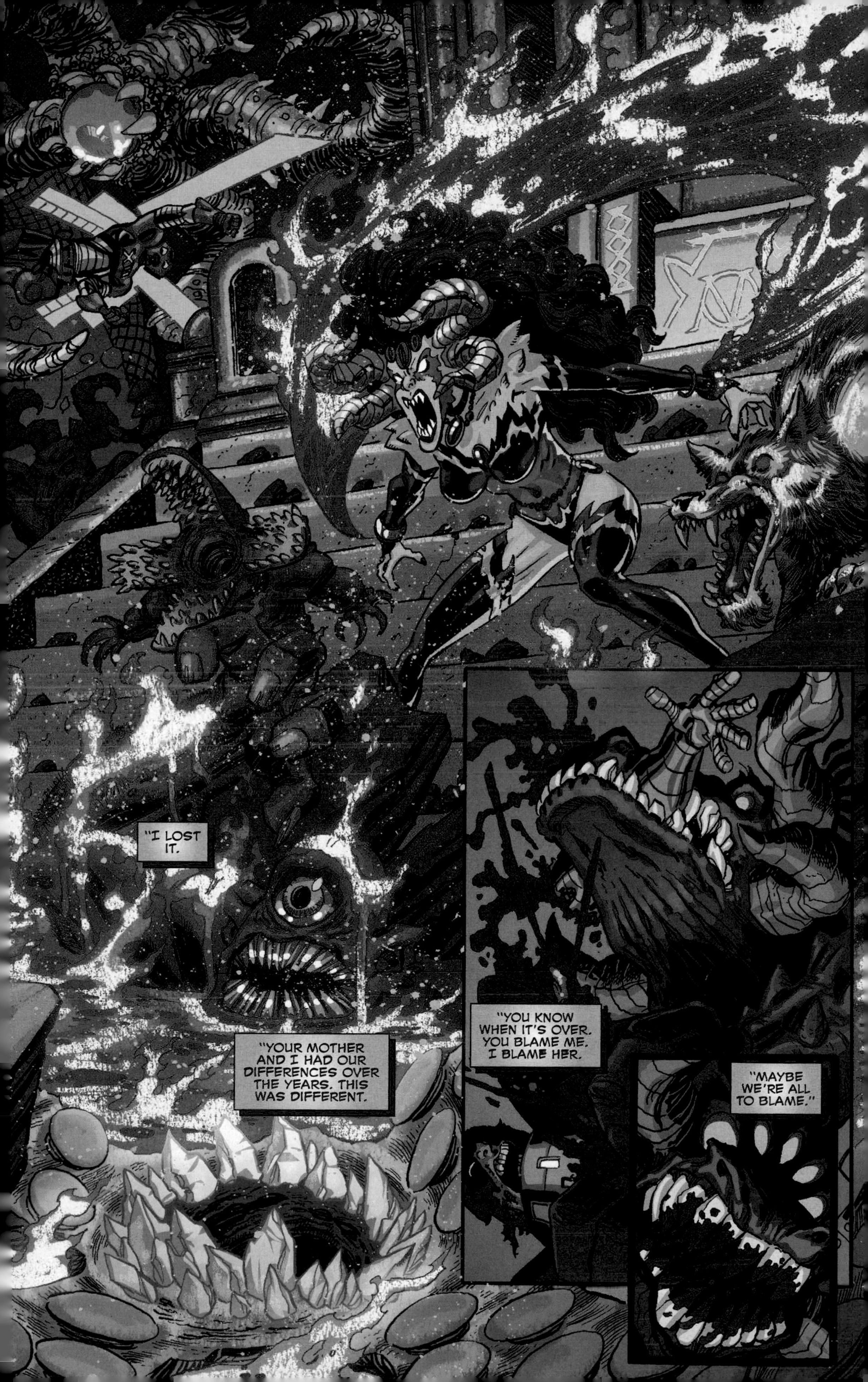
"I LOST IT.
"YOUR MOTHER AND I HAD OUR DIFFERENCES OVER THE YEARS. THIS WAS DIFFERENT.
"YOU KNOW WHEN IT'S OVER. YOU BLAME ME. I BLAME HER.
"MAYBE WE'RE ALL TO BLAME."

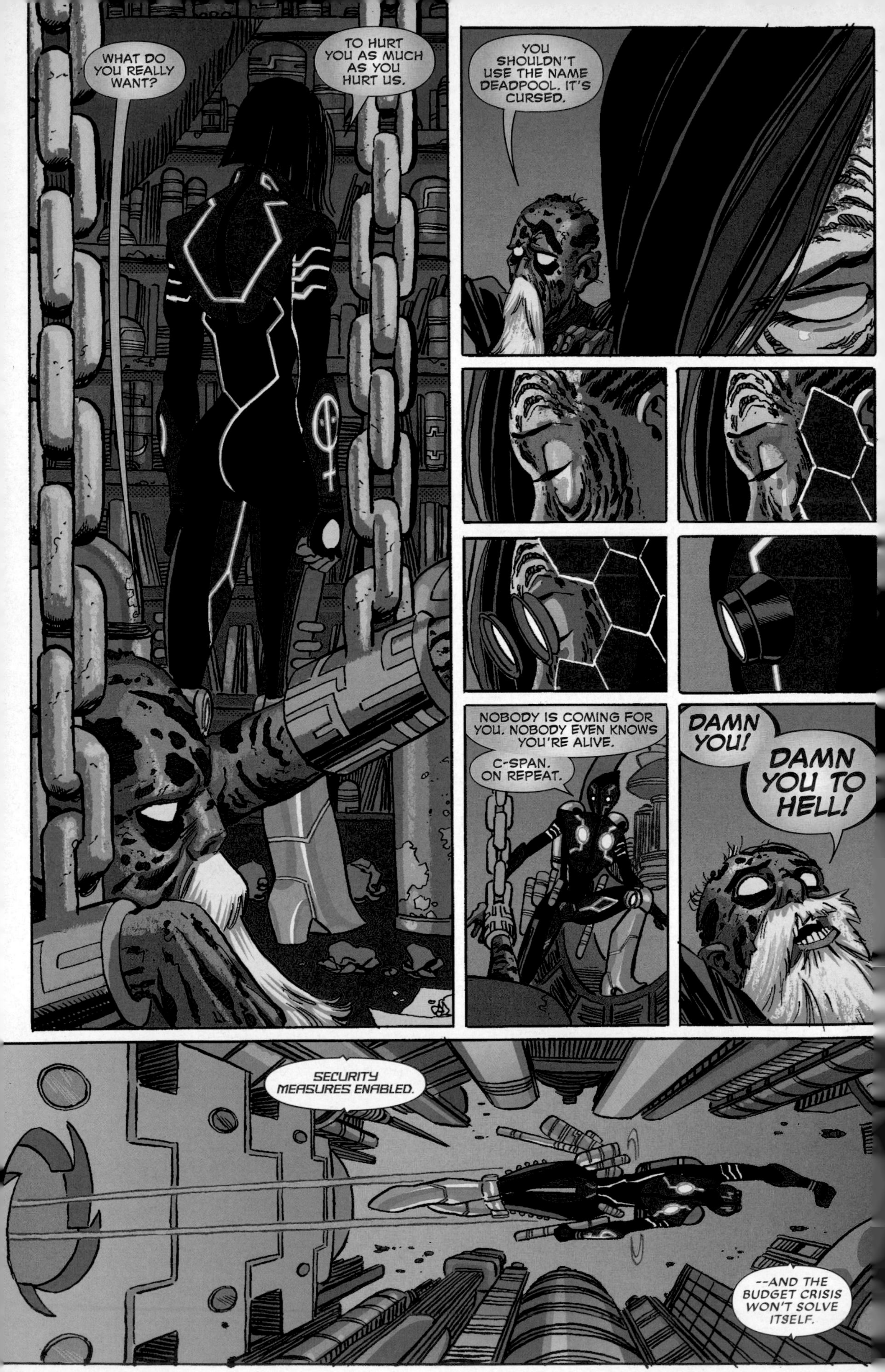
WHAT DO YOU REALLY WANT?
TO HURT YOU AS MUCH AS YOU HURT US.
YOU SHOULDN'T USE THE NAME DEADPOOL. IT'S CURSED.
NOBODY IS COMING FOR YOU. NOBODY EVEN KNOWS YOU'RE ALIVE.
C-SPAN. ON REPEAT.
DAMN YOU!
DAMN YOU TO HELL!
SECURITY MEASURES ENABLED.
--AND THE BUDGET CRISIS WON'T SOLVE ITSELF.

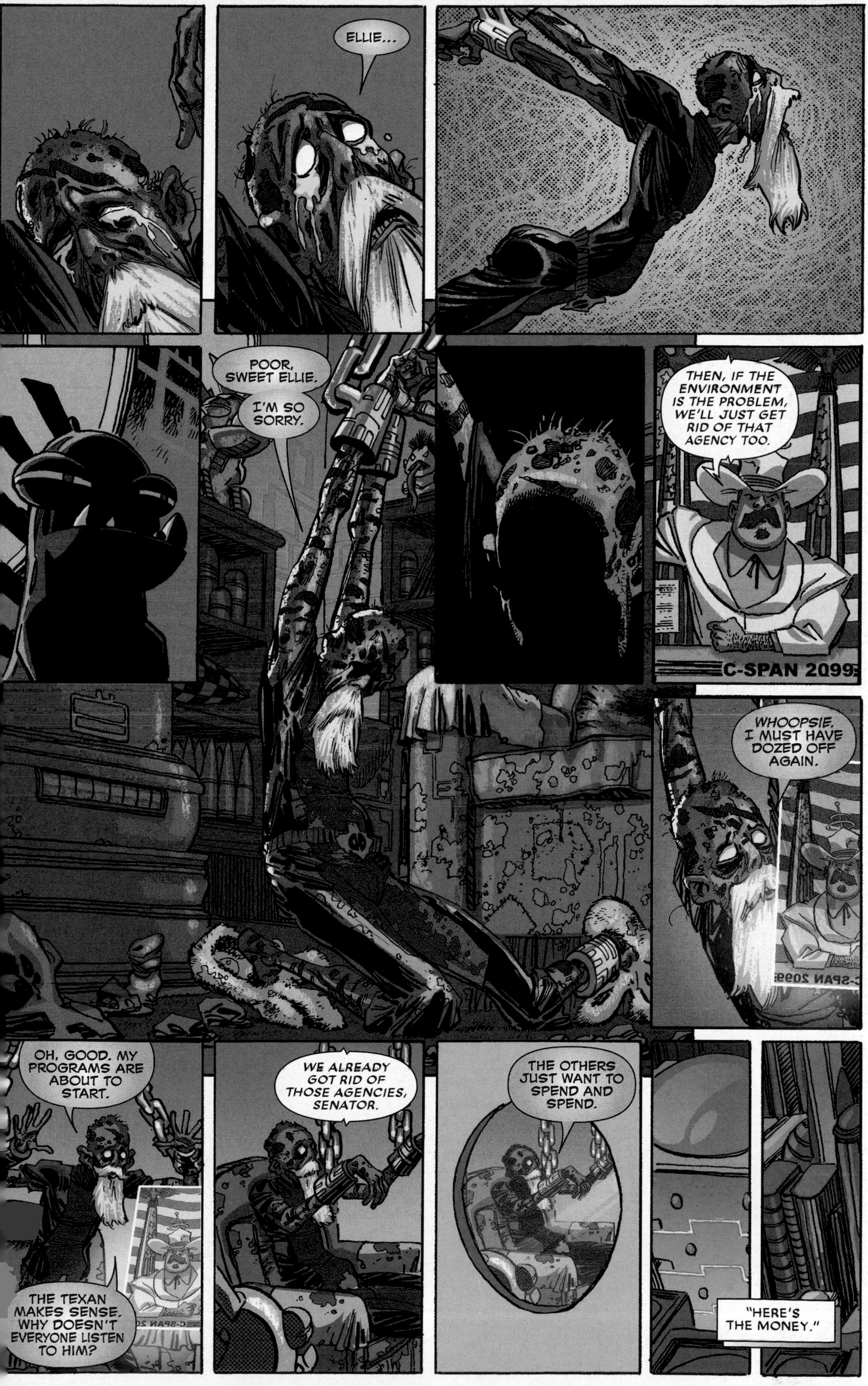
ELLIE...
POOR, SWEET ELLIE.
I'M SO SORRY.
THEN, IF THE ENVIRONMENT IS THE PROBLEM, WE'LL JUST GET RID OF THAT AGENCY TOO.
C-SPAN 2099
WHOOPSIE. I MUST HAVE DOZED OFF AGAIN.
OH, GOOD. MY PROGRAMS ARE ABOUT TO START.
THE TEXAN MAKES SENSE. WHY DOESN'T EVERYONE LISTEN TO HIM?
WE ALREADY GOT RID OF THOSE AGENCIES, SENATOR.
THE OTHERS JUST WANT TO SPEND AND SPEND.
"HERE'S THE MONEY."

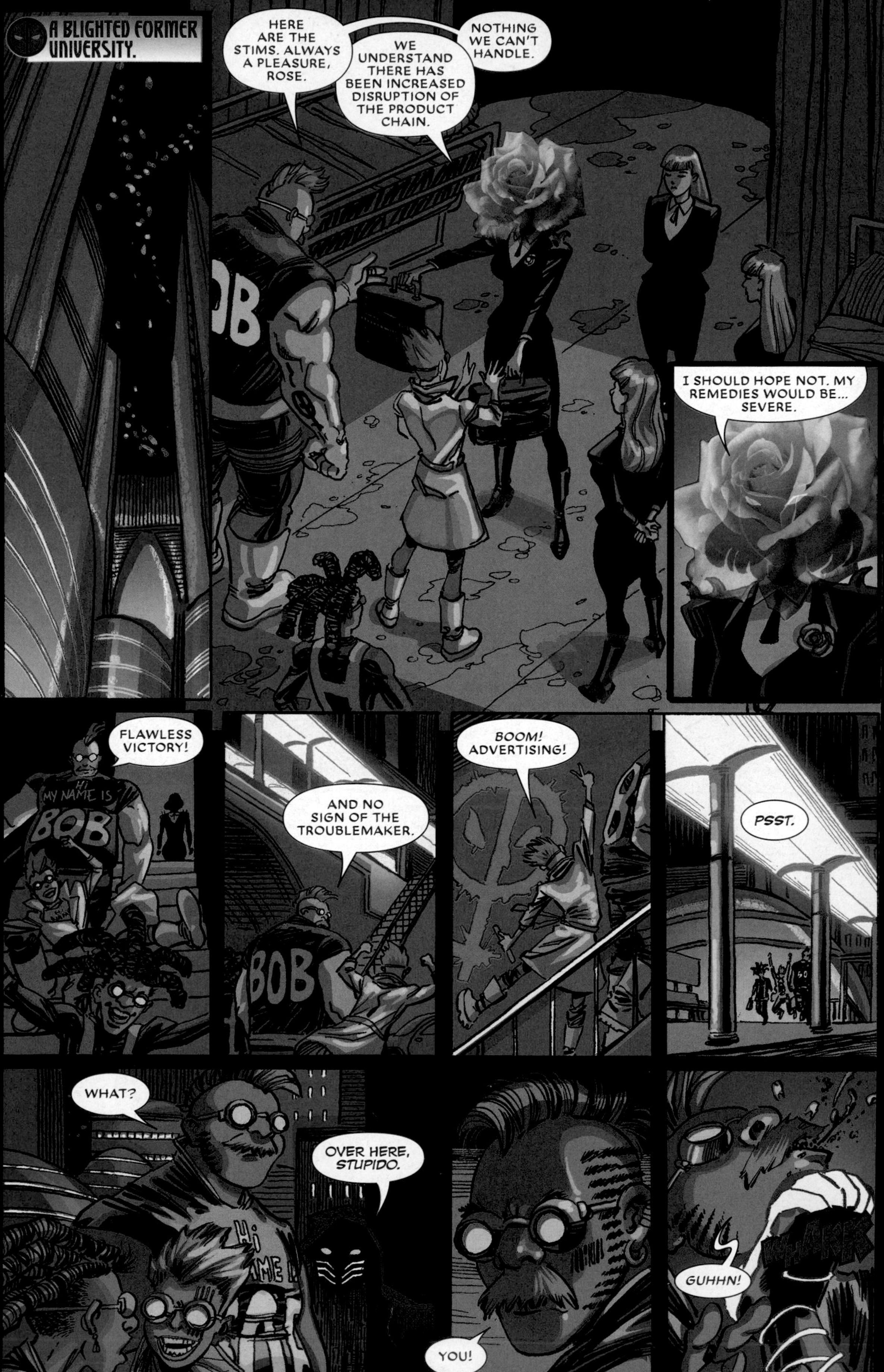
A BLIGHTED FORMER UNIVERSITY.
HERE ARE THE STIMS. ALWAYS A PLEASURE, ROSE.
NOTHING WE CAN'T HANDLE.
WE UNDERSTAND THERE HAS BEEN INCREASED DISRUPTION OF THE PRODUCT CHAIN.
I SHOULD HOPE NOT. MY REMEDIES WOULD BE... SEVERE.
FLAWLESS VICTORY!
MY NAME IS BOB
AND NO SIGN OF THE TROUBLEMAKER.
BOOM! ADVERTISING!
PSST.
WHAT?
OVER HERE, STUPIDO.
YOU!
GUHHN!

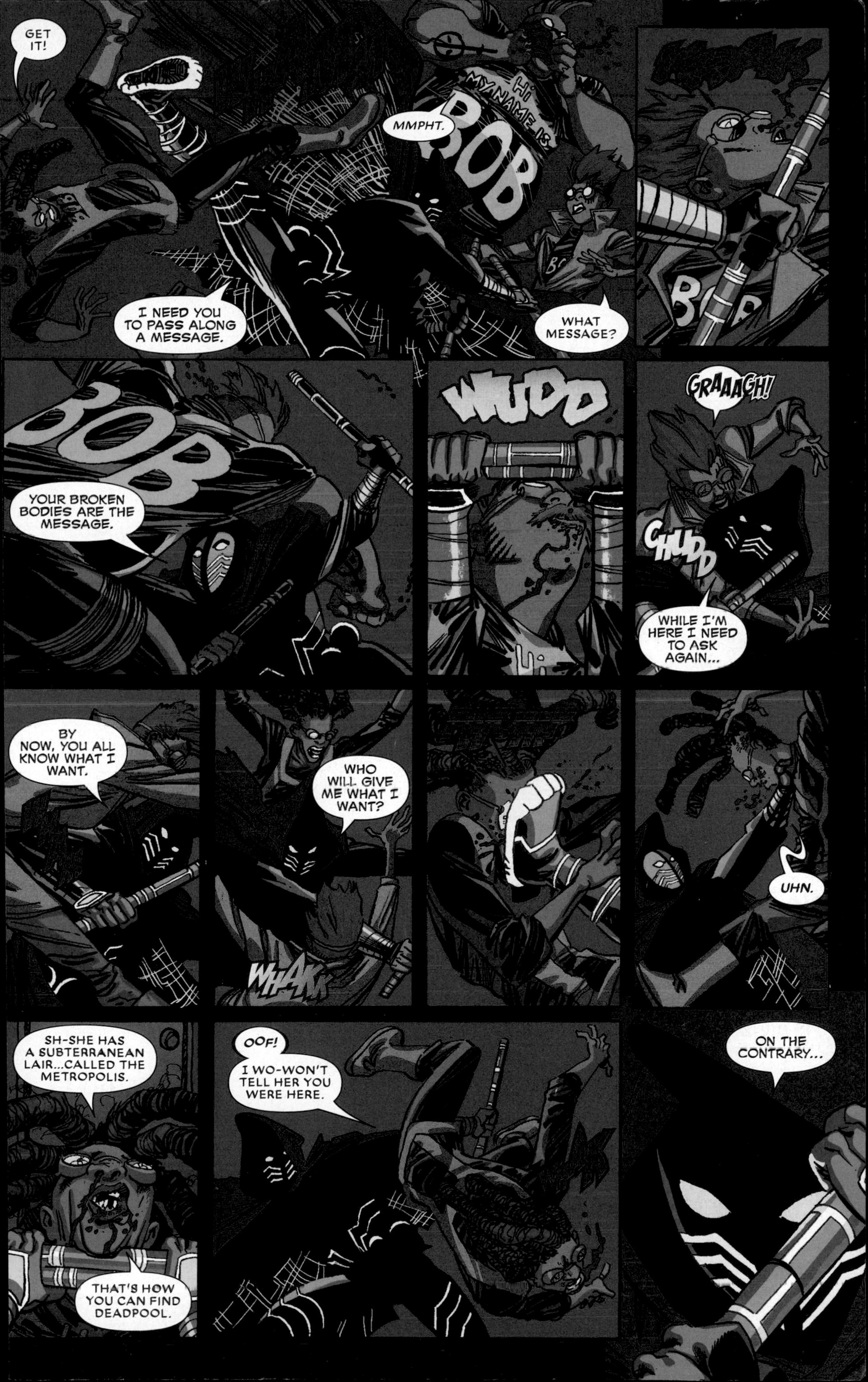
GET IT!
HI MY NAME IS BOB
MMPHT.
I NEED YOU TO PASS ALONG A MESSAGE.
WHAT MESSAGE?
BOB
YOUR BROKEN BODIES ARE THE MESSAGE.
WUDD
GRAAAGH!
CHUDD
WHILE I'M HERE I NEED TO ASK AGAIN...
BY NOW, YOU ALL KNOW WHAT I WANT.
WHO WILL GIVE ME WHAT I WANT?
WHAK
UHN.
SH-SHE HAS A SUBTERRANEAN LAIR...CALLED THE METROPOLIS.
THAT'S HOW YOU CAN FIND DEADPOOL.
OOF!
I WO-WON'T TELL HER YOU WERE HERE.
ON THE CONTRARY...

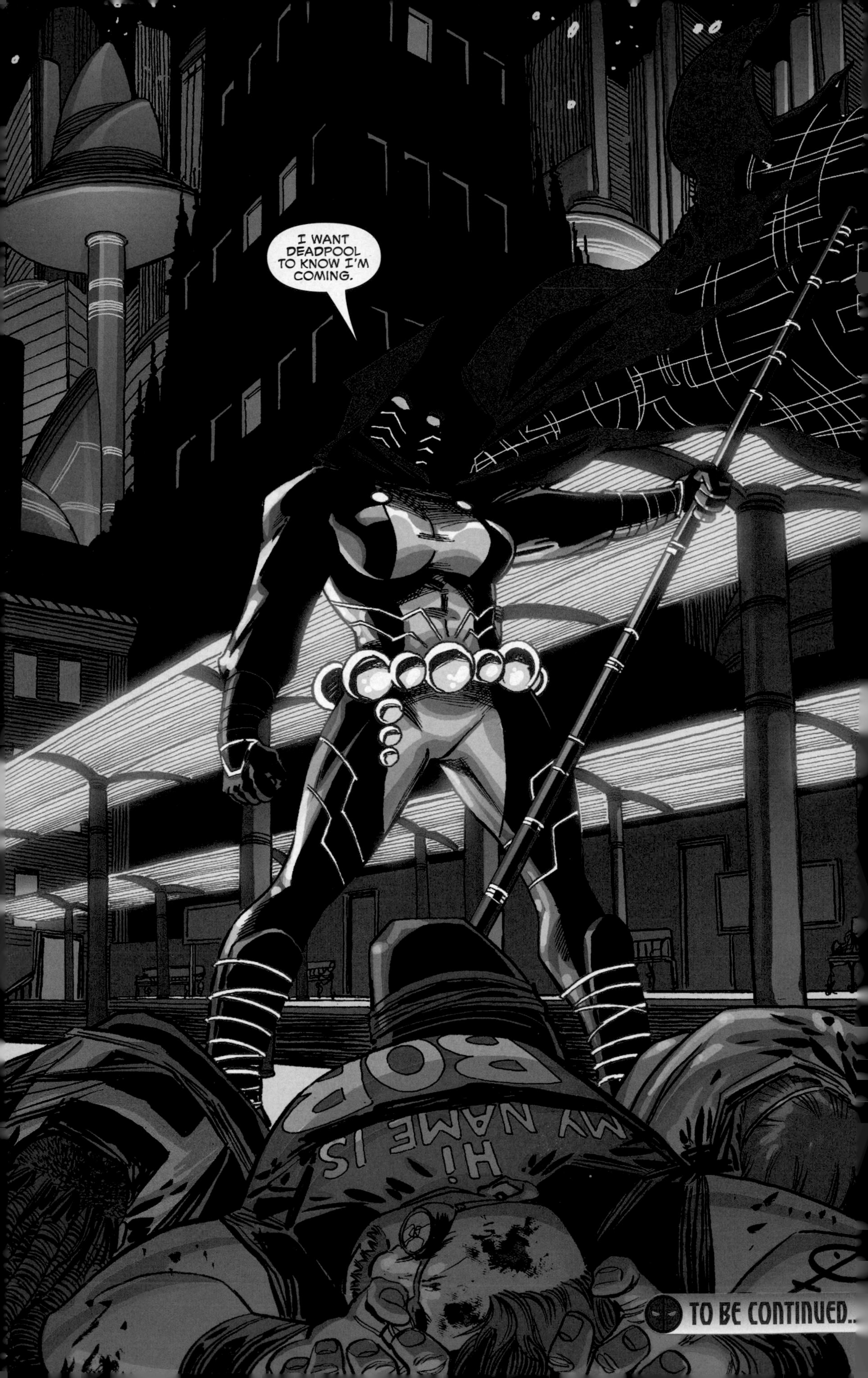
I WANT DEADPOOL TO KNOW I'M COMING.
HI MY NAME IS BOB
TO BE CONTINUED..

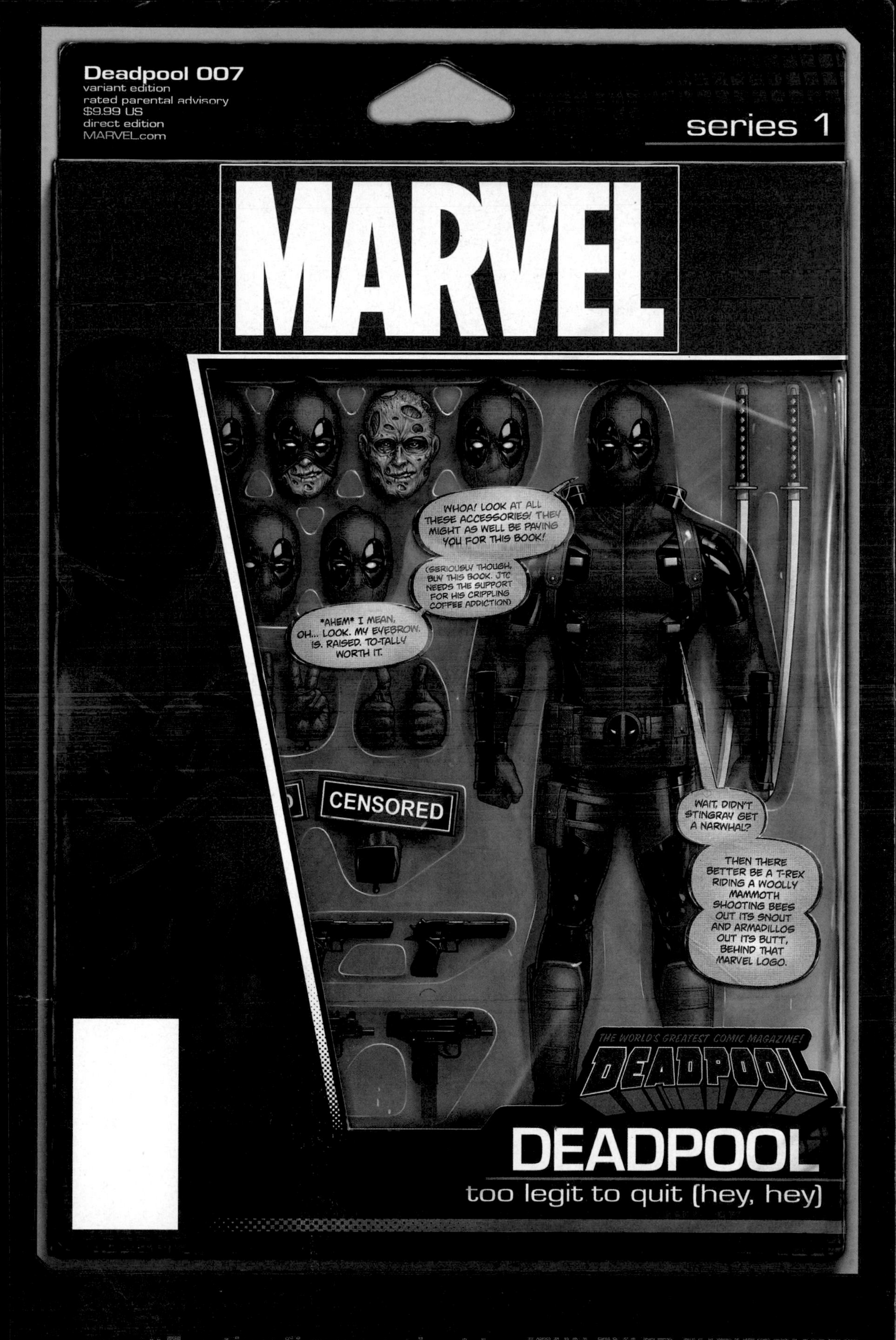
Deadpool 007
variant edition
rated parental advisory
$9.99 US
direct edition
MARVEL.com
series 1
MARVEL
WHOA! LOOK AT ALL THESE ACCESSORIES! THEY MIGHT AS WELL BE PAYING YOU FOR THIS BOOK!
(SERIOUSLY THOUGH, BUY THIS BOOK. JTC NEEDS THE SUPPORT FOR HIS CRIPPLING COFFEE ADDICTION)
*AHEM* I MEAN, OH... LOOK. MY EYEBROW. IS. RAISED. TO-TALLY WORTH IT.
CENSORED
WAIT, DIDN'T STINGRAY GET A NARWHAL?
THEN THERE BETTER BE A T-REX RIDING A WOOLLY MAMMOTH SHOOTING BEES OUT ITS SNOUT AND ARMADILLOS OUT ITS BUTT, BEHIND THAT MARVEL LOGO.
THE WORLD'S GREATEST COMIC MAGAZINE!
DEADPOOL
DEADPOOL
too legit to quit (hey, hey)

#7 action figure variant by JOHN TYLER CHRISTOHPER

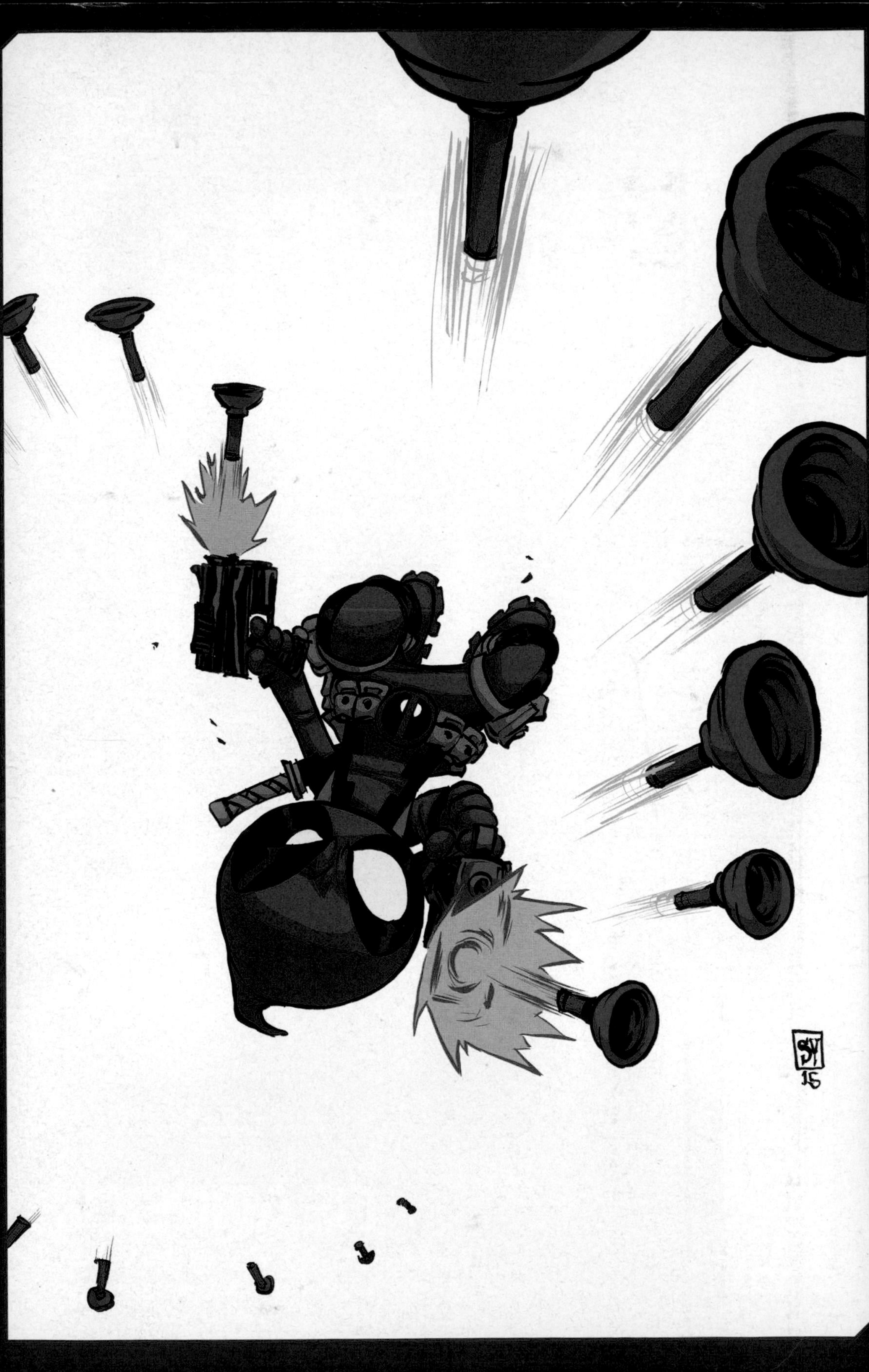
SY
15

#7 variant by SKOTTIE YOUNG

Deadpool

ILL

#7 hip-hop variant by RAHZZAH